KUMBH MELA

KUMBH MELA

Mapping the Ephemeral MEGACITY

Edited by
RAHUL MEHROTRA & FELIPE VERA

With texts by
DIANA ECK
TARUN KHANNA
JENNIFER LEANING
JOHN MACOMBER

Photography by
DINESH MEHTA
supported by DIPTI MEHTA

HARVARD University
South Asia Institute

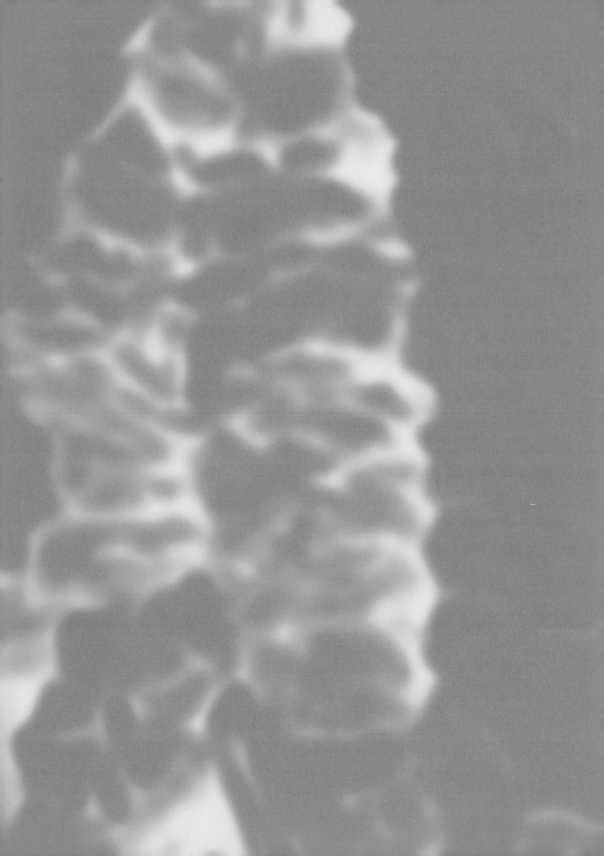

PREAMBLE

The wonderful thing about the Kumbh Mela was that it was so unusual that no one really knew what to expect and I think that's what allowed the collaboration.

—RAHUL MEHROTRA
Professor of Urban Design and Planning and Chair of the Department of
Urban Planning and Design, Harvard Graduate School of Design

What struck me about the Kumbh Mela was the sheer number of people and seeing the scale manage itself or be managed by select interventions on the part of different entities.

—TARUN KHANNA
Jorge Paulo Lemann Professor, Harvard Business School, Director,
Harvard University South Asia Institute

I have learned an entirely different way that one could look at mass gatherings.
Let them happen. Release rather than control.

—JENNIFER LEANING
François-Xavier Bagnoud Professor of the Practice
of Health and Human Rights and Director, FXB Center for Health
and Human Rights, Harvard School of Public Health (HSPH)

The Kumbh Mela is a Hindu religious fair that occurs every twelve years at the confluence of the Ganga and Yamuna rivers on the plains of northern India. Since its inception, early in the first millennium CE, the Kumbh Mela has become the largest public gathering in the world. Today, it draws tens of millions of pilgrims over the course of a few weeks. The most recent observance of the festival took place from January 14 to March 10, 2013 in Allahabad, with an estimated attendance of seventy million people. Due to its size and complexity, the 2013 Kumbh Mela inspired interdisciplinary research in a number of complementary fields at Harvard University, including business, technology and communications, urban studies and design, religious and cultural studies, and public health.

On the broad sandy flats left by the receding rivers after the rainy season, a temporary city is built for the Kumbh Mela. This "pop-up megacity" houses the Kumbh Mela's many short-term pilgrims as well as the Hindu faithful and working personnel who stay for the duration of the festival. The city is laid out on a grid, which is constructed and deconstructed within a matter of weeks. Creating a huge encampment of tents entailing multiple aspects of contemporary urbanism: city planning and management, engineering and spatial zoning, land allocation, an electricity grid, water lines and sanitation systems, food and water distribution plans, hospitals and vaccination centers, police and fire stations, and public gathering spaces for entertainment. The public health challenges and opportunities of the Kumbh Mela are enormous. Pollution abatement is necessary to keep the water quality of the Ganga and Yamuna within acceptable limits for bathing. Sanitation systems must be put in place with enough hired workers to provide waste removal. There are also sites for mass vaccination campaigns at the railway stations and on the grounds in an attempt to thwart disease. From a business perspective, the festival provides the opportunity to examine collaborations between private companies and the Indian government. Technology, media, Internet connectivity, and cellular networks played unprecedented logistical roles in the 2013 Kumbh Mela. Finally, the religious aspect of the festival is important as we try to understand the social, cultural, and religious independency and interdependency of Hindus from many different places, sects, and social strata.

Keeping this in mind, the Harvard University South Asia Institute (SAI) served as the coordinating unit for this multi-year research project titled, *Mapping the Kumbh Mela*. SAI's mission is to connect faculty across disciplines to conduct research on issues critical to the region. The study of the Kumbh Mela was seen as a keystone project to undertake. While faculty published their own research on the Kumbh Mela specific to their respective disciplines, it was agreed that it would be beneficial to have Harvard's cross-disciplinary perspectives in one book. Prior to this effort, SAI faculty identified three types of literature that existed on the festival: 1) academic work by scholars, 2) memoirs from administrators, and 3) photo collections by photographers. This book aims to examine the festival through these listed lenses.

Beginning in July 2012 and continuing through the fall semester, SAI hosted several meetings at Harvard where faculty gathered to discuss the different directions their disciplinary foci would take them. From the end of July 2012 until the visit to the Kumbh in January 2013, the project grew from two faculty and a few student participants to over fifty faculty, staff, and students from five different disciplines across the University, including the Harvard School of Public Health (HSPH), the Harvard Graduate School of Design (GSD), the Harvard Business School (HBS), the Harvard Faculty of Arts and Sciences (FAS), and the Harvard Divinity School (HDS). The conversations at the meetings provided faculty with the opportunity to frame their own research questions bearing in mind the inquiry of others.

Prior to the SAI group meetings, beginning in March 2012, a team from the GSD traveled to Allahabad, the site of the Kumbh Mela, for preliminary research. There, they met with officials, gathered materials outlining the organization of the Kumbh, and documented the processes leading up to the construction of the pop-up megacity. For the students, researching appropriation of the terrain was as important as what would eventually happen at the festival. Subsequently, faculty members used the initial information to hone their research questions and revise their research plans.

SAI continued to coordinate the growing interest in the project and partnered with the Harvard Global Health Institute (HGHI) to provide administrative support. This resulted in the production of a website with content that included research on the Kumbh Mela, contact information of Harvard team members, maps of the site, and other internal resources generated during preliminary research. The website served as a nexus for various research teams to connect and share their progress with each other.

SAI took on the responsibility for raising and managing the funds for this growing project. Working during the summer and into the beginning of the fall semester, funding was secured from a variety of sources: the President's January Innovation Fund, the Provost's Fund for Interfaculty Collaboration, HGHI, and the Harvard University Asia Center. The François-Xavier Bagnoud (FXB) Center for Health and Human Rights, HBS, and the Harvard Center for the Environment (HUCE) also contributed funds for students to travel to the Kumbh site.

As this project began to take shape, SAI's role in coordinating logistics became vital. Responsibilities included ensuring vaccinations and visas, booking domestic and international travel, taking personal information in various forms to report to the Harvard Travel Services and the US Consulate; the collection of risk and release forms from students, making contact lists and name tags with photos for each participant and securing cell phones and internet dongles for use in India. SAI also liaised with officials to secure permission for faculty and students to interview the Kumbh Mela administration and have access to important information and documents for their research.

Over fifty Harvard professors, students, administrative staff, doctors, and researchers made the pilgrimage to the Kumbh Mela site. The duration of stay on the site varied from two days to multiple weeks. A few members of the team travelled over a period of a year, documenting and photographing how the terrain was appropriated, speaking with fabricators and construction workers, and interviewing the festival's administrators. An important role for SAI was to develop a partnership between the Kumbh Mela administration and the Harvard team in order to streamline research in a way that is free of administrative bottlenecks.

 The architecture and urban planning team systematically documented the various sectors at the Kumbh site, revealing a rich and sophisticated urban typology—the components of which can be useful in the future for more precarious contexts relating to disaster response, public health, and sustainability.

The public health team gathered data about onsite, temporary hospitals, mapped and documented the various kinds of toilets being used, and studied provisions made by public health officials for potable drinking water.

The team studying religion and culture focused on the concerns participants and planners had about the pollution produced throughout the course of this festival. One group of researchers examined the use of trees and plants at the Kumbh Mela. Another group gathered data on how flowers used in worship at the festival, point to a burgeoning concern of their wider-scaled use in India. This led to a deeper analysis of the effects religious practices have on the environment.

Business teams studied the ways in which vendors and suppliers managed risks and uncertainties in this temporary, ad-hoc, ever-changing marketplace. The lessons learned from this research could serve as a model for global markets, especially in urban and temporary settings. Another business team created a case study to examine massive and rapid urbanization. They looked into the problems of excess traffic and pollution, the scarcity

of basic resources such as clean air, water, electricity, and the role of the government in effectively addressing these problems. A third business team analyzed data from cell phones used at the Kumbh to understand the patterns that emerge in large scale social networks within a bound timeframe and undefined boundaries.

Coordination of the various research teams over a short period of time relied upon careful planning and preparation by SAI throughout the duration of the project. SAI managed the media during and after the Harvard visit and also collected the accumulated materials required for precise oversight. Upon return of the research teams from the festival, SAI coordinated several additional meetings where the faculty and students gathered to outline their next steps.

A critical "working meeting" in August 2013 was funded by the Radcliffe Institute of Advanced Study at Harvard. The workshop brought together five government officials from the Indian state of Uttar Pradesh, who were responsible for planning and managing the Kumbh Mela, with the Harvard faculty, students, and administrators to discuss what each team learned, and to share each other's research findings. The spirit of interdisciplinary collaboration and academic curiosity that made Harvard's Kumbh Mela study so successful was on vivid display at this session.

By analyzing the problems that emerge in any large-scale human gathering, pilgrimage, or cultural event, *Kumbh Mela, January 2013: Mapping the Ephemeral Megacity* serves as an example of sophisticated, interdisciplinary research that produced a rich set of teaching tools useful across the disciplines of public health, data science, architecture, urban planning, business, religion, and culture. The project serves as a model for research focused on geography rather than a discipline or one particular issue. It demonstrates that the role of an institute such as SAI can serve as a catalyst in bringing the professional schools together. Over the last thirty years, geographic knowledge has been deemphasized at Harvard. This notion, however, is changing with schools such as HBS requiring all incoming students to travel to another country with the idea that bringing back their field experiences enriches classroom learning. Ultimately, the Kumbh Mela project leaves the institution with a critical question: is there more to gain from insights specific to geography or should the emphasis be on disciplinary specialties?

MEENA SONEA HEWETT
Executive Director, South Asia Institute

 TARUN KHANNA, MEENA HEWETT,
JENNY BORDO, TODD MOSTAK,
DEONNIE MOODIE, NAMRATA ARORA,
NORA MAGINN

The SOUTH ASIA INSTITUTE at Harvard University

 Harvard University
Graduate School of Design

RAHUL MEHROTRA, CHUAN
HAO CHEN, NAMITA DHARIA,
ANEESHA DHARWADKER, VINEET
DIWADKAR, OSCAR MALASPINA,
ALYKHAN MOHAMED, JOSÉ
MAYORAL MORATILLA, BENJAMIN
SCHEERBARTH, JOHANNES STAUDT,
JUSTIN STERN, FELIPE VERA,
JAMES WHITTEN

 Harvard University
School of Public Health

RICHARD CASH, CANDACE BROWN,
STEPHANIE CHENG,
JUKKA-PEKKA ONNELA

 Global Health Institute

SUSAN R. HOLMAN, AMANDA
BREWSTER, SUE J. GOLDIE

 FXB Center for
Health and Human Rights

JENNIFER LEANING, GREGG
GREENOUGH, SATCHIT BALSARI,
POOJA AGRAWAL, AARON HEERBOTH,
DHRUV KAZI, RISHI MADHOK,
NEIL MURTHY, LOGAN PLASTER,
MICHAEL VORTMANN

 Harvard University
Faculty of Arts & Sciences

DIANA ECK, KALPESH BHATT,
DOROTHY AUSTIN, ISAAC DAYNO,
FELIX DE ROSEN, ANNA KNEIFEL,
BRENNA MCDUFFIE, NICHOLAS
ROTH, LEILA SHAYEGAN,
RACHEL TAYLOR, NED WHITMAN

 Harvard University
Business School

TARUN KHANNA, JOHN MACOMBER,
SALONI CHATURVEDI,
VAUGHN TAN, TIONA ZUZUL

HARVARD UNIVERSITY RESEARCHERS DURING A MAJOR FIELD VISIT

WHAT happens when a disturbance breaks out?

WHAT pathways open up to let a sick person move out of the crowd and seek medical assistance?

WHAT is the layout for appropriate sources of water and sanitation and waste management?

WHAT are the placements, numbers, and personnel relating to health clinics of all kinds?

WHAT organizational and leadership structures exist for helping and preventing large crowd emergencies?

WHAT is the relationship between the physical structures and the temporal events that occur?

WHAT are the physical boundaries of the festival? Do they change from festival to festival?

WHAT are the ways in which the Kumbh Mela challenges traditional methods in which cities are designed and built?

WHAT is the relationship between pedestrians and vehicles during the festival?

WHAT is the relationship between the Kumbh Mela and the broader landscape that contains it?

WHAT are the timetables and routes of public transportation in the surrounding cities? Do they change?

WHAT is the business model of he Kumbh Mela? Is it considered a not-for-profit venture?

WHAT is the relationship between the government, private sector, and communities in the festival?

WHAT are the changes in air quality and air pollution during the festival?

WHAT is the overall environmental impact of the festival?

WHAT is the structure of authority (organizational and legal) and how are levels of authority designated?

WHAT is the relationship with the army besides the construction of the city?

WHAT laws formally exist?

WHAT is the overarching economic system?

WHAT is the history of technology at the festival?

WHAT is the balance between temporary and permanent technologies?

WHAT is the scope of Internet access in terms of pilgrims and tourist populations?

WHAT is the reason for the grid?

WHAT are the physical, political, and economic variations of the Kumbh Mela over time?

WHAT is the relationship between pilgrims, tourists, press, and governing institutions?

HOW are vaccinations and other available medications distributed to Kumbh visitors?

HOW are such large numbers of people organized in relatively peaceful and secure ways?

HOW are proper procedures for hand-washing, bathing, drinking, and cooking managed?

HOW is the vaccination process organized, announced, and conducted?

HOW does the Kumbh negotiate the tensions between self-identity and national and religious identity?

HOW do groups of pilgrims from different economic and social backgrounds relate to each other?

HOW does the weather affect the site daily, monthly, and yearly?

HOW do we visually and spatially document temporary urbanism?

HOW is land allocated?

HOW can the spatial systems that emerge from this festival inform other temporal settlements?

HOW is the city zoned between "public" and "private" spaces?

HOW has the land use evolved over the years in the site and surrounding territories?

HOW do partnerships between public sector and private actors emerge in short order?

HOW large is the presence of informal methods of business?

HOW do institutions of information exchange and mediation emerge?

HOW can we map infrastructure engineering, traffic patterns, and food and water delivery?

HOW is the physical infrastructure designed, planned, and deployed at the festival?

HOW are pontoon bridges built and displayed on site and HOW do they perform?

HOW is law enforcement carried out?

HOW are different zones, such as tourism, religious institutions, press, and different castes of pilgrims designated?

HOW are cell phones charged?

HOW is the technology for the festival chosen and why? Is there anything conspicuously missing?

HOW has the technology for the festival evolved over the years?

HOW are collective infrastructures for shelter, utilities, communication, sanitation, and food constructed and deconstructed?

WHERE are pop-up hospitals located in the city?

WHERE are police stations and officers settled?

WHERE do pilgrims come from and how do they travel?

WHERE and how are religious institutions allocated space?

WHERE are Internet stands at the festival, who runs them, and how effective is the access?

WHO participates in vaccination initiatives and at what scale do they expect to continue?

WHO decides where different visitors live, eat, and pray?

WHO pays for the costs of implementation?

WHO pays for the water, public amenities, public toilets, and other services delivered during the festival?

WHO receives the money from advertising and other private investments carried out during the festival?

WHO are the major religious individuals and institutions at the festival and what is their impact on the larger population?

WHEN were different technological systems (grid, power lines, toilets, Internet, etc.) introduced and why?

WHEN is everything put in place and to which existing systems is the festival attached?

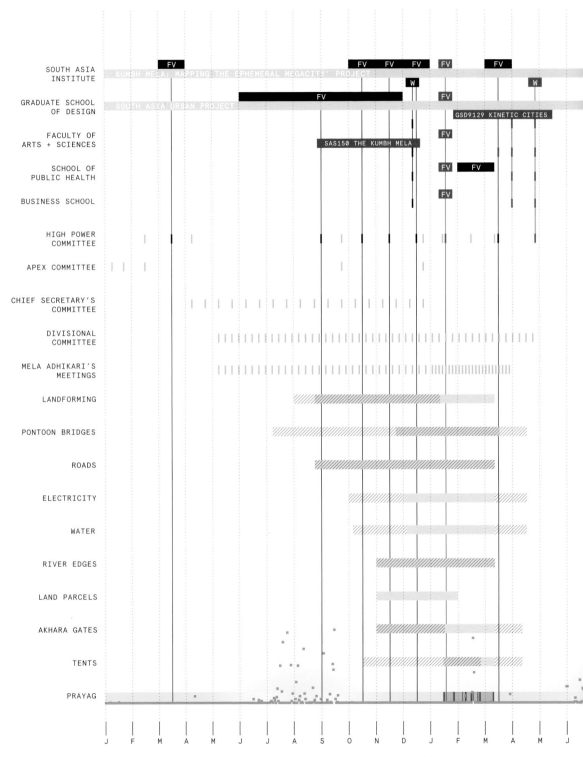

SOUTH ASIA
INSTITUTE

FV

'KUMBH MELA: MAPPING THE EPHEMERAL MEGACITY' PROJECT

FV   FV   FV   FV   FV

W

GRADUATE SCHOOL
OF DESIGN

SOUTH ASIA URBAN PROJECT

FV

FV

W

GSD9129 KINETIC CITIES

FACULTY OF
ARTS + SCIENCES

SAS150 THE KUMBH MELA

FV

SCHOOL OF
PUBLIC HEALTH

FV   FV

BUSINESS SCHOOL

FV

HIGH POWER
COMMITTEE

APEX COMMITTEE

CHIEF SECRETARY'S
COMMITTEE

DIVISIONAL
COMMITTEE

MELA ADHIKARI'S
MEETINGS

LANDFORMING

PONTOON BRIDGES

ROADS

ELECTRICITY

WATER

RIVER EDGES

LAND PARCELS

AKHARA GATES

TENTS

PRAYAG

J F M A M J J A S O N D J F M A M J

2012   2013

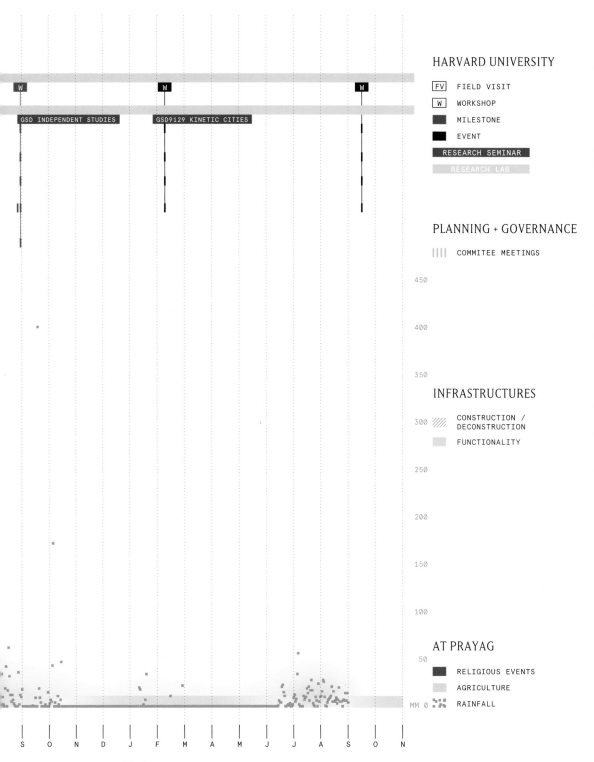

HARVARD UNIVERSITY

FV FIELD VISIT
W   WORKSHOP
▪   MILESTONE
■   EVENT
███ RESEARCH SEMINAR
░░░ RESEARCH LAB

PLANNING + GOVERNANCE

|||| COMMITEE MEETINGS

450

400

350

INFRASTRUCTURES

300 //// CONSTRUCTION /
          DECONSTRUCTION
     ░░░ FUNCTIONALITY

250

200

150

100

AT PRAYAG

50

■ RELIGIOUS EVENTS
░ AGRICULTURE
▪▪ RAINFALL

MM 0

W

W

W

GSD INDEPENDENT STUDIES

GSD9129 KINETIC CITIES

S O N D J F M A M J J A S O N

2014

PURPOSE

Understanding the KUMBH MELA

DIANA ECK & KALPESH BHATT

The Kumbh Mela is a great religious bathing fair and pilgrimage in India, said to be the largest religious gathering on earth. For more than a month every twelve years, this sacred tradition brings tens of millions of people to the confluence of the Ganga, Yamuna, and Sarasvati rivers at Allahabad. The size of this pilgrimage, especially on the three main bathing days, has long been the focus of wide-scale astonishment, amplified in the age of multimedia communication. The focus of this amazement stems from images of the vast tent city sprung up on the delta of the three rivers; the royal processions of holy men and naked ascetics, first in line for bathing in the river on the most "auspicious" (holiest) days; and the densely packed pilgrims who press toward the riverbank by the millions. Vivid color photographs of these re-markable phenomena rocket around the world, creating the global image of an exotic spectacle.

But the Kumbh Mela is far more than a media spectacle. The sheer human achievement of creating the temporary and yet complex infrastructure of the twenty-square-mile "Kumbh City" (almost two-thirds the size of Man-hattan) on the dry flood plain of the rivers is astonishing. There are tents to house millions of people and like any permanent city there are roads and bridges, power stations and electricity, sanitation facilities and clinics, po-lice and fire departments, and transportation and telecommunications. And this occurs every twelfth year, prompting the most important question: Why do they all come? What is the significance of this great pilgrimage for the thousands of ascetics who encamp here for a month and for the pilgrims who come for but a day?

The place the Kumbh Mela holds in Hindu religious life must be under-stood within the context of the pilgrimage networks, religious fairs known as *melas*, that span the length and breadth of India. It is part of a centuries-long tradition that brings Hindus to holy sites throughout the country. In modern India, technological advances in transportation and communications have made the practice of pilgrimage more popular than ever.

TIRTHA: Spiritual Ford

Across India, pilgrimages draw Hindus to bathe in the sacred rivers and to experience the festive life of a *mela*. There are thousands of places of pil-grimage across India, called *tirthas*, literally "crossing places." Many *tirthas* are located along the banks of the seven sacred rivers of India representing both literal and symbolic places of crossing or "fords." They are sites where religious rites, simple or elaborate, yield more powerful spiritual fruit. They are places where one's prayers are more readily heard, where one's generosity is amplified, where one's penitential moments are more effective. They are spiritual crossings, where the river of this earthly life enables one to reach the far shore of immortality.

Prayag, the ancient name of Allahabad, is classically called the Tirtha Raja, meaning "King of Tirthas." It is said that other riverside *tirthas* absorb the sins and sorrows of countless pilgrims. The *tirthas* themselves, seeking a place to deposit this load of human burdens also come to Prayag, where they too are cleansed. While there are certainly many important temples in Prayag, the primary "altar" of this sacred place is the riverbank, where the rivers meet and flow together, where people come for the simple rites of bathing, and according to legend, where other *tirthas* come to bathe as well. This is the power of Prayag.

The traditional pilgrim's map of the city focuses on the meeting rivers, with all the Hindu gods congregated in the landscape and river setting. It is a map where divine presence and the earthly city are depicted together.

SANGAM: Meeting Rivers

India's great rivers are said to be of divine origin and the waters of these rivers are understood to be a liquid form of the Goddess Shakti, who is

GANGOTRI

PRAYAG

the energy of creation itself. The Ganga and Yamuna rivers both come from high in the Himalayas at Gangotri and Yamunotri, places visited by pilgrims from throughout India. Many sources of India's other sacred rivers are considered holy as well, including the headwaters of the Godavari, called the Godavari Ganga, near Nashik, in today's Maharashtra; the source of the Narmada at Amarakantaka in the Maikala Hills of eastern India; and the source of the Kaveri at Talakaveri, in the Coorg hills of southwestern Karnataka.

The confluence where two rivers meet is known as a Sangam and it is especially sacred for bathing. As the Ganga—called the Mandakini (meaning "the River of Heaven") courses down the Himalayan mountain ravines, it joins with two other rivers, the Alakananda at Rudra Prayag and the Bhagirathi at Deva Prayag. At both Sangams, chains are sunk into the steep cement steps at the river's edge to enable pilgrims to bathe safely in the swift current of the meeting rivers. The greatest of the Sangams along the Ganga is at Prayag. This is where the Ganga and the Yamuna Rivers meet the invisible but venerable, Sarasvati River. This place where the three rivers meet is called the *triveni*, the "triple-braid" of rivers. When the rivers connect at Prayag, they are broad and swollen with floodwaters from the rainy season. From here, the Ganga flows past Varanasi, and on through what is now Bihar and Bengal. Finally, a thousand miles downstream, there is a great confluence at the delta, where the Ganga meets the sea in the Bay of Bengal. This is the place of the famous Ganga Sagara Island, which hosts a three-day *mela* of approximately a million people every January.

The great destination of pilgrims to the Kumbh Mela is the Sangam at Prayag. For pilgrims, bathing at this very location marks the precise holy moment they are seeking. Here, the rivers are said to flow with *amrit*, "the nectar of immortality," during the auspicious period of the Kumbh Mela.

ARCHIVAL IMAGE OF THE KUMBH MELA SETTLEMENT, ALLAHABAD IN 1953

AMRIT: Nectar of Immortality

"From untruth, lead us to truth; from darkness, lead us to light; from death, lead us to immortality." This oft-quoted prayer from the Upanishads reveals a more universal truth that spans cultures and religions—the yearning for immortality. In the Hindu story associated with the Kumbh Mela, even the gods seek to overcome death, and according to legend, a drop of *amrit* fell upon the earth at Prayag. Of old, so they say, the gods sought for themselves the nectar of immortality that was to be found deep in the ocean of milk. They decided to churn the ocean to bring it forth from the deep. Vishnu obliged and became a tortoise and his shell became the base on which the churn could be placed. The Himalayan Mount Mandara became the churning stick and the serpent Vasuki became the rope with which to churn. Yet to gain that nectar, the gods needed the help of the anti-gods, the *asuras,* to pull one end of the churning rope while they pulled the other. And so they all exerted themselves, each side pulling mightily until the *kumbh,* the "pot," containing the *amrit* came forth from the ocean. It was immediately seized by the *asuras.* It seemed all was lost until Vishnu took the form of an enchanting maiden named Mohini, the deluder, and beguiled the *asuras* into letting her hold the *kumbh.* She delivered it immediately to the gods who swept it away to heaven. As they sped off with the pot, four drops of *amrit* fell upon the earth. According to tradition, these drops landed in the four locations where the Kumbh Mela is observed today: 1) Haridwar where the Ganga enters the plains,

2) Prayag at the Triveni Sangam, 3) Nashik on the Godavari River in Maharashtra, and 4) Ujjain on the Kshipra River in Madhya Pradesh. Each place hosts a *mela* every twelve years in an astrologically determined, cyclic sequence that enables the Kumbh Mela to occur in approximately three-year intervals.

The story of the churning of the ocean and the battle over the immortal nectar is told in the *Puranas*, the "old stories," passed down and amplified in one version after another. While the Kumbh Mela is not mentioned by name, its connection with the churning of the ocean is so widely known today that the official website of the 2013 Kumbh Mela portrays the gods and asuras churning the sea on the banner of its homepage.

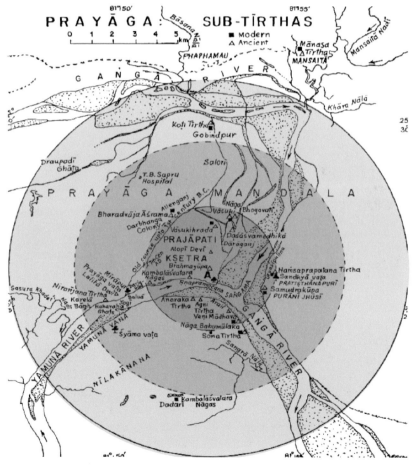

PRAYAG MANDALA

Scholars who have looked for the origins of the *mela* in classical texts have been disappointed, although one scholar who has studied Prayag's history has found a text attached to the Skanda Purana that contains the story and links it to the astrological conjunctions when the four Kumbh Melas take place and the places where the drops of nectar were spilled.[1] It is generally agreed that the mention of a large astrologically determined *mela* occurred first in relation to the Kumbh Mela at Haridwar. According to Prayag scholar D.P. Dubey, "It appears that the Kumbha Parva derives its name from an auspicious occasion of ritual bathing that used to take place at Haridvara, every twelfth year, when Jupiter was in Aquarius, and the sun entered Aries."[2]

The legend of the immortal nectar aside, the praises of bathing in the Sangam and sipping its waters are ubiquitous in the Puranas. Two examples of many hundreds may suffice:

> If one bathes and sips water where the Ganga, Yamuna, and Sarasvati meet, he enjoys liberation, and of this there is no doubt (*Padma Purana* Uttara Khanda 23.14).

> Those who bathe in the bright waters of the Ganga where they meet the dark waters of the Yamuna during the month of Magh will not be reborn, even in thousands of years (*Matsya Purana* 107.7).

PILGRIMS GATHER TO EAT AT THE AKHARA'S MAIN GATE

History

While the Kumbh Mela is often said to be "ageless" and "ancient," those who have studied the history of the large *mela* in Allahabad see it as being more or less continuous since the Gupta period from the fourth to the sixth centuries. Perhaps the first historical description of a great *mela* in this region was in 643 CE, written by the Chinese, Buddhist monk Hsuan Tsang, who had travelled to India to find Buddhist sacred texts. Hsuan Tsang wrote of a gathering of pilgrims to an "age-long festival" in the month of Magh (January–February). He explained how King Harsha displayed his generosity by giving away goods to all classes of people until he himself possessed nothing and returned to his capital wearing only single piece of cloth.[3] The Narasimha Purana, dated to the fifth or sixth centuries, also gives evidence that a month-long *mela* was known during the Gupta period. Sages are said to come from different orders assembling from various parts of India during the month of Magh.[4] One aspect of today's Kumbh Mela that truly seems to be ancient is this gathering during the winter month of Magh. This Magh Mela may well have taken place annually, as it does today.

It was during the time of the Mughal emperor Akbar that Prayag was renamed Ilahabad, which later became Allahabad. The emperor visited the city in 1582 and asked that a fort be built at this strategic location where the two waterways converged. The fort remains to this day, a lofty sentinel at one end of the Kumbh Mela grounds. Historians of the Islamicate kings give notice of this gathering through the years and, subsequently, British writers have added their descriptive accounts. Reading their descriptions, D.P. Dubey concludes, "The traditional scene of the *mela* has remained almost unchanged: the ascetics' exhibitions of yogic performance, the recitation of religious texts, discourses on socio-religious problems, and sectarian propaganda continue to be the main attractions of the fair."[5]

The Kumbh Mela name seems to have been adopted by Prayag from the Kumbh Mela that took place, as it does today, at Haridwar. Historian Kama Maclean's careful analysis has concluded that prior to the eighteen-sixties there is no mention in textual sources of a *kumbh* in Allahabad or of a special *mela* occurring every twelve years, although the Magh Mela was well known. The first modern Kumbh Mela was likely in 1870. Since the mid-nineteenth century, the festival has expanded in size and scope. Ironically, the attempt of the British colonial state to regulate the seemingly chaotic and possible dangerous practice of such a pilgrimage contributed to its success. Maclean writes, "Colonial government intervention in *melas*, though often controversial, generally made them safer, which consequently encouraged pilgrimage attendance."[6]

MELA: Festival

It has been said that one must understand the *mela* to really know India. A *mela* is a great religious fair where spiritual life and the robust world of commerce and entertainment come together. It is a confluence of people from all walks of life and from all over India, and it is a microcosm of Hindu India's spiritual life.

Many of India's *melas* last but a few days. The annual *mela* at Prayag every winter lasts for the whole month of Magh. The Kumbh Mela of 2013 stretched out for fifty-five days, from Makar Sankranti (January 14, 2013) to Mahashivaratri (March 10, 2013). The Magh Mela is about a quarter the size of the Kumbh Mela. However, like the Kumbh Mela, the Magh Mela brings day pilgrims as well as the *kalpavasis*—the devout ones who take a vow to stay for the entire month. They bathe in the rivers daily, praying, meditating, and listening to the discourses of teachers. The grid of streets, the tent city, and the combination of religious life and festivity is an annual smaller version of the great Kumbh Mela. "What attracts them as a magnet, all at one time, to the same place, is the still vital strength of religious tradition," writes Dubey. "A miniature spiritual India is represented on the dry flood plain between the Ganga and the Yamuna during the shivering cold month of Magha."[7]

The great Kumbh Mela is of a far greater magnitude and scale than other *melas*, but has some of the same elements. The pavilions constructed along the main streets of the Kumbh City have colorful gateways, decorated with flags, flashing lights, and spinning fluorescent pinwheels. Crowds of pilgrims are welcomed into large halls where hundreds may sit for the discourses of a famous teacher for whom the great *mela* is a chance to gather their followers and recruit new ones. Gurus sit with their disciples and interpret sacred texts. Yogis demonstrate their spiritual accomplishments. Popular singers and musical artists are invited to perform. Some of the great pavilions are built especially to house the theater troupes that perform the *lilas*, the religious plays in which actors enact favorite scenes from the Ramayana or the life of Krishna. These performances occur twice a day, in the morning and evening, and conclude with worship, religious songs, and a ceremonial lamp and flower offering to the principal actors who portray the deities. *Lilas* incorporate a multimedia approach that provides vibrancy and energy to the *mela*.

Outside, along the streets of the Kumbh Mela's encampment, sit hundreds of merchants, selling both daily necessities and various wares and trinkets of religious life. They spread their merchandise on the ground or wheel it along the streets in carts. For them, the *mela* is a great opportunity for business.

PILGRIMS BATHE AT A SANGAM

In short, a *mela* combines the festivity of a festival and a fair with the intention and devotion of a pilgrimage. For pilgrims, it is a family affair. On the quieter days of the *mela*, bathing in the sacred rivers might be followed by a moment of reading and reflection and perhaps a family picnic on the riverbank, with cotton candy and pinwheels for the children.

SNAN and SHAHI SNAN

What is the spiritual pull of the Kumbh Mela? For most pilgrims, a holy dip in the rivers holds the most spiritual value. They dip fully into the waters once, twice, three times, and then take the waters in their cupped hands to pour it again into the river as an offering to the gods and to the ancestors. They make offerings of flowers and oil lamps, floating them into the current of the mother waters. In the evening, the pilgrims might come to the riverbank for one of the *aratis* (lamp offerings) that are performed by *pujaris* (priests) who raise huge, multi-wicked oil lamps to the river. The rites are simple, but absolutely central to the spiritual experience of the Kumbh Mela. This is what they have come for. For those *kalpavasis* who have vowed to stay for a whole month, Ganga Snan is a once or twice-a-day rite.

On an ordinary day, bathing is a constant activity along the riverbank, beginning before dawn. The riverfront mud *ghats* have been reinforced with sandbags to allow secure footing. In some places, bamboo guardrails and fences have been anchored in the river to protect pilgrims from the press of crowds that might push them too far into the current. Many pilgrims take a boat into the river where a makeshift dock enables them to bathe in the actual waters where the rivers join. Shahi Snan, the Royal Bathing Days, are astrologically auspicious, so on these days the power and magnetism of the holy waters is amplified, and the crowds swell. On these days, the ordinary bathing of pilgrims takes place in a crowd as many as twenty million.

There are three traditional Shahi Snan days: Makar Sankranti (January 14, 2013), Mauni Amavasya (February 10, 2013) and Vasant Panchami (February 15, 2013). There are other spiritually auspicious bathing days, but these three are the great days of the Royal Procession. The heads of the Akharas, the monastic orders of renunciants, are the kings of the Kumbh Mela. They ride atop elephants, tractors, or flatbed trucks, elaborately decorated with flowers and surmounted by the umbrella of royalty. Behind them follow the members of the Akhara, carrying the insignia of their order, their scantily clad or completely naked bodies besmeared with ash for the sacred bathing.

The orders of Akharas are given priority and exclusive rights to bathing at the Sangam on these auspicious days. In the past, especially in Haridwar, there were often battles between Akharas for precedence to bathe at the most sacred time. However, today the bathing order has been fixed. James Lochtefeld writes about the Haridwar Kumbh Mela, "Since the early eighteen hundreds, the Mela authorities—first British, and later Indian—have maintained the established bathing order, freezing into custom and privilege what had once been claimed solely by force of arms."[8]

AKHARAS: Ascetic Encampments

Pilgrims are drawn by the prospect of *darshan*, the "sacred sight" of the saints, which is the power of simply beholding them and receiving their blessing. Dilip Kumar Roy and Indira Devi, urban pilgrims to the Kumbh Mela, found that "it was possible to see . . . the heart of India, anchored still to her faith in *sadhus* [the holy men, the ascetics] and to her veneration for spiritual values."[9] What characterizes the Kumbh Mela every twelve years is not only its vast size, but also the massive presence of the orders of the sadhus. These orders are referred to as Akharas and there are thirteen represented at the Kumbh Mela, both Shaivite and Vaishnavite. According to tradition, again without written record, it was the great eighth-century philosopher Shankara who instigated the gathering of ascetic orders at the *mela*. He is said to have established *mathas*, the headquarters of orders of ascetics, at the four compass points of India. Coming together in conclaves on a regular basis has become part of *melas*, here as well as elsewhere in India. It was estimated by authorities that some 200,000 ascetics were present at the 2013 Kumbh Mela.

The ascetics also participate in the yearning for immortality. Strictly speaking, they have already died. Initiation into an ascetic order includes symbolically lying upon one's own cremation pyre. *Diksha*—the initiation into the Akhara orders takes place at the Kumbh Mela. When their bodies are adorned with ashes, they are the ashes of another life, or perhaps the ashes of the fire that they keep constantly burning in their tent compounds. They are conquerors of death.

At the Kumbh Mela, some of the most flamboyant ascetics enact their indifference to discomfort and pain, holding one arm in the air for years, lying on a bed of nails, or sitting in meditation in an iron swing, hung over a burning fire. Typically, they go barefoot winter and summer, conquering cold and heat. Their flagrant rejection of the comforts of settled life empowers them in a world dominated by consumerism and the concept of what they call "getting and keeping."

Pilgrims flock to the Kumbh Mela by the hundreds of thousands, not only to bathe in the sacred waters, but also to receive the blessings of the ascetics whom they have never seen in such numbers. They press forward to glimpse the *babas*, as they call them, in the great Shahi Snan processions. Many

SADHUS IN THEIR CAMP

pilgrims aspire for *darshan* of the holy ones. To see the *babas* up close, pilgrims may venture into the dense neighborhood of the Akharas, to perhaps converse with them, or simply to have their silent blessing.

As the dates of the Kumbh Mela approach, each of the orders receives a formal invitation to the *mela* from the government authorities in charge. The event is called Pravesh, or the "Entrance," and it begins when the Akharas and their generals, the Mahamandaleshvars make their processional entry into the Kumbh Mela grounds. This signals the beginning of the encampment that will last for nearly two months. In the build-up to this moment, however, workers have already set up camp. In 2013 the Akharas' allotments of land, called "Sector 4," were in the choicest area of the Kumbh Mela grounds, nearly adjacent to the riverbank. The perimeter of each encampment is laid out and each order has a *bhumi puja* (earth prayer), to sanctify the ground at the central altar of the camp. Each camp raises a huge flagpole to symbolize the deity of the Akhara. Great gateways are built along one of the main roads to mark the entryway into the Akhara.

Both in numbers and in real estate, the largest Akhara of the Kumbh Mela encampment is the Juna Akhara. Like others, this was formerly a militarized monastic order that included traders and warrior ascetics. They would compete for precedence at each *mela*, including bathing rights and rights to receive the

SWAMI CHIDANANDA AND FOLLOWERS TALKING ABOUT THE GREEN KUMBH

alms of pilgrims. Of course, asceticism has to do with power: the particular kind of power called *tapas* is associated with renunciation and ascetic practice. The power of the great ascetics is very much a counterpoint to kingly power, an alternative that is asserted, as we have seen, in the Shahi Snan processions.

The Kumbh Mela is a time when renouncers and ascetics gather as an order. They initiate members, and the initiation ceremonies in which the new members are shaven and naked as newborns, constitute one of the important iconic moments of the *mela*. In their *mela* conclaves, the Akharas also discuss policies. They elect officers. Indeed, at the *melas*, the Akharas demonstrate an astonishing display of complex, hierarchical organization despite commonly held misconceptions that they are a loose band of other-worldly and usually solitary renouncers.

GURUS and TEACHINGS: Spiritual, National, Social, and Environmental

The sector of the Akharas is a densely populated area not unlike the ancient urban heart of an old Indian city. On the other hand, the broad avenues that crisscross the flood plain are lined with camps of another kind—the pavilions and halls and housing of the teachers, *acharyas*, and their followers. In the vast Kumbh city, some of the teachers have real estate in both the Akhara sector and in the more spacious "suburbs." For instance, one of the most prominent camps is that of Avdeshanand Giri Maharaj, the Acharya Mahamandaleshvar of the Juna Akhara. Spread over acres, his camp includes a capacious assembly hall, a traditional fire pit to perform Vedic rituals, a huge dining hall and kitchen that feeds thousands of ascetics and pilgrims every day, a free medical clinic, a shop selling essentials at cost, and a bookstore. The camp is managed entirely by volunteers from across the world. Their quarters are of temporary but sturdy construction, with basic electricity and water. The administrative offices and the residence of Avdeshanand himself are in a large central compound.

The Camp of Radha Raman Prem Samsthan at the edge of the Kumbh Mela grounds provides a different glimpse into the meanings of the *mela*. The perimeter of the camp is a series of tents housing those who have come for the month-long discipline of the Kalpavas. There are also tents for toilets and showers, and there is a kitchen refectory tent. In the center is a spacious meeting hall tent with a raised platform on one side for the daily teachings from the Bhagavata Purana. The teachers, Srivatsa Goswami and his wife Sandhya, intersperse the narratives of Krishna with devotional classical

singing. The crowd includes many Bengalis, the followers of this form of Krishna devotion based in Brindavan, as well as devotees from all over India. During the opening weeks, this camp hosts an interfaith dialogue conference offering teachings by Jewish, Buddhist, Muslim, Christian, and Sikh leaders, enabling an interfaith experience in the heart of the Kumbh Mela.

Green KUMBH

The 2013 Kumbh Mela authorities called it a "Green Kumbh." They banned polythene plastic bags from the site and called on NGOs, educational institutions, and religious leaders to spread environmental awareness at the gathering. The internationally known teacher, Swami Chidananda from Paramarth Niketan ashram in Rishikesh, launched a series of green initiatives. Noting the ineffectiveness of the Government of India's Ganga Action Plan, Chidananda took the GAP acronym for the Ganga Action Parivar (*parivar* meaning "family"). He said it would be necessary for Indians to act together on behalf of Mother Ganga, with the urgency of a family protecting the health of their mother. During the Kumbh Mela, Chidananda hosted a two-day meeting of stakeholders, including the Muslim chief minister of Uttarakhand, Dr. Aziz Qureshi (who advocated for the endangered Himalayan landscape), as well as the mayors of the major cities along the Ganga that could make the biggest difference in stemming river pollution through sewage and industrial waste.

Throughout the *mela,* Green Kumbh efforts were visible. There were paid sanitation workers with red aprons and long nets, fishing litter and marigold offerings out of the river. Thin cotton reusable bags were offered as substitutes for plastic. Chidananda also piloted a program for repurposing the eco-friendly toilets used during the *mela* for other pilgrimage sites. Along with members of his community, Chidananda made daily sweeps along the riverbank, picking up litter and marigold garlands, making the cleaning of the Ganga a visible reality. Their tips for pilgrims, with the do's and don'ts of pilgrimage included, "If your offering (to the Ganga) is in a plastic bag, make sure to take the offering out of the bag before offering it to the Sangam, and recycle the plastic bag. The Sangam is a great purifier, but plastics kill all the life in Her waters and along Her banks!"

PRAYAG: Meanings of Sacrifice

The name Prayag refers to the *yajna* or *yaga,* "the sacrifice," the greatest of Vedic rites, said to have been performed by the creator at the time of creation. The triangular area between the two rivers is the great sacrificial ground, the earth-altar called the *vedi.* The ancient sacrifice was the elaborate and expensive rite of kings and wealthy sponsors. At this place, however, as with other great *tirthas,* the meaning and power of the sacrifice is ascribed to simpler and more widely accessible acts of faith, namely pilgrimage and bathing in the sacred waters. One contemporary *sadhu* at the 2013 Kumbh Mela put it this way in an interview in his tent headquarters, next to his *dhuni* or fire pit: The significance of this whole thing is in the word *prayag* itself. The prefix "pra" means the first, the foremost, the original; and "yag" is yajna, the sacrifice. So, Prayag, where we are sitting, is the foremost place of sacrifice. This is the best place to make sacrifice and this is the best time to sacrifice. The Kumbh Mela is a macrocosm of sacrifice. In the microcosm, in the family, you have the same thing, taking place. For example, the mother sacrifices her individuality and her self-interest to make the baby as healthy as possible. Here in the ascetic community, we also make sacrifice of our self-interest, our individuality, toward the collective interest, and we become one limb of the collective. This is the sacrifice. This is Prayag.

The ones who have offered sacrifice here are many. Of old, the kings and patrons who sponsored great sacrificial rites did so for the benefit of the whole society. The ascetics, sadhus, and *sannyasis* (ascetic renouncers) cast off the life and wealth of the householder, to live a life of renunciation. The pilgrims who come sacrifice the comfort of home and often take on great hardship in order to bathe at the Sangam and receive the *darshan* of the saints.

Sacrifice of Personal WEALTH

There is another kind of *yajna* associated with the Kumbh Mela: the offering of personal wealth by donors and sponsors in order to make it possible. The administration in Allahabad sought a government budget of about INR 1.55 billion, about 300 million dollars, to put in place the infrastructure and staff for the 2013 Kumbh Mela. But beyond the roadways, bridges, and power stations, there is an enormous cost in erecting and running the temporary city of the Kumbh Mela, which comprises hundreds of large encampments constructed and maintained by traditional Akharas and religious, social, or cultural organizations. Many of these encampments are spread over tens of acres of soft river sand, and provide lodgings and boarding to thousands of ascetics and devotees for fifty-five days. They feed thousands of pilgrims two or three times a day, free of cost. Camps maintain huge pavilions with canopies and marquees for hosting religious discourses and cultural performances. In the camps of many traditional Akharas, such as the Juna Akhara, thousands of male and female ascetics burn hundreds of quintals of wood to keep their *dhunis* smoldering twenty-four hours a day.

Who covers the expenses of the Kumbh Mela? Who pays the company that supplies the tents? What about food deliveries and wood deliveries? Baba Rampuri of the Juna Akhara has been to more than a dozen Kumbh Melas

PILGRIMS IN AN ALLOTMENT FOR OPEN CAMPING

here in Allahabad as well as the other three Kumbh Mela sites. He tells us that a system of patronage has usurped the traditional role of royalty from the time of kingdoms and rajas. As the Kumbh Mela approaches, wealthy patrons usually donate to the Akharas and religious organizations to construct the encampments, which comprise makeshift accommodations, temples, assembly halls, performance areas, kitchens, and drainage and sewage systems. Once it is all in place, they donate again to maintain daily operations. In addition, many wealthy and middleclass members affiliated with gurus and the great leaders of the Akharas not only make donations, but become volunteers. Some people support the gatherings because they view it as their social responsibility, whereas others support the charities for religious reasons. In the Hindu tradition, performing acts of charity has been associated with *yajna* (sacrifice) since Vedic times. The word *yajna* is derived from the Sanskrit verb root *yaj*, which has a three-fold meaning: worship, unity, and charity.[1] In Vedic times, many kings performed royal sacrifices, such as the *ashvamedha* (horse sacrifice), in order to earn *punya*, or religious merit, and to increase the prosperity of the kingdom and its subjects. In addition, the term *dana* is used to speak of charity. Dana is the "religious gift" and in the Hindu ethos, the most powerful and fruitful gifts are what are called *gupt dan*, meaning the secret and anonymous.

There is no question that *dana*, whether anonymous or named, is what maintains the life of the Kumbh Mela. Many donors may not be inclined to share their fortunes with others for non-religious reasons. Their sacrifices and philanthropic contributions help promote humanitarian tendencies. Many of these wealthy patrons also believe that by engaging in charitable giving they earn religious merit, while at the same time help the local community socially and economically. Ultimately, these charitable sacrifices make possible the running of a fifty-five daylong event that facilitates the coexistence of millions of people from diverse religious traditions. The Kumbh Mela nourishes their faith, rejuvenates their social bonding, and helps foster a harmonious society. Moreover, the local economy is bolstered by the increase in monetary transactions that occur among thousands of businesses large and small, ranging from the construction of the temporary city to the many hawkers selling trinkets. Thus, the sacrifice of personal wealth for the Kumbh Mela helps the donor as well as society.

Sacrifice of Personal COMFORT

There is also a sacrifice on the part of those who come as pilgrims and *kalpavasis*. Millions of pilgrims who faithfully flock to the Kumbh Mela with the hope of acquiring everlasting peace are usually greeted by dust, smoke, noise, the cold, and chaos. As morning dawns over shimmering waters and sandy riverbeds, thousands of shivering pilgrims emerge from tattered tents, thatched huts, or elaborate shelters to perform rituals and to seek wisdom from the multitude of sadhus. They must make their way through the overcrowded, muddy, makeshift roads made of unevenly laid steel plates to reach the confluence and bathe in the spine-chilling water. They change clothes outdoors, and when required, use one of the 35,000 portable toilets that facilitate this huge, popup megacity. At this sacred carnival, along with the sanctity of the atmosphere, millions of participants also inhale the fine, sandy particles of ashy smog.

The hardships and adversities of the Kumbh Mela for the pilgrims are multiplied many times over for the *kalpavasis*, the spiritual aspirants who vow to spend the entire month of Magh at the Kumbh Mela devoting themselves to prayer, meditation, and *satsang* (devotional group singing.) They temporarily leave their families, stay in flimsy tents with no heating, follow a vow of celibacy, abstain from enjoying worldly pleasures, eat non-spicy vegetarian food once a day, and try to live a Spartan life of renunciation and devotion. They immerse themselves twice daily—morning and evening—in the waters of the confluence, listen to spiritual discourses, and participate in religious rituals. They also help in the daily operations of the camp.

Why do an estimated 2.5 million *kalpavasis* and tens of millions of pilgrims willingly sacrifice personal comforts and endure hardships at the Kumbh Mela? What do they receive in return? While many respond "to attain *moksa* (liberation)" or "to live a successful, prosperous life," a few responses are strikingly divergent. One volunteer at the camp of Swami Chidananda explained, "Here, I learn how to live with others, understand their viewpoints, and make adjustments so that we can work together cooperatively. We also help society. We go out every day to clean the riverfront and participate in work to preserve our environment." Laura, a *kalpavasi* from Denver, Colorado in the camp of Sai Maa Mataji said, "Sixty of us from all over the world are staying here throughout the Kumbh Mela to learn the lessons of how to dissolve our ego." Nalini, a volunteer at the Swami Avadheshanand Giri's camp, observed, "We need to practice how to be fully attached and fully detached at the same time. We spent weeks here enthusiastically erecting the whole camp, then we spent almost two months running it successfully, and then almost overnight we will need to dismantle it and leave—with total detachment. Here, we practice how to live with equanimity in this perishable world."

SWAMI AVDESHANANDA

Sacrifice of Personal BONDS

While the *kalpavasis* and pilgrims of the Kumbh renounce personal comforts for a few weeks, the hundreds of thousands of ascetics who throng the Kumbh Mela not only renounce personal comforts but also personal property, familial bonds, and communal connections for a lifetime. For many hundreds of years, ascetics have wandered the sacred geography of India, from the high Himalayas to the southern seashores, from the populated plains to the dense forests, in pursuit of this-worldly and otherworldly ends. In the fourth century BCE, during his brief incursion into northwest India, Alexander the Great is said to have been impressed after his encounter with ten Naga sadhus who pursued asceticism to the point of regarding food and clothing as detrimental to purity of thought.

The goal of the Hindu ascetics has been to acquire unusual temporal skills or abilities (*siddhis*), to experience imperturbable tranquility, or to attain the blissful beatitude in the state of liberation (*moksa*). Many are initiated into the Akhara orders during the Kumbh Mela itself. There are innumerable variations in ideologies, practices, and attire of ascetics in the different Akharas. As a group, they may be called ascetics, renouncers, saints, *sadhus*, yogis, *babas*, or *sannyasins*. What they have in common, however, is the renunciation of personal bonds.

The Bhagavad Gita teaches the practice of four physical and mental disciplines or yogas: *karmayoga* (yoga of action), *jnanayoga* (yoga of knowledge),

INITIATES ARE ADDRESSED BY SWAMI AVDESHANANDA

bhaktiyoga (yoga of devotion), and *dhyanayoga* (yoga of meditation). The ultimate goal of most yogis, whatever path they may take, is to unite with the divine. However, Sondra Hausner, who studies the wandering sadhus of the Himalayas, argues that, "Ironically, the fusion with the divine is only possible through fission, or by breaking apart from the trap of material reality, with its seeming social and physical laws of differentiation."[10] The physical, social, and psychological worlds of these renouncers are often symbolized by metaphors of sacrifice.

Most renouncers of the traditional Akharas live around *dhunis*, the personal sacred fire pits that are slow-burning symbols of the continual sacrifice they need to make in order to achieve their goals. Based upon her conversations with many renouncers, Hausner explains that a proper *dhuni* includes all five essential elements of the universe: the elements of earth, water, fire, air, and space. The mud of the fire pit represents earth; the water is kept in a small pot by the pit; the mantras recited by the sadhus represent air; fire, of course, is kindled in the *dhuni*; and space pervades and sustains the four other elements. The world of five elements present in a *dhuni* represents both the outer physical body of the renouncer and the inner psychological body, both of which will be burned one day and turned into ashes.[11]

Thus, the sacrifices of thousands of *dhunis* at the Kumbh Mela represent the macrocosm and microcosm of Hindu renouncers. The ash produced by the fire, known as *vibhuti* or *bhasma*, signifies the fact that all substances reduce to the same grey dust one day. It reminds the renouncers as well as

others of the impermanence of all material forms. The fire at a *dhuni* keeps
a renouncer's sacrifice alive by reminding him to break away from the outer
world of social relations and material gratifications as well as from the inner
world of thoughts and cognitions, the fission with the mundane required for
the fusion with divine.

What do ascetics do at the Kumbh Mela? Apart from the ritualistic bathing
and public blessing for which they are famous, they in fact pursue their spiritual endeavors in a myriad of ways. Sri Sri Ravishankar explains:

> There are various methods and ways of worshipping in the Hindu
> tradition. Some do satsang, some simply sit with the dhuni, some
> sit in vairagya that is total dispassion, some just bless those who
> come to them, and some don't do anything. They are just there.
> You find all sorts of sadhus at the Kumbh Mela. It is like a spiritual
> expo. In some places, you find that it is beyond reason. You can't
> reason out why they do what they are doing. That is freedom of
> worship. Everybody is free to find their own path, their own way.
> There is no saying whether it is correct or not correct. Everybody
> is free to explore their way into spirituality. An explorer doesn't
> say this is right and that is wrong. He just wants to experiment with

SWAMI CHIDANANDA, SWAMI AVDESHANANDA, AND OTHER PROMINENT RELIGIOUS LEADERS

his life, experiment with truth. In the process of experimentation you may make wrong turns, and learn from that as well. That is a beauty of Hinduism. Hinduism is basically liberal. It doesn't say that you have to believe in just one book or one thing. It gives individual freedom of thinking, freedom of practicing rituals the way they would like. So, it is an inherent characteristic of Hinduism—harmony in diversity.[12]

The Kumbh Mela facilitates the coming together of ascetics, scholars, practitioners, volunteers, and pilgrims from diverse traditions. Most participate in discourses, discussions, reflections, and meditation with the positive intention of elevating the self and benefiting society. People cannot visit all the different places ascetics and scholars come from, but they can all converge in one place to share their thoughts and experiences, and learn from one another.

Sacrifice of Differences: Ingathering of HINDU INDIA

One common meaning of the word sacrifice in the English language is "an act of giving up something valued for the sake of something else

BABA RAM PURI

regarded as more important or worthy."[13] In this context, the sacrifice of differences may well engender the more important and worthy value of human harmony. Yet, as we know, many people are not willing to sacrifice their differences for the sake of social cohesion and peace. Even if we wish to accommodate the religious other, we are sometimes too preoccupied with our perceptions to act in a manner that respects diversity. Despite knowing the flipside of our differences, many of us are not ready to let go of even small things or ideas of ours that might cause divisiveness. Hence, it takes a conscious effort to let go, to sacrifice our personal opinions, beliefs, and differences, even temporarily, for the larger good of society.

Renouncers at the Kumbh Mela are no exception to this human tendency to become quarrelsome over differences. Factional feuds among the orders of ascetics come up occasionally on issues such as which Akhara ascetics will be first in line for the Shahi Snana, the royal ritual bathing on the most auspicious days. Sometimes an Akhara threatens to boycott the Shahi Snana if it is not allowed to take part in a certain order, at a certain place, or at a certain time. Kama Maclean refers to the discordant impasse between the Juna Akhara and the Mela administration at the 1998 Haridwar Kumbh Mela.[14] However, three years later, at the 2001 Maha Kumbh Mela at Allahabad, the mela administration and Akharas reached a historic agreement on the sequencing and timing of the Shahi Snan. Hailing it as one of the most significant achievements of the Kumbh Mela, J.S. Mishra notes, "The mutual respect, understanding and the overwhelming sense of accommodation on both the sides shall be regarded as the most important milestone in the management of this Mahakumbh of the new millennium."[15]

The fact that there is agreement at one level, however, does not necessarily mean that there will be concord at other levels. Occasional inter- and intra-Akhara conflicts arise, as do disputes between the Akharas and the *mela* administration. Considering the demographic, spatial, and spiritual vastness of the Kumbh Mela, conflicts are bound to come up, especially about space allocation. Nevertheless, these conflicts do not diminish the sense of commonality that is the basis for religious, social, and communal harmony. One common belief among many pilgrims is that the divine power of the confluence of the three rivers is so redemptive that regardless of one's imperfections, just bathing here during the auspicious times bestows *moksa* in this lifetime. Similarly, most religious discourse stresses the common Hindu ideology that all living beings are essentially *atman*, the inner breath—the spirit that pervades all experience. While similarities bind the ascetics and pilgrims through unifying threads, there is no need to resolve differences in order to live together.

Baba Rampuri of Juna Akhara offers many examples to illustrate the dissolution of theological and ideological differences. The Juna Akhara, one of the largest with about 400,000 ascetics, is divided into fifty-two lineages. It is fundamentally a Shaivite tradition established by Adi Shankaracarya, the commonly held first guru and yet the chosen deity of all 52 lineages is Guru Dattatreya, who is regarded as an avatara of Lord Vishnu. Hence, the ascetics of the Juna Akhara greet each other with "Om Namo Narayana," invoking one of the names of Vishnu even though they worship Lord Shiva.

The Juna Akhara tradition has not only embraced diverse Hindu deities and gurus, but has also accommodated Buddhists and Muslims within the tradition and exalted them as the head of their lineages. Baba Rampuri notes that one of the fifty-two lineages of the Juna Akhara was established by Padmasambhava, also known as Guru Rinpoche "Precious Guru." Padmasambhava was instrumental in transmitting Vajrayana Buddhism to Tibet and is considered an emanation of Buddha Amitabha. Recognizing that the Juna Akhara includes a lineage associated with the Vajrayana Buddhist tradition, the Dalai Lama often visits the Juna Akhara camp during Kumbh Melas. In addition, the lineage to which Rampuri himself belongs is known as the Multani Marhi of the Juna Akhara. It is called Multani Marhi because a Hindu-Sufi saint called Multani Baba, also known by Hindus as Keshav Puri Baba and by Muslims as Pir Shah Shams-i Tabriz, the teacher of Rumi, established it. The tomb of Multani Baba is located just outside the city of Multan, Pakistan with which his name is connected. Multani Baba had Hindu as well as Muslim disciples. He wrote books on both Sufi and Hindu subjects. When he left his body, he gave instructions that he be interred in a traditional Hindu sannyasi way, sitting in a meditative posture in an underground cave, with mala in hand. He maintained, however, that a *qabr*, a Muslim grave, even if empty, should be built next to the *samadhi*. Beyond the Juna Akhara, however, it is important to note that there are three Udasin Akharas, comprised of Sikhs following Guru Nanak and guided by the Sikh scripture, the Guru Granth Sahib. These Udasin ascetics are also an integral part of the traditional Akharas present at the Kumbh Mela.

In so many ways, the Kumbh Mela facilitates the coexistence of diverse traditions that have partially sacrificed their theological, ideological, cultural, and social differences in order to engage with one another and to seek understanding and even harmony.

Religious teachers from heterogeneous traditions converge in this multicultural, multi-faith event with their own perspectives, purposes, and prejudices. While they share the same space with each other, many of them also share sentiments of mutual acceptance and assimilation and thereby impart the spirit of pluralism through their discourses at the Kumbh Mela.

Many religious leaders expressed one common theme: that the Kumbh is a place where one should learn to get rid of one's ego. Ego, the sense of "I" and "me," is the root cause of arrogance, intolerance, fear, jealousy, tension, and stress. How does the Kumbh Mela help let go of ego? Sadhu Brahmaviharidas explains:

> The Kumbh is such an overwhelming experience that makes a person humble. The spiritual leaders who come to the Kumbh may have a great ashram, a permanent ashram. But here, everything is temporary and everybody is on the same plane. Spiritual leaders who come to the Kumbh realize that they are not the only one; there are hundreds out there who are leading the masses. Whether they say it or not, in their heart they accept it. Before the grandeur of the Ganga and Yamuna, in the eternity of the sands of time, before the cosmic force, everybody is on the same earth, on the same level. And they also accept the fact that other people are doing good work. So, even spiritual leaders are humbled, which is very important for a leader. Even the followers are humbled when they see thousands of other followers. So, this gathering itself, which humbles both the devotees and the spiritual leaders before the energy of God, leads perforce to harmony. Ego leads to disharmony, humility leads to harmony. They carry back with them a lot of faith, a lot of hope, and also a lot of humility. For whatever reason you come to the Kumbh, whether you are searching for a guru, or whether you are a guru searching for more disciples, you are humbled. And this humility leads to harmony.[16]

Conclusion

The Kumbh Mela is a confluence of sacred rivers and sacred time, with a colossal number of people. Millions of lay pilgrims, religious practitioners, volunteers, and ascetics live together in the tent city created on the huge expanse of sandy riverbeds. Adherents of many Indian traditions sometimes antithetical to each other, converge to observe a single ritual—bathing in the rivers. And they come, as well, to benefit from the company of spiritual teachers and aspirants. There is no other ecumenical event in the world, held on such a vast scale, where ascetics and lay people from theologically disparate traditions coexist and coalesce. The Kumbh Mela pragmatically promotes the pluralism inherent in Indian civilization by creating the spatial and psychological conditions in which followers of disparate traditions live together, reflecting the spirit, "By whatever path you go, you will have to lose yourself in the one."

1   Giorgio Bonazzoli, "Prayaga and its Kumbha Mela," *Purana*, vol. XIX, no. 1 (January 1977), pp. 113–15.

2   D.P. Dubey, *Prayaga: the Site of Kumbha Mela* (New Delhi: Aryan Books International, 2001), p. 133.

3   Ibid., p. 124.

4   Ibid., p. 123.

5   Ibid., p. 124.

6   Kama Maclean, *Pilgrimage and Power: the Kumbh Mela in Allahabad, 1765–1954* (Oxford: Oxford University Press, 2008). p. 104.

7   Dubey 2001 (see note 2), p. 121.

8   James Lochtefeld, "The Construction of the Kumbha Mela," *South Asian Popular Culture*, vol. 2, no. 2 (Oct 2004), p. 104.

9   Dilip Kumar Roy and Indira Devi, *Kumbha: India's Ageless Festival* (Mumbai: Bharatiya Vidya Bhavan, 2009), p. xvi.

10 Sondra L. Hausner, *Wandering with Sadhus: Ascetics in the Hindu Himalayas* (Bloomington: Indiana University Press, 2007), p. 36.

11 Ibid., p. 121.

12 Sri Sri Ravishankarji, *The Art of Living*, http://sris-riravishankar.org, http://www.artofliving.org/ Interview: 2-10-2013.

13 "Sacrifice." *Oxford Dictionaries*, http://oxforddictionaries.com/definition/english/sacrifice?q=sacrifice.

14 Maclean 2008 (see note 6), p. 5.

15 J.S. Mishra, *Mahakumbh, the Greatest Show on Earth* (Allahabad: Har-Anand Publications, 2004), p. 90.

16 Sadhu Brahmaviharidas, BAPS Swaminarayan Sanstha, interview on January 26, 2013, http://www.baps.org.

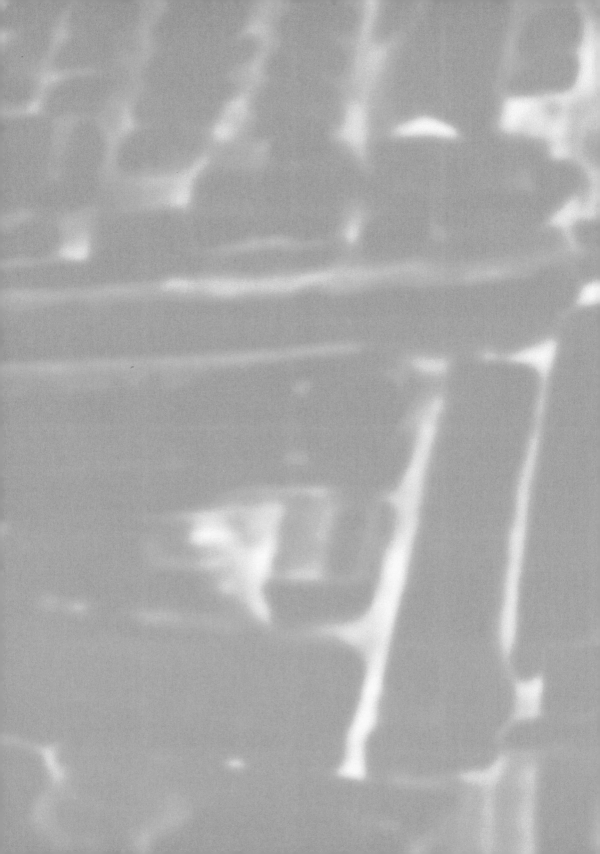

URBANISM

The Ephemeral
MEGACITY

RAHUL MEHROTRA & FELIPE VERA

THE KUMBH MELA:
A City with an Expiration Date

The Kumbh Mela, a Hindu festival held every twelve years, is an extreme example of a religious congregation that generates a temporary settlement. Approximately five million people gather for fifty-five days, with an additional flux of ten to twenty million people coming for twenty-four-hour cycles on the six main bathing dates. The aggregation of units converges in an endless texture of cotton, plastic, plywood, and other materials all of which is organized by a smart infrastructural grid for roads, electricity, and waste, configuring the biggest ephemeral megacity in the world.[1]

The ephemeral city of the Kumbh Mela is not only framed by a strong cultural ecology, but also located in a highly dynamic physical geography, affected seasonally by the monsoon, which moves over the Indian peninsula into the dense network of sacred nodes across the sacred landscape. By superimposing these two networks—religious settlements and different forms of hydrology—one can realize how this sacred geography is affected by the displacement of rainwater across the Indian subcontinent. Hydrological flows are at the very core of almost every sacred settlement in the region.

Looking closer at the state of Uttar Pradesh, one can clearly understand how the presence of the sacred rivers Ganges and Yamuna enable the occurrence of the Kumbh Mela. The rivers are key geographic features that define the towns they run through—they serve as major transportation routes for people and goods and shape the entire system of roads and regional infrastructure. Both of these sacred rivers configure the floodplain on which the temporary city for the Kumbh Mela settles. This temporary city has extremely elastic boundaries because of the monsoon's effect on the amount of water that moves through the shifting rivers. The vacant space, especially along the riverbanks of the Ganges (Ganga in previous and pursuant sections), changes completely with the drastic expansion of the river's surface during the monsoon season. From the month of May until late October, the whole plain is inundated, leaving less than eight weeks in between for the deployment of the ephemeral megacity. This short timeframe creates many design and planning challenges for the construction and administration of the Kumbh Mela.

How can we even start to manage this rapid, unprecedented process of urbanization that aims to assemble a city in a matter of weeks, on an area that is no larger than the span between the North End and Roxbury in Boston or the northernmost extreme of Central Park and the southernmost extreme of

VIEW OF KUMBH MELA STREET. ALLAHABAD 2013

Manhattan Island in New York City? How are these practical issues, such as the aggregation and displacement of millions of people toward the Sangam on major bathing days, managed by the administration?

The modulation of time in the process of deployment, as well as ritualistic thresholds set on the bathing days, must be managed in relation to natural cycles, most notably the monsoon season. These are the logistical dilemmas that strongly define the forms in which the ephemeral city is erected. Unlike a more permanent city where the construction of the physical environment happens as a simultaneous aggregation of relatively permanent parts that progressively materialize the space, the Kumbh Mela takes form like a choreographic process of temporal urbanization, happening in coordination with environmental dynamics. It comprises five stages: 1) planning, 2) construction, 3) assembly, 4) operation and disassembly, and 5) deconstruction. These stages are directly linked to the makeshift context and timings determined by the presence of the monsoon in the region. Therefore the diagrams and maps in this book show, among other things, how the deployment of the city unfolds over time and in particular how the fluxes of people and the monsoon are coordinated. Large fluctuations of people and the shifting of the river make the Kumbh Mela site an unpredictable environment for addressing even the most basic design challenges.

Right after the level of the Ganges recedes, when the monsoon season is over, the ephemeral city is assembled over the course of a few weeks. Once completed, it provides for the biggest public gathering in the world—

a pop-up megacity of roads, bridges, shelter, as well as a plethora of social infrastructures such as temporary hospitals, markets, police stations, and social centers, each replicating the functions of a permanent city. Issues of social inclusion, urban diversity, and even expressions of democracy arise under the framework of neutralizing grids of roads that differ in structure, module, and geometry. The accumulation of units converge in an endless texture of textiles, plastic, plywood, and several other materials, each organized by a smart infrastructural grid that articulates roads, electricity, and waste.

In the following section of this essay, we will try to provide a glimpse at possible answers to the fundamental questions surrounding governance, power structures, the potential of the grid as a neutralizing design element, and diverse layers of infrastructure.

Governance

The banks of the rivers that are normally configured into a rural landscape, full of seasonal crops, are transformed into a temporary city of extreme proportions that lasts as long as the duration of the festival. The Kumbh Mela, similar to most permanent cities, is subject to the complex political dynamics that operate at both the national and regional levels. Administrative oversight during the Kumbh Mela forms from a normative framework that is similar to any urban context or to any other city in India. This ephemeral governance intentionally allows the land surrounding the confluence of the Ganges and the Yamuna to quickly transform from a simple, rural landscape into one of the most densely populated and rapidly urbanized spaces on earth.

After the waters of the Ganges river retreats, the riverbank becomes an interstitial space between three distinct locales—the city of Allahabad from one side, the small industrial village of Jhunsi from the other, and a still undeveloped span of rural land between. The coordination among these three settings normally works as a balanced and integrated regional system. However, during the Kumbh Mela process, these areas experience a temporary expansion of infrastructure in the form of railway stations, street and bridge connections, and other mobility infrastructures all to accommodate the massive influx of people and goods that demand special coordination and management. This coordination is resolved by the creation of a special regulatory framework that provides for the appointment of a *Mela Adhikari* (district magistrate) who has the power to administrate the site through an ephemeral jurisdictional framework that exists during and after the event. Besides taking care of the logistical and management aspects of the deployment of the temporary city, the Mela Adhikari is in charge of developing partnerships with religious institutions that participate in the Kumbh. The Mela Adhikari also coordinates the allocation of land and negotiates with different groups and orders. By the time the Ganges has retreated, the administration must have transformed this complex spatial and political landscape into a simple grid that divides the space into 14 self-sufficient sectors, upon which the grid and infrastructure of the Kumbh Mela is deployed. (This is represented in a map on page 14 that captures the spatial parcelization).

Metrics

The extent of the deployment is enormous. The whole area of the Kumbh Mela, commonly referred to as *nagri*,[2] covered 23.5 square kilometers, a measurement that includes the rivers. However, the floodplain, once the river recedes, offers an additional fifteen square kilometers of land for the temporary tent city to be constructed. Official figures given by the administration estimated that 100 million people were projected to visit the 2013 Kumbh Mela throughout the course of the festival.[3]

It is difficult to think of other temporary settlements that are planned to host such an increment of thirty times its regular size. Moreover, it is even more difficult to find another case of a temporary urban configuration that can host roughly the same number of people as other permanent megacities like New York or Delhi. The sense of elastic accommodation within the temporary settlement is outstanding and unique.

In early March, people start leaving the Kumbh Mela and with them the different pieces of the city, which are progressively disassembled and recycled, while softer organic materials are left in the ground to be reabsorbed, either by the same agricultural fields or washed by the river in the next monsoon. However, most of the pieces, as we will discuss later, will be reincorporated into regional economies of construction or stored in order to serve future versions of the festival. One can understand the true extent the Kumbh Mela has by closely examining the metrics. For instance, by tracing the aerial Google image, it shows how different elements were added to the preexisting layers of infrastructure in Allahabad. Another eighteen pontoon bridges were built to supplement the existing bridges that connect the floodplain. Within the city, the grid gets its structure by the deployment of more than 150 kilometers of temporary roads. The transport infrastructure in the city organizes vehicles in more than ninety parking lots that are mostly open in the periphery of the settlement. In addition, five temporary bus stations were set up, along with seven train stations that were used as a primary means of entry and egress for visitors. Similarly, more than 3,500 buses were deployed during the bathing days to transport the influx of millions of additional pilgrims that visit the Kumbh on the five auspicious dates. Additionally, a grid comprised of thirty police stations and thirty fire stations operates in parcels of 20 x 20 meters, each assigned to a security official that oversees the event. Throughout the area, eighty-five closed-circuit cameras were deployed, as well as fifty-six watchtowers. In short, a fine grid of infrastructure becomes the defining matrix for the temporary settlement.

Grid

The question of how the floodplain is subdivided and how the area of the river gets occupied takes us to another important dimension in the planning—the incorporation and refinement of "the grid" as a basic planning instrument. From archival documents it is clear that since the mid-nineteenth-century, British colonial influences utilized the grid as the main rationalization for infrastructural deployments and the organization of the space. The implementation of a grid was incorporated as an artifact designed and managed by the state. The grid as an abstract construct is widely utilized

TENTS IN THE KUMBH MELA. ALLAHABAD 2013

VIEW OF THE KUMBH MELA AT NIGHT. ALLAHABAD 2013

in cities as a neutralizing mechanism that supports diversity within regular patterns, becoming the only constant in the evolution of cities. However, at the Kumbh Mela it is not only the built fabric that continues to change as the city develops; it is also the grounded territory on which the grid is deployed. Therefore, the geometry of the grid for each version of the Kumbh Mela must be adapted to a new morphology that informs both its structure and internal organization.

As the final morphology of the floodplain is unknown until the river actually recedes, most of the design is based on a certain level of structural flexibility and the ability to adapt to uncertain contexts. Other than the need for connecting with the pre-existing and more permanent infrastructures of Allahabad, there are no other constrains on the deployment of the network. Therefore, the final form of the city is the result of a progression of uncertainties, ranging from speculation about the possible physical forms that the floodplain might take once the river recedes, to the estimation of the timespan of the monsoon, and the approximation of the expected number of people that would arrive to the city on the major bathing days.

Very early in the process, before the exact location of the streets is even determined, the whole *nagri* gets divided into sectors—fourteen in the case of the 2013 Kumbh Mela. Camps are located in each of these sectors, thus creating a well-thought grid for basic infrastructures such as water is imperative to the overall functionality. The physical division of the space gets reflected in the administrative structure. The Sector Magistrate—the principal authority that deals with negotiations during the design process and oversees the deployment and management of the infrastructure within the space—conceived each section as an independent and almost self-sufficient unit. Although sectors are intended to work independently, different sectors accomplish different functions that facilitate the ephemeral city as a whole. Some sectors, like sector four located near the Sangam, are more socially active and culturally relevant while other sectors, such as sector eleven, which is located more in the periphery, serve as logistical nodes or transportation hubs that receive the city's provisions before they are distributed across the grid.

Unlike other temporary cities where the grids are repetitious in a way that erases originality and identity, the basic idea of the Kumbh Mela provides for unique, open areas with camps that are constructed without preconceived internal regulation over religious communities. This gives each community the organizational authority over their own space in a way that enables the expression of their internal structure and identity by advocating for spatial singularity. The variable spatial organization can be seen walking within the *nagri*—some camps are more spontaneously and incrementally arranged, while others are more systematically structured into rigid grids. This is how the grid's neutralizing potential to facilitate

TENTS IN THE KUMBH MELA. ALLAHABAD 2013

democratic self-expression is employed in the initial planning strategies at the Kumbh Mela. Unlike other temporal configurations seen in some refugee camps or natural-disaster shelters, the temporary condition of the Kumbh Mela space does not remove individuality, which ultimately provides for the construction of several identities within the city. One example of this sort of originality is on display in the form of the gardens created during the forty-four-day duration—they provide a temporary yet personalized aesthetic in the face of the fact that the ground in which they are planted will be flooded again.

The grid not only organizes the residential space, but it also forms the diverse layers of infrastructure such as water, electricity, sewerage, roads, and bridges—built more as relational fluxes than as a collection of superimposed elements. While the word "infrastructure" typically conveys the images of heavy and corporeal constructions, at the Kumbh Mela, smart processes of incremental aggregation reach the scale of the interventions by presenting a soft infrastructure. The roads, for instance, are constructed from steel plates that can be carried by local people without any heavy machinery. The unspecific and adjustable technology of simple metal clamps used for connecting pieces of infrastructure provides for an easy disassembly. These pieces of metal are then reintroduced into the regional construction economies once the festival is over. On account of the ease that this infrastructure can be dismantled, there is prompt and effective recycling of any material used to construct the city. The paraphernalia that is not reused is typically degradable thatch or bamboo and gets incorporated or merged with the natural terrain through organic decomposition. This allows for the seamless return of the space from a temporal city to agricultural fields.

DEPLOYMENT Process

Standing at the Kumbh Mela at night looking towards an endless functioning city where the temporary construction of the *nagri* is fused with the city of Allahabad, there are two things that one cannot avoid asking: 1) How was this enormous city planned in terms of scale and complexity? 2) How is the city actually constructed? One of the most interesting elements about the construction process of the city is that unlike more static and permanent cities—where the whole is comprised of the aggregations of smaller parts, constructed in different moments that are tied together by pre-existing and connecting urban infrastructure—the city of the Kumbh Mela is planned and built all at once, as a unitary effort.

The flow of the deployment process is very dynamic. Even though the 2013 Kumbh Mela was held from January 14, 2013 (the day of Makar Sankranti) to March 10, 2013 (the day of Maha Shivratri), the preparations for deploying the settlement started several months in advance. During the monsoon season, meetings were held in different offices outside the boundaries of the Kumbh Mela while materials were transported into vacant spaces near the floodplain for the fabrication process to start. When the water receded at the end of October 2012, the ground was leveled and the roads were marked, signaling the initial deployment of the grid on the ground. The only part that was constructed beforehand was sector one, which is located outside the floodplain. This sector hosted the administrative apparatus and different governmental institutions. When the river level subsided, the materials were brought in and the pontoons were built. By early November 2012, the layers of infrastructure were in place. Electric poles, sandbags for containing the shifting river, and the temporary walls for the different sectors were all organized from plans drawn up by the administration. Later in November, the road assembly started and the perimeters of the *nagri* were plotted. In early December 2012, construction started and a settlement rich with texture, using different kinds of fabric, clad over bamboo enclosures began to take form. By January 2013, the city was completed and operative.

In March 2013, all of the constructions were dismantled into parts and taken back to storage or resold. At some point the river will flood the traces of the city until the following October, when the river will again reach its lowest levels and the landscape will become a productive, agricultural site that endures for twelve Ganges cycles, until a new version of the Kumbh Mela emerges again in 2024.

The construction process is made more complex by the short construction and deconstruction timeframes as well as the city's enormity in terms of the deployment. Given the compressed timeframes and the scale of the city, all decisions necessitate a precise and productive balance that leaves space for readjustment and maneuverability. The design, planning, and implementation of what becomes the city of the Kumbh Mela are led by a specific team, which coordinates the whole as a single project in a very centralized design process. This enables the team to address many complex issues, such as the design response for effective construction delivery; the capacity to allocate people and goods; the management of risks and resources; and the oversight of handling diverse economies driven by public and private agents. The plan coordinates most of the material components that conform the settlement. Vertical limits, pontoon bridges, streets, electricity lines, and health facilities are all deployed systematically,

VIEW OF THE ROADS OF THE KUMBH MELA. ALLAHABAD 2013

in coordination with the cycles of the river. This process runs in parallel with the development of governance and management structures that drive the negotiations with the anticipated needs of the different religious groups and devotees that attend.

The Kumbh Mela's administration has empirically come to develop a vast knowledge of the infrastructural necessities of an ephemeral city. Through repetition and incorporation after every version of the festival, the administration manages high magnitudes of tension with utmost efficiency, providing configurations that function properly in conditions that a more permanent settlement could collapse and become dysfunctional. Each function of the city calls for thick infrastructure, specific in its design and scale. Different layers of groundwork are planned and deployed by various agents. Some are completely financed and managed by the state, while others are financed by public-private partnership systems or via concessions, involving the private sector development. Generally speaking, the infrastructural demands are an exclusive responsibility of the Kumbh Mela's administration. They are charged with the responsibility of providing electricity, mobility, waste management, and facilities to manage health and risk. On the other side, the deployment of the uncountable tents for habitation is left to the private sector.

The deployment of these overlapping, structural layers is what jumpstarts the temporary city. However, the construction process starts much earlier than most on the ground realize. According to J. D. Mishra, the planning of the Maha Kumbh Mela in 2001 began in 1998, thirty-one months before the fifty-five-day festival was to start. This preparatory time span was more or less repeated for the 2013 version.

According to onsite interviews, it takes about two months for total deconstruction of the Kumbh Mela. Some of the materials are put in storage in Uttar Pradesh, so they can be reused in future iterations. Each Kumbh Mela provides its subsequent iterations fresh ideas—always trying to rethink deficiencies. When it came to decisions about the quantity, dimensions, and organization of key infrastructural elements, one of the most interesting strategies incorporated in the planning of the city was the implementation of resilience redundancy, instead of optimization. The seventeen pontoon bridges that connected both sides of the river are great examples of this, as they allowed the grid to operate effectively under extreme conditions of flux.

Following the wiring of the whole flood plain, the construction of thin membranes functioning as walls, define the space of the city in more concrete ways. These walls are built from canvas or corrugated sheets or textiles. The physical divisions of the space, defined by the Adhikari who is the district magistrate and his team, designate the structures of the sectors and the camps inside the *nagri*. The construction of vertical limits begins once the river recedes, defining the area.

By September 20, 2012, the material started arriving. On September 30, 2012 the order to start working was given. It takes five minutes to lift a dividing wall consisting of two pieces of tin and two bamboo planks as part of the enclosure walls. These are used as separating elements for social groups and activities during the Kumbh Mela.

Subunits

The distribution of risk among infrastructural subcomponents is a strategy for building resilience in the way that spatial substructures are organized inside the *nagri* or settlement. Similar to how Le Corbusier's plan of Chandigarh works in the organization of space in discrete subunits, the Kumbh Mela subdivides the space in basic operative areas called sectors, defined by the grid. Complexities relative to size are resolved by dividing the city—administratively and functionally—into self-organized camps that form an interconnected network that support the functioning of the city in a way that avoids systemic collapse in situations of crises.

Only general principles remain from one Kumbh Mela to the next because every version of the festival must be adjusted to new environmental conditions, a different number of visitors, altered economic contexts, and an ever-transforming geography that depends on the river. Newer trends in spatial organization and planning might also be incorporated. For example, the idea for the sectors is clearly something that emerged post Chandigarh. Before that festival, town planning and subdivision were implemented by more traditional methods.

The whole is divided into smaller sectors, each of which is divided into camps containing various operating parts. The 2001 Kumbh Mela comprised eleven sectors while the 2013 edition had fourteen. Most constructions within *nagri* were built out of bamboo pieces and tin. More permanent areas, like hospitals, were constructed of plywood. The government invests what is necessary to flatten the sandy ground on the banks of the Ganges and on the Yamuna, which is where the tents were located. The same contractors that build for the government also build for the Akharas, who typically receive considerable discounts.

Besides traditional religious groups like the Akharas, individual groups also bring their own contractors. For instance, many tourist agencies hire their own construction teams. The entire architecture of the Kumbh Mela is outsourced. It is the Mela Adhikari who determines discounts for holy men and fixes subcontract fees. For example, a plot of land for one tent costs approximately 1,000 rupees (20 USD). It is worth noting that in early March, almost a year before the festival began, the equipment used to build enclosures and tents is checked and repaired—it is being reused from other festivals held throughout the year across India.

Roads

The Public Works Department of the State of Uttar Pradesh is responsible for the construction of bridges and streets. It is in charge of managing both their construction and their maintenance. The team includes a head engineer who leads all operations; and on the field, there is an engineer in chief, an engineer superintendent, an executive engineer, an assistant engineer, an engineer in training, as well as other agents and unskilled laborers. Construction is supervised by the Motilal Nehru National Institute of Technology (MNIT), which performs periodic inspections. Since its last iteration, the Kumbh Mela has had to widen the major arteries that enter the city from other regions or cities such as Lucknow, Shringarpur, and Benares. The work was affected in a radius of twenty to twenty-five kilometers. This is one of several synergies between the administration of the Kumbh Mela and that of the fixed city of Allahabad.

In each version of the festival, part of the funding comes from the central and regional governments and is designated for road improvements and enhanced accessibility.

The network of roads can be classified by functionality. Two types of roads connect to the streets that serve the fixed city, some of which are local and some of which connect Allahabad to Varanasi, like the Civil Line that divides its sector in two. Other streets in the Kumbh Mela are more permanent. Known as *pucca*, they are built with bitumen, in flattened ground outside flooding areas—temporary streets made out of sand tread. The streets that cross the center of *nagri* are historic. They have remained where they are through earlier versions of the festival, and although their lines have been erased, their names remain in the memory of the inhabitants of Allahabad, even when it isn't time for the Kumbh Mela. The paths between the main streets are known as *gattas*. The main street is centrally positioned, elevated approximately twenty-four inches above ground level, with slight slopes descending from either side. In the latest edition of the Kumbh Mela these streets were made with tractors, although in previous versions they were made by hand. A series of square metal plates are laid in two lines for vehicle tires to have traction. These form the basis for the vehicular transit. Each plate is about 1 x 1 meters and six millimeters thick. An estimated total of 116 kilometers of plates were used.

Bridges

The different sectors are connected by elements that articulate mobility in an ephemeral city. The floating bridges are one of the most prominent layers of infrastructure. Their function is to provide accessibility to the camps and to help connect the edges of the Ganges River. Seventeen floating bridges were built for the 2013 Kumbh Mela. Fifteen of these bridges were set across the Ganges River and two were set across the Yamuna River. Each bridge rests on *pipas*, which are huge steel structures designed to float. 2,692 new *pipas* were built for the most recent Kumbh Mela, and 1,510 were reused from previous versions of the festival in Haridwar, Nashik, and Ujjain. Each *pipa* is thirty-two feet long, eight feet across, and weighs 5.459 tons. They are made of a very thin layer of steel that contains a large volume of air inside and each has two inspection cameras on top. The cameras are approximately sixty to seventy centimeters wide, and they are essential to inspections on the quality and performance of waterproofing systems. Inspections were conducted once the pipes were on the river to ensure the safety of the multitudes of people who crossed them. The volume of water displaced by all of the *pipas* minus the weight of the bridge determines the resistance of each bridge and therefore their capacity.

The *pipas* are placed on the water by flat trucks that incorporate elements to help them work like a lever. The pontoons have two kinds of cables connecting them. One is made of steel and goes above the water, connecting one support to another. The other is made of coir rope and goes beneath the water. A bamboo tripod is built as a structure, which becomes a transient network on which river sand-filled bags are loaded. These tripods are converted into anchors and embedded at the bottom of the river. Each pontoon is anchored separately on both sides. A distance of five meters is left between each *pipa*. Once in the water, the pontoons are connected with screwed-in beams and their surfaces were plated with wood (the same sort used for sleepers cars on trains). At the height of the Kumbh Mela, every bridge has between thirty and thirty-five persons responsible for inspecting and repairing them, in addition to two junior engineers and an assistant engineer to lead the group. Though a list of registered contractors is available, the reality is that contractors who participated in previous Kumbh Melas have the monopoly on the contracts. The bright side of this, however, is that since every new edition of the festival seems to be larger, with increased dimensions, new contractors are always finding ways to become

TENTS IN THE KUMBH MELA. ALLAHABAD 2013

incorporated. Most large contractors subcontract smaller ones, and because of this, the field displays a great fragmentation of actors. In the stages prior to the mounting of the bridges, most of the workforce hails from Allahabad, but once the assembly begins and the work gets more intense, labor is summoned from different parts of Uttar Pradesh. Both qualified and unskilled workers receive a salary in daily wages, with the wages of the former being higher.

Electricity

Electricity is one of the earliest needs in the assemblage of the city. In 2001, the Kumbh Mela accounted for 135,000 electric connections. All of the work was completed on the last day of November and tested between November 15 and December 15, as soon as the Akharas provided their energy load requirements. The grid of streets designed by Kumbh Mela's management determines the design of the electrical wiring. The government mostly finances electricity and, as is the case with almost all public expenses for the festival, 30% of the funding comes from the federal government and 70% comes from the state government. However, the state government refused to provide the funds required for the electricity during the most recent 2013 Kumbh Mela, arguing that the energy commission of the central government should pay for it. Local residents receive fixed charges per connection, instead of by the amount of electricity utilized. In previous years, a charge of forty rupees (0.8 USD) was used per electrical connection, but in 2013, the price was raised to 150 rupees (3 USD) since it used a new and more expensive energy supply system. Electricity has two types of contractors, one for materials and another for installations. The 2013 Kumbh Mela had twelve contractors working simultaneously. Implementation and maintenance are negotiated as one joint contract so that necessary repairs during the festival is covered in advance.

At the moment in which the city starts to function, the connections need to be in place in order to provide electricity to camp users. Two types of electrical infrastructures make this possible: on the one hand, there are the permanent installations that cover the entire periphery of the Kumbh Mela and which benefit the entire city. These could be considered a non-ephemeral part of the fixed city. But then there are the temporary installations that are deployed for the ephemeral city in particular. The system is organized by incorporating several substations to different camps. Once the Kumbh Mela is up and functioning, the electricity is cut during the day to prevent accidents. This measure ensures that the use of energy and electrically motored elements are minimized, reserving the use of electricity mostly for lighting and sound amplification. It is important to mention that wiring starts on October 20, 2012 after the monsoon has ended. Before that, electrical materials began to arrive in January 2012 the same month in which a final estimate of the amount of materials required is completed.

Tents

Once the infrastructure is in place, the focus shifts to creating the residences that house the pilgrims. The company Lalooji and Sons stands out from all the other contractors because it is the one that brings all the construction materials, including the tents and furniture, to the site. It has several subsidiaries managed by relatives who compete with each other. These same companies are represented in the four cities in which the Kumbh Mela occurs, and the respective contractors (Lalooji and Brothers or Cousins) are used again once the sites have been designated. Together they plan out the various components of the camp. There are different design units available, such as 1) Kitchen; 2) Area bathrooms (luxury bathrooms or separate latrines); 3) Tents of various types; 4) Tin; and 5) Areas covered, parliamentary enclosures. Different types of fences are made of *ballis* (bamboo), while pipes or trusses are used to save great lights. The dimensions of the lights covered by trusses can range from seventy-two to 120 feet. The typologies of available tents have different sizes: 1) Darbaru (VIP) 45′x 30′ 2′; 2) Swiss Cottage 30′ x 30′; 3) Staff Tent 24′ x 25′; 4) Choldary 18′ x 18′.

Everything provided in the Kumbh Mela is directed to very different classes of people, with different levels of luxury depending on the class to which the product is oriented, (e.g., presidential bed sheets or ordinary sheets; padded high chairs or wooden chairs; and for VIP customers, nothing can be reused and everything must be purchased specifically for each iteration of the Kumbh Mela).

Social INFRASTRUCTURE

Besides the construction of the tents, the Kumbh Mela has several buildings that replicate the functionality of permanent cities. There is a network of health infrastructure comprised by temporary hospitals and diagnosis points spread across the festival grounds. There are twenty-two administrative health sectors conducting different "health programs." People from the administration were very emphatic when it came to making the distinction between hospitals and health programs. Hospitals are meant to receive and

EDGES OF THE SANGAM, KUMBH MELA. ALLAHABAD 2013

treat people for very minor health issues, and do not operate or perform complex procedures. The health programs have a broader agenda, serving not just the needs of the sick attending the Kumbh Mela, but also to provide vaccinations and health-awareness programs for the population. The state takes the opportunity to have so many people gathered in one a place to optimize resources for the public interest.

Spatially speaking, there are two divisions within the area of health provision—the permanent structures such as the GT Hospital and the temporary hospitals, with equipment created specifically for the Kumbh Mela. These temporary facilities provide no medical units for complex treatments, so that in the case of an emergency, there is a system of ambulances to transport people to full-service hospitals in Allahabad.

The organization of the health division has three wings: one for public health, which works in sanitation and inspects key infection points; another for the main clinic, where a doctor deals with disease; and a third one known as Vector Terminal Disease Control, which is specifically designated for the control of pandemics or aggressive infectious outbreaks.

Security SYSTEMS

It is also interesting to analyze how the infrastructure for security and control is manifested. The 2013 Kumbh Mela had thirty police posts, strategically positioned in the different sectors. The police arrived in the area in three deployments: the first on October 15, 2012, the second on November 15, 2012, and the last on December 15, 2012. One of the functions of the police at the Kumbh Mela is to manage the river baths. Given the high risk in having such large crowds, the bathing police is responsible for getting people out of the river once they have been immersed, which is allowed just once a day during the sacred bath. Among other safety measures, police handle traffic stops within a radius of seven kilometers around Kumbh Nagri, after which people have to walk up the designated area.

Sanitation

To carry out the discharge of the daily volume of waste, between 35,000 and 45,000 sanitation facilities (toilets, latrines, etc.) were constructed. The vast majority of toilets are built under a shed, with bamboo upon a cement platform. The flushable toilet in the majority of bathrooms, stylistic to India, has a plastic faucet and the trench is made of bricks. Most of the times there is no drain available, so the installation ends up being just a well. When there are drains, they are usually covered with bamboo trellises, which are covered with dry grass to prevent gases from escaping. A layer of clay is placed between the bamboo grid and the dry grass. The system includes subsidiary moats as back up, in the case of overflow. When the soil is sandstone, barrels of tin are placed upside down to act as septic tanks. Most of the visitors come from rural areas and are not used to toilets. There is a large percentage of open defecation, which is collected and carried into wells where it accumulates in large amounts and then burned. Sweepers are also working as separators since they must extract the feces from plastic and other recyclable items prior to burning. With 45,000 sanitation facilities built, the amount of waste that can be evacuated by the equipment would be in the order of sixty-five liters serving 388 people. Needless to say, it is unlikely that the sanitation facilities serve all attendees. If we consider that they were used sixteen hours a day, then each person would need to evacuate in 2.5 minutes. It is for this reason that we can assume that much of the defecation will be done out in the open, leading to major health concerns.

Therefore, to best manage the evacuation of this waste, the administration considered twenty-two groups of sweepers that ratchet common areas during the night. These same workers dig holes in large open areas on the outskirts of the Kumbh Mela and transport waste in carrels, where they apply an antibacterial chemical. There is no clarity on whether waste is simply buried or burned, although it is assumed that it is burned, since this is the how trash is traditionally dealt with in India. Each group of eleven sweepers has a leader, and it is presumed that approximately 9,000 people worked as sweepers in 2013.

All of the previously described deployment happens within an infrastructural mesh of very interesting characteristics. Unlike traditional network of infrastructure operating in permanent cities, at the Kumbh Mela, goods and mobility provision, consumption, and waste management are structured around discrete units, of low complexity, that form a robust chain, which is highly efficient. Every component is quick and easy to deploy and built from low technology protocols. Infrastructural systems presented at the Kumbh Mela range from layers of very simple elements made out of organic and absorbable materials, to the more complex and sophisticated constructions such as the bridges.

Envoi

The Kumbh Mela presents a distilled narrative surrounding the deployment of a city in a short timeframe that demonstrates an extreme case of ephemeral urbanism. Issues that are negotiated in this form of ephemeral urbanism are as diverse as cultural memory, geography, infrastructure, sanitation, public health, governance, and ecology. As a fecund example in elastic urban planning, it has much to teach us about planning and design, flow management, elements that support the accelerated urban metabolism, and deployment of infrastructure. It also offers insights about cultural identity, adjustment, and elasticity in temporary urban conditions. These parameters unfold with projective potential, offering alternatives not only for rethinking cases within the boundaries of ephemeral urbanism, but also of how to embed softer, more malleable yet more robust systems in permanent cities. This case exposes a very sharp illustration of how the light, indeterminate, and unspecific instruments empower agents and could be useful tools in the generation of robustness and in allowing a highly complex process to flow seamlessly.

As architects, planners, and designers we are interested in this case as one example of urban ephemeral landscape that fires a fruitful dialogue with other more permanent urbanisms. A thick description and deep analysis of the Kumbh Mela can contribute to reflection on several questions. How can we more flexibly accommodate things while providing the space for rapid transitions, frugality, and the increasing fluidity that cities require? How can we move toward a more adjustable urbanism that is capable of anticipating and hosting the impermanent?

KUMBH MELA. ALLAHABAD 2013

In order to successfully depict the nuances involved in everything that goes into planning the Kumbh Mela, a first challenge is to understand the dynamic context, sacred spatiality, temporal heterogeneity, and the structures of power that situate the festival while developing a conceptual language for thinking about a city that strays from orthodox approaches that are heavily grounded in time, rather than space. One needs to look more closely at the very description of a city and then examine its capability for being disassembled. Rethinking the urban form in a way that understands rhythm is more important than predicting growth. This is where the management of intensities is critical for the establishment of physical densities. A city is a place where adjustment mechanisms are sometimes more interesting to understand and develop than the impeccable anticipation strategies implemented.

The architect, Andrea Branzi advises us on how to think of cities of the future. He suggests that we need to learn to implement reversibility, avoiding rigid solutions and definitive decisions. He also suggests approaches that allow space to be adjusted and reprogrammed with the yet-to-be discovered. Branzi suggests that we should use material technologies that could find new modalities of use afterwards. He is referring to the materials that can be reused and reformulated, therefore giving them an afterlife. In order to be more widely considered as a productive alternative to contemporary paradigms, urbanism of the ephemeral has to be considered as an idea that acknowledges the need for reexamining permanent solutions in cities as the only mode for the formulation of urban imaginaries. We must imagine new protocols that are constantly reformulated, readapted and projected in an iterative search for a temporary equilibrium, instead of reacting to a permanent state of crises that, according to Branzi, has become our contemporary condition by default.

The scale and pace of contemporary urbanization challenges the notion of permanence as a basic condition of cities. Ephemeral landscapes of pop-up settlements are constantly increasing in scale and confronting the notion of "the city" as a stable and permanent entity. In response to this condition, there are emerging discussions about how the discourse on urbanism would benefit if the false perception of the division between ephemeral versus stable components in cities were dissolved. For in reality, when cities are analyzed over large temporal spans, ephemerality emerges as an important condition in the life cycle of every built environment—perhaps the only constant. Peter Bishop and Lesley Williams recently asked: "Given overwhelming evidence that cities are a complex overlay of buildings and activities that are, in one way or another, temporary, why have urbanists been so focused on permanence?"[4] Taking this argument further, more radical authors such as Giorgio Agamben, argue that it is fundamental to "recognize the structure of the camp in all its metamorphoses."[5] This is the case not only because of the need for emphasis on the temporal dimension of cities but also because, as Agamben explains, "today it is not the city but rather the camp [that is] the

KUMBH MELA. ALLAHABAD 2013

fundamental biopolitical paradigm of the West."6 It is in this context that the exploration of temporal landscapes opens a potent avenue for research, by questioning the illusion of permanence that shrouds cities. The idea is to enable opportunities that trigger discussions about both permanent and explicitly impermanent configurations within the urban condition.

The growing attention that environmental and ecological issues have garnered in urban discourses, articulated through the anxiety surrounding the relatively recent emergence of landscape as a model for urbanism, is making it evident that we need to evolve more nuanced discussions for the city—discussions that overcome its limited representation. As Richard Sennett's image of "the open city" suggests, cities should be seen as more than just the complex aggregation of discrete static objects. They are, among other things, the result of overlapping social and material flows that generate open metabolic processes, which operate and transform at different rates. In contemporary urbanism around the world, it is becoming clearer that in order to be sustainable, cities will have to facilitate active fluxes in motion rather than static material configurations. To embrace this condition, we must shift our gaze from just problems of space to those that also factor in time, allowing more complex and nuanced readings to be deployed and new conditions to be included as part of the repertoire that surrounds discussions about urbanism more generally.

Consequently, thinking of a gradient from more permanent toward more ephemeral configurations, we could focus on the impermanent end of the spectrum, bringing into the discussion cases of cities or urban conditions that are explicitly ephemeral, allowing us to observe extreme conditions of temporary space occupation grounded in the territory. In this context, however, the distinction between permanent and ephemeral is not binary. Rather, it refers to what remains versus what vanishes. It activates a broader concept of permanence in its meaning of what is more stable, static, and persistent in relation to what is impermanent. Impermanence is the constant process of internal transformation, renewal, and reinvention, allowing for greater levels of instability. This approach embraces a longer temporal scale from the effervescent forces of growth to the tendencies of shrinkage, depopulation, and reabsorption.

To expand the terrain of study and learn from temporary cities, the first challenge is how to organize an increasingly growing archipelago of heterogeneous cases. A useful organization strategy could focus on the fact that temporary cities, unlike more permanent ones that have a range of elements that simultaneously support their continuity, are structured around one main purpose. This operates as a central force that not only defines their dimensions and complexity but also determines essential characteristics such as the life cycle of the settlement, its material composition, and the land it occupies in both physical space and cultural memory.

It is therefore possible to categorize ephemeral cities in clusters of configured cases in diverse taxonomies, fused by their commonality of temporality. Inside every group of cases we find similarities such as time spans of deployment processes, supportive institutional structures, and morphological geometries, among several other possible shared attributes.

The understanding of the Kumbh Mela in the context of ephemeral urbanism can teach us how to reintroduce temporality to urbanism's imagination by anticipating spaces for impermanence, curating meaningful urban rites, and inviting us to ponder more pragmatic aspects of material temporality. Dematerialization and disassembly must become an integral part of the design of buildings and cities. This research is a call to go beyond physical density and bolster urban intensity in the production of settlements. An invitation to move toward a more holistic brand of what could be called a more "(w)holly" urbanism, meaning inclusive and open to embrace that which is outside material outcomes.

1   The festival happens in four cities where sacred Indian texts say that the *amrit* (sacred nectar of immortality) fell. Therefore, every three years, following astrological calendars, crowds of people will take sacred baths in one of four designated places: Ujjain, Nashik, Haridwar, and Allahabad, next to a holy body of water, a sacred river that acquires great potential for providing spiritual benefits. Every twelve years, "the festival of the pot" is celebrated at the Tirtharaja, the king of all *tirthas*, in Allahabad, which becomes the most sacred and, provisionally, the most populated and expanded congregation of pilgrims out of all four locations of the Kumbh Mela. For more information about the origin of the festival, refer to the essay written by Diana Eck and Kalpesh Bhatt.

2   *Nagri* is the name that the area of the ephemeral city receives.

3   Other interesting metrics are related with the total headcount of visitors. It is highly difficult to ensure that the official numbers are accurate. A workshop was held at the Radcliffe Institute for Advanced Studies at Harvard University in which different authorities were involved in the planning and management process. During this working session, Devesh Chaturvedi, Commissioner of Allahabad explained how a series of different images and video cameras were used to estimate the number of people that attended the massive gathering. After talking with Mr. Chaturvedi and the inspector general of Allahabad Police, we realized that if we followed their headcounts, the total number of people would be around forty to sixty million, instead of the 120 million reported in the official figures. In any case, the number supposes a high level of infrastructural stress during the main days—for instance, in the opening day of the Kumbh Mela around 8 million people arrived.

4   Peter Bishop and Lesley Williams, *The Temporary City* (New York: Routledge, 2010), p. 10.

5   Giorgio Agamben, "The Camp as Nomos," *Homo Sacer: Sovereign Power and Bare Life*, trans. Daniel Heller-Roazen (Stanford: Stanford University Press, 1998), p. 176.

6   Ibid., p. 181.

89

Setting the Megacity VIGNETTE

JAMES WHITTEN, OSCAR MALASPINA & VINEET DIWADKAR

This vignette focuses on the urban form of the Kumbh Mela. As the biggest public gathering in the world, this extreme case reveals certain characteristics that are unique, as well as others that can be applied to the broader family of temporary settlements. The specific focus of this vignette lies in the fluid nature of the territory it is grounded in and the nature of the grid as a structuring device. This "Urbanism" vignette focuses on the urban grid as a physical strategy to coordinate the large scale of the entire Kumbh Mela down to the small scale of the individual tent or bathing area. The "Governance" chapter focuses on the urban grid as an administrative tool (sectors, Akharas, institutions), while the "Deployment" chapter focuses on the grid to manage specific material flows (water, sanitation, circulation, river stabilization, food, etc.) through construction and labor practices. The "Purpose" chapter focuses on the appropriation of the grid for the cultural, social and religious activity for which the grid is designed.

The shifting spatial and temporal contexts of planning a settlement within an active monsoon riverbed call for flexible planning and design strategies. The flexible open urban grid functions as such a planning tool to respond to the unpredictable location of river migration and as a delivery mechanism for infrastructures. The graphic visualizations within this chapter investigate the monsoon as a shifting ground condition and the use of the urban grid as a planning tool for the Kumbh Mela. This vignette examines the large-scale hydrological context and the national and regional geography in which the Kumbh Mela is embedded. This large analysis introduces three scales of hydrological mapping: 1) the monsoon and elevation producing South Asian hydrological systems; 2) water management, damming and land use (cropland and settlement anthromes) within the Ganges watershed; and 3) the river migration of the Yamuna and Ganges at the Allahabad / Kumbh Mela scale. The results of this monsoon cycle are then analyzed in their immediate impact on the riverbed site of the area. This shifting context is mapped and compared to previous incarnations of the Kumbh Mela. The grid, as a structuring and mediating device that is superimposed over the emerging landscape, is introduced as both a conceptual and physical tool. The following analysis focuses on the ensuing design of the 2013 sectors, urban grid, and form. The grid as a conceptual tool serves to administer sadhus, pilgrims, and residents, in line with the sector-based planning more famously seen in Chandigarh. The grid as a physical tool provides multi-scaled infrastructural networks (electricity, circulation, water, and sanitation); ample circulation routes, bathing, and queuing areas on major bathing days, in line with dominant engineering attitudes / paradigms; and serves as a land allotment structure for appropriation by sects and pilgrims. A further analysis of the grid shows its malleability to the given territory. The grid is analyzed as a sequence, with a focus on temporal deployment as a binary of both preexisting infrastructure

and the Kumbh Mela infrastructure. Once the administrative, conceptual, and physical forms of the grid have been introduced, the focus then moves to the individual camps. As an example, the Juna Akhara sector is shown and analyzed in further detail. The confluence of the two rivers, the Ganges and the Yamuna, constitutes the floodplain, a terrain with elastic boundaries, determined by these shifting waters. During the monsoon, from May to late October, the rivers expand dramatically, inundating the riverbanks completely. Once the water recedes, a large sandy surface is revealed. This area provides the ground for the deployment of this temporary megacity. The cyclical environmental dynamics of the monsoon confines the construction and deconstruction of this massive settlement. The sequence of diagrams and maps in this vignette show how the deployment of the city unfolds over time. Meticulous tracing of aerial images was a key component in analyzing the Kumbh Mela as an urban aggregation, which successively revealed the deployment on through to the peak operation, and the gradual return of the land to its previous state. These deployment maps show the relationship of the more permanent infrastructure of Allahabad and its surroundings with the temporary, low-tech macro-scaled infrastructures that plug into these preexisting layers and form the grid for the duration of the Kumbh Mela. The origins of the grid as the fundamental physical planning device can be traced to mid-nineteenth-century British colonialism. In the case of the Kumbh Mela, the planning process starts with an abstract grid that serves as a framework for the structure and internal organization. The final form of the city is the result of a progressive resolution of uncertainties ranging from the geology of the riverbed to speculations on the numbers of people anticipated to visit on major bathing days. As more information is available, the master plan for the city evolves progressively while adjusting accordingly to the grid's geometry. The final geometry of this grid gets adapted to the morphology of the floodplain, which is only revealed once the river has actually receded. By the time the Ganges retreats, the administration must have transformed this complex spatial and political landscape into a simple grid that, in the case of the 2013 Kumbh Mela, divides the space into fourteen self-sufficient sectors, upon which the infrastructure is deployed. These sectors are the spatial translation of an administrative structure. Each of these sectors is conceived as an independent and almost self-sufficient unit. Although sectors aim to work independently, different sectors accomplish different functions within the ephemeral city as a whole. This subdivision is represented in a map that captures the spatial parcelization of the sectors and camps. The areas contained by the grid differ in structure, module, and geometry. Unlike other temporary settlements, the basic grain of the Kumbh Mela is not the repetition of a unique structure, like a tent, but the definition of bigger open areas—the camps. These camps are given to religious communities without preconceived internal regulation. This grants authority to each community to organize their space creatively, in ways that express their individual identities, resulting in the emergence of various forms of spatial organization. This network of roads, bridges, shelters, as well as social infrastructures—such as temporary hospitals, markets, police stations, and social centers—replicates the functions of a permanent city. The grid is initially transcribed onto the sandy riverbed initiated by a sacred ceremony. This abstract grid finds its physical manifestation in the form of diverse layers of infrastructure such as water, electricity, sewage, and for mobility, such as roads and bridges. Not unlike the grids of more permanent cities like Chandigarh or Manhattan, these administrative and infrastructural lines contain a neutral field for the evolution of diverse residential, commercial, and cultural activities. The eighteen pontoon bridges, built to supplement the existing bridges, are core components of the physical infrastructure. While bridges in conventional cities tend to be limited to specific points, the large number of these floating bridges ties the grid across the two sides of the river like a continuous seam. While the existing infrastructure such as the bridges, roads, railway lines, train stations, power lines, etc. are heavy and rigid constructions that support the continuity of processes over time, the Kumbh Mela's specific infrastructure is soft and adapts dynamically to the existing flow of people, water, and energy. The roads, for example, are made of steel plates that can be carried by a number of workers without any heavy machinery or simply by laying down thatch to stabilize the ground. The connections of pieces are unspecific and adjustable, resulting in an aggregation of self-similar units that converge into an

endless aggregation of elements made of wood, steel, textiles, plastic, plywood, etc. The limited number of necessary pieces works to maximize the potential for reconfiguration and future use beyond the Kumbh Mela. Many of the more durable and complex components are stored or reincorporated into regional economies of construction in order to serve other festivals or disaster relief in other parts of the state, resulting in a seamless feedback of material flow. The reusable elements of the temporary city get progressively disassembled and recycled, while softer organic materials, such as thatch or bamboo, are left in the ground to be reabsorbed, either by the same agricultural fields or to be washed by the river in the next monsoon.

HARIDWAR

ALLAHABAD

UJJAIN

NASIK

GANGES WATERSHED BASIN

DAMS & HYDROPOWER
PROJECTS

RIVERS & STREAMS

Monsoon in movement

The monsoon changes the flows in the water shed of the subcontinent. Rivers, which are usually considered as sacred places, drastically change in morphology, configuring a highly dynamic sacred landscape.

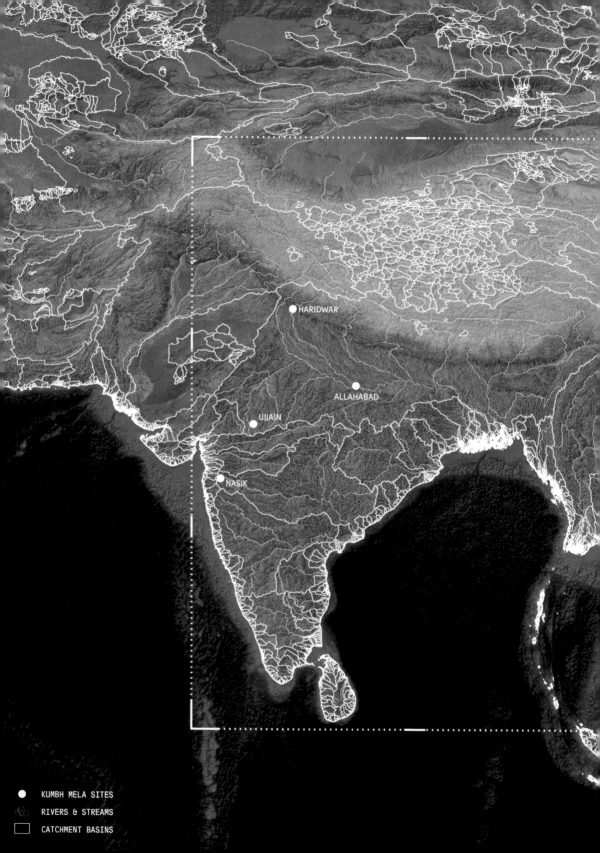

HARIDWAR

ALLAHABAD

UJJAIN

NASIK

● KUMBH MELA SITES

RIVERS & STREAMS

CATCHMENT BASINS

Shifting river

The shifting of the river, year after year, does
not allow the city of the Kumbh Mela to have
a constant layout. The morphology of the ground
varies, and with that the scheme of the grids
becomes a structure that constantly adapts to
an unpredictable ground.

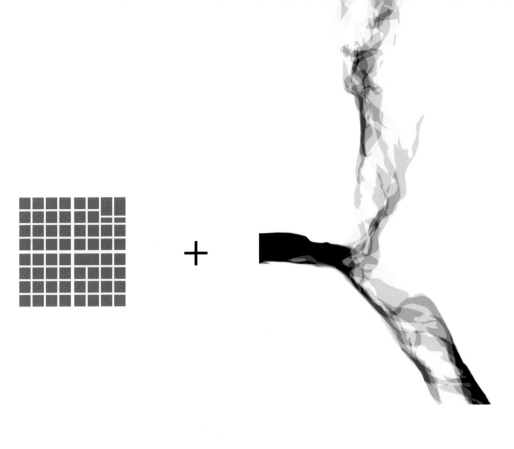

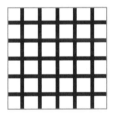

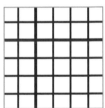

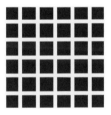

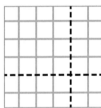

ROADS

TRAFFIC,
CROWD CONTROL,
PUBLIC SPACE

FIGURE GROUND

URBAN FORM,
CULTURAL ACTIVITY,
SETTLEMENT

INFRASTRUCTURE

MATERIAL,
TECHNOLOGY

SECTORS

GOVERNANCE,
ADMINISTRATION

Shifting context and grid

The grid as a neutralizing field meets the fluid
landscape of the constantly shifting riverbed.
This adjustable grid also mediates between the
existing infrastructure and the changing form of
the temporary city. It is both an administrative
tool and a physical mesh of infrastructures that
delivers services to the areas it contains.

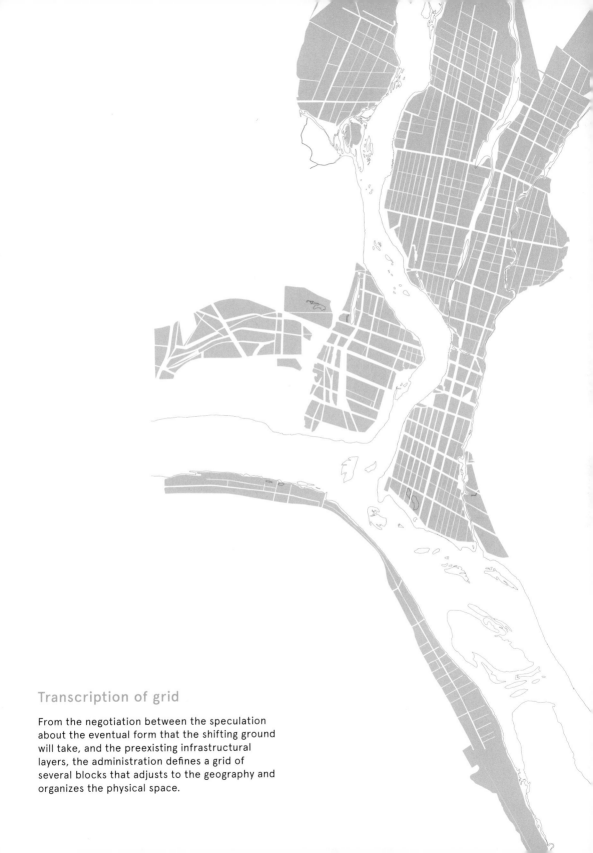

Transcription of grid

From the negotiation between the speculation
about the eventual form that the shifting ground
will take, and the preexisting infrastructural
layers, the administration defines a grid of
several blocks that adjusts to the geography and
organizes the physical space.

JULY 2012   OCTOBER 2012

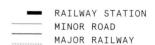
RAILWAY STATION
MINOR ROAD
MAJOR RAILWAY

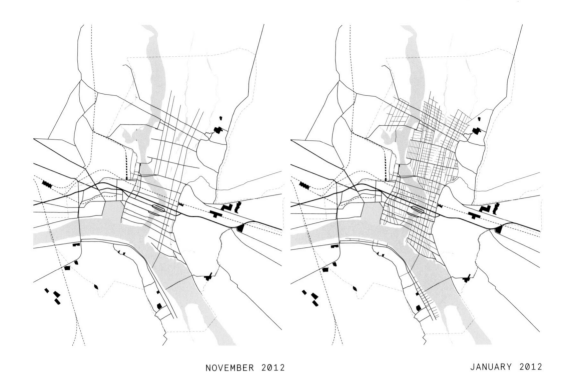

NOVEMBER 2012   JANUARY 2012

Grid sequence

The specific location of the Kumbh Mela in the
River delta of the Ganga and Yamuna rivers
presents the planners of the Kumbh with a
constantly changing hydrological context. Every
year, the rivers leave behind a changing riverbed
when the water recedes after the monsoon.
This shifting context, in combination with the
administrative borders, outlines the canvas for
the deployment of the settlement.

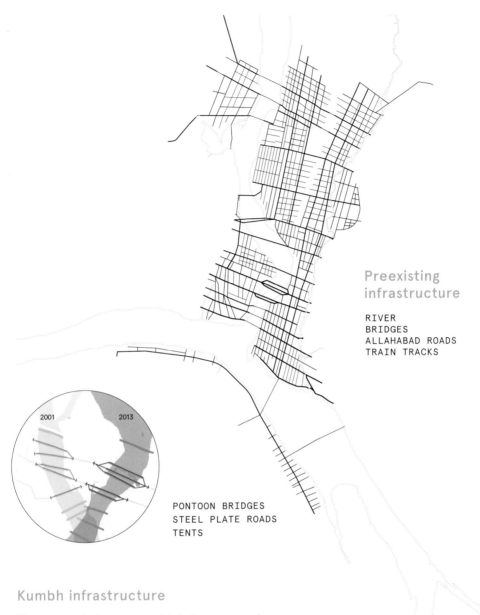

2001   2013

PONTOON BRIDGES
STEEL PLATE ROADS
TENTS

Kumbh infrastructure

The same spot changes completely from one version
of the Kumbh Mela to another. In this diagram, we
can see an overlapping between the figure ground
of the river in 2013 and 2001 with the bridges that
are deployed for each version. Some of the bridges
have almost the same location in order to match
the preexisting permanent infrastructure. The texture
of the Kumbh city is the result of several overlapping
layers that sit on the grid. Some of those layers
grow incrementally throughout the evolution of the
festival, whereas others are deployed all once.

111

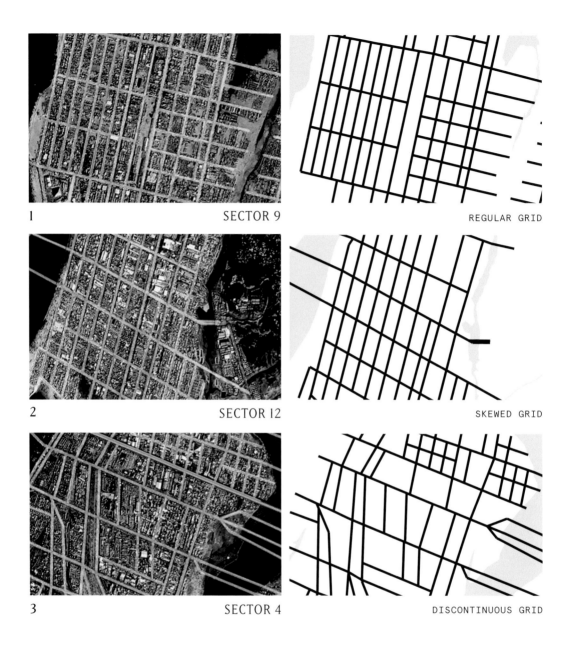

1	SECTOR 9	REGULAR GRID
2	SECTOR 12	SKEWED GRID
3	SECTOR 4	DISCONTINUOUS GRID

Adaptable street grid

Depending on the nature of each sector, different grids are configured, some following a more strict and neutralizing logic while others seek to provide adjustment to the terrain. The street grid implemented in the Kumbh is flexible enough to adapt to the given geography and can be adjusted to contain areas within the grid suitable to the various uses required.

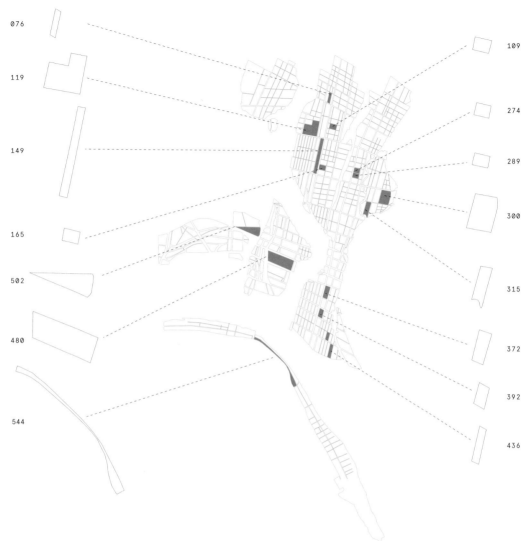

076

119

149

165

502

480

544

109

274

289

300

315

372

392

436

Grid analysis

An analysis of the urban structure of the Kumbh Mela reveals a great variety of block shapes. Starting from more regular shapes for the blocks in the center with the main Akharas and their dense religious and residential uses, the blocks become increasingly skewed and / or chopped as the abstract grid hits the natural and manmade boundaries. A taxonomy of blocks reveals this transformation of more dense and regular blocks to strange irregular types. These building blocks form the basic DNA of the Kumbh. Many of these patterns break with conventional formal guidelines, yet successfully combine to create a remarkably walkable city.

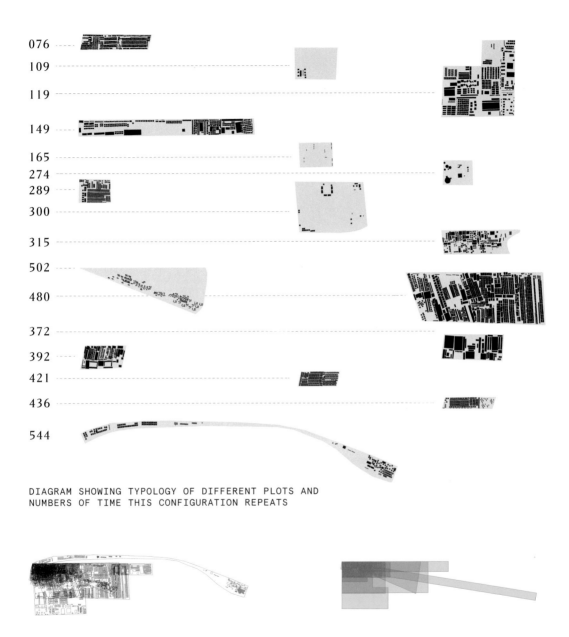

076
109
119
149
165
274
289
300
315
502
480
372
392
421
436
544

DIAGRAM SHOWING TYPOLOGY OF DIFFERENT PLOTS AND
NUMBERS OF TIME THIS CONFIGURATION REPEATS

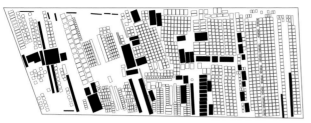

PUBLIC FABRIC

RESIDENTIAL FABRIC

PUBLIC SPACE

GROUPING WITHIN THE BLOCK

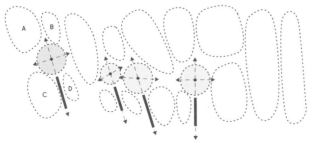

SPATIAL STRUCTURE OF THE JUNA AKHARA

BLOCK STRUCTURE

The Akharas

The Akharas (parcels) limit what is alotted by the governing bodies of the Kumbh. Within the Akharas, the various sects and religious groups appropriate the land by building tents and other structures for their specific needs.

In January 2012, the Akharas started applying for land. Starting on November 28, 2012, the government started allocating land.

The various Akharas vary significantly in texture but tend to follow similar basic structural principles.

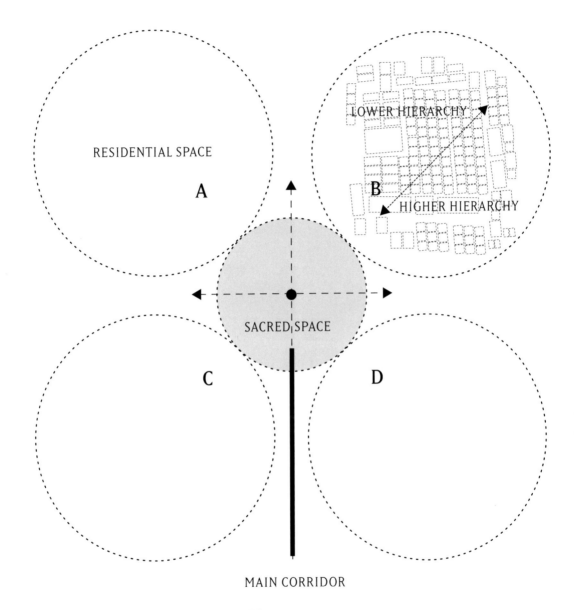

RESIDENTIAL SPACE

A

B

LOWER HIERARCHY

HIGHER HIERARCHY

SACRED SPACE

C

D

MAIN CORRIDOR

Spatial structure of the Juna Akhara

As can be seen in the case of the Juna Akhara, the
central space is marked by a flag. This religious core
is surrounded by open, public space. The axis leading
to this space is the most attractive, desirable space
with maximum exposure. The proximity to the central
sacred space determines the spatial hierarchy.

DURING
THE
KUMBH MELA:
JANUARY 14
TO
MARCH 22

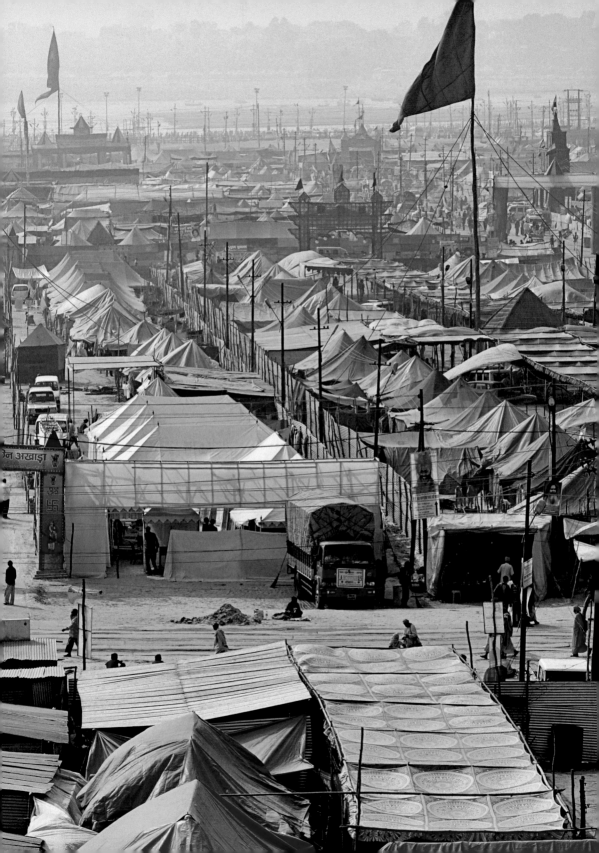

During the
KUMBH MELA
Photo Essay

DINESH MEHTA

This photo essay focuses on the period of the Kumbh Mela itself, taking place from January 14, the day of Makar Sankranti to March 10, the day of Maha Shivratri. Dinesh Mehta's kite-aerial and on-the-ground photography spans the urban scale down to the finer grain of individual tents and the public spaces in between. The aerial photographs capture a synoptic view of the terrain and a more three-dimensional spatial understanding of the two-dimensional analytical drawings and maps. The street level photographs show the interactions on the ground, impressions of everyday life, and add an atmospheric depth to the research project. While revealing the nature of the urban grid and urban form as larger-scaled systems, these photographs also show the social and cultural dimensions of the Kumbh Mela.

Health and Safety at the KUMBH MELA

SATCHIT BALSARI
in collaboration with
JENNIFER LEANING

A mobile digital surveillance tool can be
rapidly and inexpensively deployed
at mass gatherings to extract critical
real-time data of great public
health significance.

Introduction

Hundreds of millions of people from across India visit the Kumbh Mela. In a short span of less than two months, they mingle in the Kumbh Nagri, celebrating, praying and eating together, and most importantly, bathing at the Sangam. The young, the old, and the infirm travel long distances to attend this great fair, to bathe in the waters of Hinduism's holy rivers and seek liberation from the cycle of rebirth and death. On auspicious days punctuating the length of the festival, their numbers swell exponentially, drawing as many as thirty million visits to the Sangam on Mauni Amavasya, the most important of all bathing days.

The unwritten mandate of the Kumbh Mela, according to Inspector General Ashok Sharma is, "to ensure that everyone reaches the Sangam safely, and has a good time at the mela." The astounding, high-density human interaction at the *mela*, occurring within the relatively confined space of the *nagri*, poses great public health challenges. The multiple threats of stampedes, epidemics, accidents, and terror strikes, none of which are unique to this mass gathering event, loom large. Their prevention is a formidable public health feat by any measure, and becomes the focus of the Kumbh Mela administration. A large number of personnel and resources are appropriated to protect the health and safety of the pilgrims attending the *mela*. The many months of meticulous planning results in a staggering array of services. Drinking water taps, working toilets, food inspections, vector-control, health clinics, wide roads, safe bathing areas, lifeguards, controlled vehicular traffic, and additional transport facilities are all geared toward protecting pilgrims from disease and accidents.

This chapter examines the public health planning and response at the Kumbh Mela. The chapter serves two objectives. Firstly, it outlines the highly nuanced, context-based planning and execution undertaken by local administrators to prevent epidemics and stampedes at the *mela*. Secondly, it situates lessons learned from the 2013 Kumbh Mela in the context of future iterations and other mass gatherings. It examines the scope, limitations, and the potential for the state to advance public health at the world's largest gathering.

Public Health Priorities at the KUMBH MELA

THE IMPETUS FOR PREPAREDNESS

The Kumbh Mela administration, albeit temporal, is a colossal enterprise, committed to protecting the safety of the pilgrims. The administrators are focused on the triggers for mass casualties with laser-like insight. Rigorous planning begins months in advance and incorporates lessons learnt from past *melas*, institutional memory, and longstanding tradition. Over the last century, large epidemics and devastating stampedes have periodically marred the Kumbh Mela.

The origins of the first cholera pandemic in the nineteenth century have, in fact, been traced to the Kumbh Mela. After the 1817 Kumbh Mela, cholera spread beyond the endemic vicinity of the *mela*, first to port cities like Calcutta and Bombay (1818), and then to China and the Mediterranean Sea. While Hindu pilgrims carried the disease over the subcontinent, the movement of the British army and navy—along with other trade and travel, including that for the annual Hajj pilgrimage—helped spread the disease across Asia and Europe. The pandemic, which eventually reached North America, ended in the harsh winter of 1824.

In 1954, at the first Kumbh Mela organized by the government of newly independent India, a rogue elephant charged a dense crowd of pilgrims near the bathing area, resulting in over 500 deaths. Since then, every subsequent Kumbh Mela administration, along with the state and central governments has been very vigilant about the risk of stampedes. The Kumbh Mela is a high profile event, and consequently, the avoidance of any mishap is given paramount importance in planning and execution.

ARCHIVAL PHOTOGRAPH OF 1953-54 KUMBH MELA IN ALLAHABAD

THE KUMBH MELA ADMINISTRATION

Historically, the central and state governments have risen to the challenge of providing financial and administrative support to this great enterprise.[1] The Kumbh Nagri is deemed a new and temporary "district" of the State of Uttar Pradesh (UP) and vested with the full administrative machinery of any district in India. It is further divided into fourteen administrative structures. Its principal coordinator, the Mela Adhikari, is appointed a year in advance, and holds the powers of a district magistrate. Working closely with the Municipal Commissioner of Allahabad, the Adhikari is ultimately responsible for the planning and execution of the *mela*.

Completely funded by the central and state governments, the 2013 event was overseen by the Adhikari's team of experienced government employees drawn from across UP, who managed a budget of $200 million[2] and supervised a workforce of 100,000. Since the Kumbh Mela only occurs once every twelve years in each of the four cities, there is little continuity in the administrative structure or personnel between events. There are no written manuals, work plans, or codes of operation. The new team relies heavily on institutional memory captured in archival government reports and on experiences of the few employees who have served at previous *melas*.

Mela planning involves a web of partnerships among a variety of players: government agencies across national, state, and city jurisdictions; the private sector; hundreds of religious groups; and thousands of individuals tasked to work the event. Various degrees of autonomy and obligations are negotiated in each of these transactions, and the scope of responsibility is strictly adhered to, once delineated.

In 2013, the gargantuan enterprise resulted in the construction of over 160 kilometers of roads, seventeen bridges, fourteen field hospitals, 35,000 toilets, countless planning meetings, and a constant heightened level of vigilance at all levels of government.

HEALTH and SANITATION

Diseases can be transmitted at the Kumbh Mela in multiple ways; pilgrims are at a risk of infection from the mass bathing rituals, from flies hovering around the defecation fields and open food stalls, from poor hand hygiene, from contaminated water sources, and from air borne transmission. The Kumbh Mela administration attempts to address and control these various modes of transmission to the best of its ability. The temporary *mela* township boasts the quality of its own water supply system, sanitation facilities, and a rather impressive two-tiered healthcare referral network.

Water, sanitation, and healthcare are almost entirely managed by the government, with limited private sector engagement.

WATER SANITATION AND HYGIENE

In 2013, over forty tube-wells dug into the banks of the Ganga supplied drinking water at the *mela* through a network of pipes and taps. Private companies like Tata and Aquaguard also dispensed free purified water at several intersections. Over 35,000 toilets were provided across the *mela* grounds. They ranged from simple squatting plates enclosed in cloth partitions, to state of the art bio-digester units. Yet, many defecated in the open, and the administration employed an army of "night-soil sweepers" to clean the defecation areas and dust them with lime. Grey-water from tap runoff was collected in sandbag-lined stilling ponds at the margins of the roads. The water was then treated and pumped into trucks, from which it was sprayed on the road to settle the dust. As early as 1895, observers of the cholera epidemic at the Kumbh Mela had concluded that stagnant or slow flowing waters that accumulated human waste were more likely to spread disease.[3] Water current is maintained at 2,500 cubic feet per second (just enough to wash away the contaminating bacteria and viruses but not strong enough to make bathing unsafe). Coliform counts (measurements of certain types of bacteria) recorded by our team were consistently below expected ranges at multiple points upstream and downstream from the Sangam. Polluting factories upstream were either barred from dumping their affluent into the river, or were made to strictly comply with existing norms.

In spite of reasonably fair water and sanitation facilities, the threat of the spread of food-borne disease was real and high. People ate in close quarters, shared very large communal meals, ate with their hands, and had poor hand hygiene.

HEALTH SERVICES

The extensive health care system specifically developed for the Kumbh Mela included thirteen field hospitals, one in each administrative sector, and a larger, centralized, referral hospital equipped with higher diagnostic and therapeutic capabilities.

Each sector hospital was staffed by a physician, a nurse, and a pharmacist and included a twenty-bed inpatient unit and a semi-open outpatient clinic. The clinics were open twenty-four hours a day and were quite busy on most days. On auspicious days of the festival, when the *mela* population multiplied significantly, several hundred patients arrived at clinics in route to the Sangam. The patient encounters at the clinic were no different from similar events occurring daily across rural and urban clinics in India;

the clinics were understaffed, and the doctor-patient interaction lasted less than a couple of minutes. The doctors had no time to take the patient's history, check vital signs like pulse, blood pressure, or temperature, or conduct a meaningful physical exam. The doctors largely prescribed medications based on the patient's presenting complaint, and the government paid for a free, three-day protocol of medications. Patients were eligible for free refills if they returned to the clinic, however most would have left the *nagri* to return home by then. Many pilgrims had limited or no access to allopathic doctors near their homes and simply availed of the opportunity to have an allopathic physician see them.

During these fleeting patient encounters, overworked clinicians juggled patient expectations, meager resources, and efficient medical practice. By way of record keeping, physicians logged the patient's symptoms and prescribed medications in blank paper notebooks provided to the clinic. The total number of patient visits recorded at the clinics were tallied daily and sent to the central hospital. These patient encounters and notebooks became a critical component of an innovative surveillance system designed by our team, whom we describe in the subsequent sections.

Patients requiring higher levels of care were referred to the central hospital, and transported there by ambulance if needed. The central hospital was comprised of several specialty clinics: cardiology, otolaryngology, gynecology, and pediatrics; facilities for obtaining x-rays and basic blood tests; a 100-bed inpatient unit; and a two-bed intensive care unit. Patients requiring surgery, interventional cardiology, or more intensive monitoring were transferred by ambulance to one of three tertiary-care hospitals in Allahabad.

The Kumbh Mela authorities had organized a fleet of 143 ambulances, conscripted from government-owned facilities across the state of Uttar Pradesh. Each ambulance arrived with its own driver, who maintained field response supplies and kits dedicated for responses to stampedes and burns. However, the ambulances lacked trained paramedics and faced severe delays due to pedestrian traffic on busy bathing days.

ANTICIPATING EPIDEMICS

Dense crowds in mass gatherings can facilitate the rapid spread of communicable diseases. As density increases, the frequency of physical contact and interactions between people increases non-linearly, allowing for the rapid transmission of vectors to a large population.[4] The high density of the *mela* favors air-borne disease transmission, allowing common cold and influenza to spread rapidly across the Kumbh Mela grounds. Similarly, a contaminated water source can affect large numbers of pilgrims very quickly. Flies, a rather constant hazard at the *mela*, were in fact kept at bay by deploying a periodic and aggressive DDT spraying campaign. Other vector-borne illnesses like Malaria, while otherwise endemic to the region, are less of a threat in the cold climes of northern India during the Kumbh Mela season. It is noteworthy that the mostly underutilized, twenty-bed, inpatient unit attached to each sector hospital is essentially a vestige of the "cholera ward" necessitated by previous epidemics at the *mela*.

In spite of these extensive measures undertaken, the threat of contagion and epidemics remains high due to the sheer volume of pilgrims, the density of the population, and the diversity of places across India from where they originate. Yet, at the start of the event, there was no organized surveillance system in place to detect outbreaks or inform a response.

INTRODUCING DISEASE SURVEILLANCE AT THE KUMBH MELA[5]

An epidemic is defined as the occurrence of disease at a rate higher than what is normally expected in a population. For example, a new case of polio in a country where polio had been eradicated would herald an epidemic, but in the case of influenza (flu), the incidence of new cases would have to be higher than the expected seasonal numbers within a population to trigger worries about an epidemic. Herein lies the problem. To look for epidemics

MEDICAL CONSULTATIONS AT A SECTOR HOSPITAL

PILGRIMS BATHE AT A SANGAM

at the Kumbh Mela, one would need to know how many new cases of a particular disease were showing up at the clinics every day and whether these
numbers were above the expected norm. New cases, by way of presenting
complaints (diarrhea, vomiting, fever, rash, etc.) were recorded in the paper
notebooks we discussed in the Health Services section. Though the information captured in the notebooks was rudimentary, it was enough to power
a syndromic surveillance system, as long as the data could be accessed and
analyzed in real time. However, several kilometers and a dense sea of humanity made access to the notebooks scattered across the thirteen clinics
difficult, and time sensitive data collation impossible.
The public health contingent of Harvard's Kumbh Mela team sought to provide a solution to this challenge of real time data gathering. Collaborating
with India's apex disaster response agency, the National Disaster Management Authority of India, we recruited an enthusiastic team of over twenty
medical and public health students from Allahabad and Mumbai to implement an innovative disease surveillance tool. These senior students, all
close to graduation in their respective specialties, were drawn from the Motilal Nehru Medical College, the Sam Higginbottom Institute of Agriculture,
Technology and Science, and the Rotaract Club of the Caduceus.
The students were divided into groups, given iPads rented locally, and assigned
to one of the five sites in which the surveillance project was piloted. Using a com-
mercially available data-collection app and a homegrown analysis program, "EM-
counter," the students were instructed to transcribe data from the paper notebooks

to their iPads. The EMcounter program allowed students to record epidemiologically relevant data such as age, gender, chief-complaint, and prescribed medications—just enough information to construct a robust disease surveillance system. At the end of each day, the teams met to debrief. Within minutes, data from the ten iPads were uploaded to a remote server using mobile hot spots. Once data upload was completed, the EMcounter tool instantaneously generated graphs showing the number of patients presenting to the clinics, the frequency and proportions of various diseases, the types of medicines prescribed, and the age and gender distribution of patients. The team plotted the data every day, allowing Kumbh Mela administrators to study the daily rise and fall of disease presentations as the population numbers ebbed and flowed. Any deviation from expected projections would signal an impending epidemic.

The surveillance team tracked over 50,000 patients for a period of three weeks that included the busiest bathing day. In addition to implementing a surveillance tool, the project provided critical information on resource allocation, service utilization, clinical practice patterns, and inventory.

The EMcounter system captured the incidence of diseases presenting to key sector hospitals close to the Sangam. In a stable city population, a rise in incidence (above the expected seasonal norm) may alert one to an impending epidemic. However, a change in disease incidence at the Kumbh Mela could merely reflect the wide swings in population, precluding, on face value, the ability to predict epidemics. The surveillance team therefore chose to monitor the relative proportion of the most common diseases presenting to the clinics. The team hypothesized that it would be possible to establish the relative proportion of diseases *in relation to each other* if the population were surveyed over time, and across a large sample size. A deviation in the expected occurrence of one disease relative to the incidence of all others could then portend an epidemic. To test this hypothesis, EMcounter tracked patients at four sector hospitals and the central hospital during a three-week run that included some of the busiest bathing days at the *mela*.

HEALTH SERVICES: SUPPLY AND DEMAND AT THE KUMBH MELA

The Kumbh Mela authorities reported 280,755 unique patient encounters at all allopathic hospitals for the duration of the *mela*. The data presented below is based on findings elicited by our digital surveillance system, which recorded 49,131 encounters during the study period.

The median age of pilgrims seeking care was forty-six years. Half the patients presenting to the central hospital were women, as compared to only a quarter in the sector hospitals. The caseload at the busiest sector hospital was 1,200% higher than in the least busy sector hospital, despite identical infrastructure and resources.

Mostly, patients presented with common ailments like musculoskeletal pain, fever, cough, coryza, and diarrhea. This disproportionately large presentation of minor ailments is strikingly similar to that seen at other transient mass gatherings, including the recent 2012 London Olympics.[6] One in 100 patients presenting to the central hospital required hospitalization, mostly for diarrhea, abdominal pain, fever, and breathing difficulties. Nine out of ten patients presenting to the sector hospitals received a prescription. The most common prescriptions were for antibiotics, pain medications, anti-allergy medications, and vitamin supplements. Close to half of the patients who reported they had a fever received an antibiotic, and over 80% received paracetamol for their fever. Six of ten patients presenting with a cough also received antibiotics.

MISSED OPPORTUNITIES FOR PUBLIC HEALTH INTERVENTIONS

Healthcare delivery at the Kumbh Mela requires a large number of human resources, infrastructure, and pharmaceuticals. Though the ailments that patients presented to the clinics were not different from presentations at other mass gatherings around the world, the pervasive, symptom-based, placebo-like prescription practice is highly problematic. A sizeable portion of the *mela* budget is spent on healthcare; yet, most of it is wasted on providing sub-optimal care. The large healthcare infrastructure could perhaps be better utilized to implement much needed public health interventions. Close to one in five patients at the clinics presented with a cough, and an equal number with fever, yet there were no systematic case-finding efforts for pulmonary tuberculosis, a major public health challenge in this population.[7] Hypertension and tobacco use are on the rise in rural India. The clinic visits provided a unique opportunity to screen for high blood pressure, or initiate tobacco cessation education. After all, if the total numbers reported are to be believed, close to 6% of India's population passed through the *mela*. Diverting resources to public health interventions targeting this large captive slice of India might yield great dividends in the future.

Stampedes at the KUMBH MELA: Preparedness and Response

Stampede prevention remains one of the foremost drivers of Kumbh Mela planning to date. Administrators spend many months debating the optimum

parameters for crowd control in the Kumbh Nagri. Their decisions impact not only the physical layout and infrastructure of the township, but also influence transport planning, river currents, and police and military staffing needs. A great number of resources were once again marshaled to prevent stampedes at the 2013 Kumbh Mela. Yet, on February 10, on Mauni Amavasya, the most auspicious bathing day, when thirty million visits were reported at the Sangam, a stampede at the Allahabad railway station resulted in thirty-six dead and twice as many injured.

Crowd models focused on inter-pedestrian and macroscopic pedestrian-environment interactions have revealed several self-organizing principles. These include bi-directional lane formation; oscillations or unidirectional, intermittent flow through narrow bottlenecks; stop-and-go waves in cases of high crowd density; and crowd turbulence when pedestrians are involuntarily jostled around with varying force.[8] The Kumbh Mela police, tasked with crowd management, have, over years of observation and intervention, taken these principles into account. Stampede mitigation strategies are built into the blue print of the Kumbh Nagri. After all, the raison d'être of the Kumbh Mela is for the pilgrim to bathe safely at the Sangam.

Mela administrators including police, civil engineers, state bureaucrats and private contractors improve each successive stampede mitigation plan with strategies learnt from having observed, attended, or planned previous

ROADS AND PONTOON BRIDGES PROVIDED ACCESS BUT CREATED CHOKE POINTS FOR CROWDS

melas. Kumbh Mela inventory and scale keep growing with each passing year. In 2013, more than 160 kilometers of roads were constructed, some as wide as sixty feet, and wider than most roads in India. Pontoon bridges (seventeen in 2013) traversing the rivers maintain the continuity of the main thoroughfares on both sides of the bank. The resulting checkered road and bridge grid is an effective town-planning design that prevents bottlenecking as crowds flow easily from one bank to another. Pedestrian traffic is tightly controlled on busy bathing days, often permitting only one-directional flow and diverting crowds through a more circuitous route across the *mela* grounds to decrease concentration.

At the waterfront, riverbanks are reinforced with thousands of sandbags and covered with a thick blanket of hay to provide traction to millions of visiting feet. Tall poles sunk into the riverbed a few feet from the shoreline demarcate the safety zone for bathing, and strategically dispersed manned lifeboats keep a vigilant eye on the bathing crowds.

State authorities adjust a series of upstream dams on the Ganga and Yamuna rivers to control the current of water reaching the Sangam. Closer to the bathing areas, a series of temporary jetties built for the *mela* jut into the water to further temper the flow and create safe areas for bathing. The current is slow enough to maintain safety but brisk enough to prevent stagnation.

Around the main bathing days, rail and bus traffic to Allahabad grows exponentially. Two hundred special trains are commissioned by Indian Railways, a federal ministry, to ferry pilgrims in and out of Allahabad throughout the duration of the *mela*. Thousands of buses coming to Allahabad are parked in special zones at varying distances from the city to prevent congestion within the city. Pilgrims then walk on foot toward the Sangam.

THE STAMPEDE

On February 10, 2013, thousands of pilgrims were gathered at the Allahabad railway station just west of the Kumbh Nagri. A significant number of additional trains had been deployed on previous auspicious bathing days prior to this date, but had not been utilized to capacity. Fearing further financial losses, the federally run Railway Ministry had cut back on the number of trains requested by the Kumbh Mela police for the main bathing day.

By evening, throngs of weary pilgrims had collected at the station to board the bustling trains home. There were no restrictions on who could enter the station, and most seats on the trains were unreserved. The cars were packed dangerously full at two to three times safe capacity.[9] By 6:30 PM, all overhead footbridges were jam-packed. People had gathered on Platform 1 for the Rajdhani Express, and on Platform 6 for one of the specially designated trains for the *mela*. For reasons still unclear, a last minute track change was announced, and masses of people, anxious not to miss their trains, surged to the newly assigned platforms. Platforms one and six were only connected via a narrow overhead footbridge.

There was virtually no room on the bridge, stairs, or platforms for anyone to move in any direction. The ensuing panic in the rush to cross the footbridge triggered a stampede that left thirty-six people dead.

RESPONSE FOR THE STAMPEDE

The teeming station was so noisy that people waiting on other platforms not too far from the stampede had no idea that it had taken place. It was impossible to move the victims through the packed platforms. Those who could walk or move with assistance managed to maneuver through the crowds to reach the railway clinic at one end of the platform. Those more grievously hurt were initially left behind, contrary to sound triage principles. The railway clinic was ill equipped for true emergencies and patients lost several hours waiting for transport to the nearby railway hospital from where they were eventually transferred to their third and final destination, the larger tertiary medical centers in the city. Most of the thirty-nine patients transferred out were sent to the Swaroop Rani Nehru Hospital, which received the last stampeded patient seven hours after the incident.

The security forces policing the city belonged to four different units—the city police, the state police, the federal Rapid Action Force, and the Indian Army, each of which functioned independently without a joint incident commander coordinating response at the scene, as is warranted during such mass casualty incidents. The lack of coordinated triage and dispersal resulted in all patients arriving at the nearest tertiary facility. Since the government had instructed the hospital that no one be turned away, less acute cases often blocked up the hospital beds, and sicker patients, arriving later had to be sent forth to more distant hospitals. Medical personnel were quickly mobilized across the city and all hospitals receiving the patients were adequately staffed in a short time. By morning, the hospitals released a list of admitted patients, and of those who were deceased.

STRENGTHENING DISASTER RESPONSE AT THE KUMBH MELA

In spite of the vast time, energy, and resources spent on crowd safety, the most auspicious bathing day of the 2013 Kumbh Mela was marked by the unfortunate stampede. The stampede was not a freak accident as it was made out to be, but was rather the inevitable result of rigid, centralized planning. The lone footbridge that bore the crush of pilgrims on February

ALLAHABAD RAILWAY STATION DURING THE KUMBH MELA

10, 2013, quite literally represented the weak link between various arms of government, each individually committed to the Kumbh Mela's success, yet inefficient together.[10]

The *mela*'s rigid planning processes—which rely heavily on institutional memory, tradition, and sometimes personal pride—fail to provide room for the nimble, facile, and rapid response required during emergencies. The railway ministry had unilaterally decided against providing the additional trains requested by the police. While crowd flow was anticipated and planned within the perimeter of the *nagri*, and on the many roads leading in and out of Allahabad, the state's jurisdiction ended where the federally operated railway ministry took over. Joint mock drills were seldom conducted across jurisdictional boundaries.

A flow study that begins in the villages from where the pilgrims begin their long journey to the Kumbh Mela, and follows the crowds through the winding corrals, across the pontoon bridges to the Sangam, back to the railway and bus stations, and finally home, may unearth several pitfalls not otherwise obvious. Similarly, strategic understanding of crowd behavior in an ethnographic context is critical. Adequate signage is always advisable, but the high levels of illiteracy in the rural population must be recognized. The subcontinent also suffers from a pervasive lack of a queuing culture, and subsequently, the frenzied rush to board unreserved train compartments is quite common and should be anticipated. By late evening, especially on busy bathing days, crowds are expected to be fatigued and anxious to get home by the earliest available means. Planning agencies would greatly benefit by closely examining these many variables. A rigorous flow analysis would include not only the quantitative metrics modeled as the subjects move in time and space, but also the more elusive, qualitative understanding of human behaviors in specific situations.[11,12] People will ascend crowded bridges, not read signs, not wait their turn—and system architects must pre-empt, observe, and learn from these behaviors. Furthermore, such analyses after disasters must transcend jurisdictions. Although both the Kumbh Mela administration and Indian Railways each focused on mass casualty mitigation, they did not do so together, a classic failure of horizontal coordination.[13]

In spite of India's rapid urbanization and wealth, emergency management in India has lacked far behind and is, at best, unpredictable. Mass casualty response is seldom coordinated, and in practice, incident command systems are not a routine component of urban disaster management plans. Pre-hospital care or Emergency Management Systems (EMS) have shown vast improvement over the last decade, with better-equipped ambulances often staffed by trained paramedics plying many of India's large cities. Yet, EMS control rooms do not seamlessly sync with the police and fire departments that are primarily responsible for coordinating the overall response.

The lack of triage, coordination, and overall absence of organized mass casualty plans within hospitals results in unacceptably delayed care and avoidable complications, suffering, and death. The 2013 Kumbh Mela stampede was a highly visible and highly reported event. However, the city's response was not far from the norm in the region.

Lessons from the KUMBH MELA

The 2013 Kumbh Mela, its shortcomings notwithstanding, was an extraordinary fete, on a scale unparalleled in the world. Millions from across India, and many from around the world, enjoyed a purifying bath at the Triveni Sangam and returned home safely. Almost two centuries of state supported *melas* have resulted in a sophisticated partnership of public and private players, religion and commerce, piety, and celebration. Millions of pilgrims traveled long distances to the *nagri*, by foot, by bus, and by train, paid obeisance to their gurus, attended religious discourses, bathed in the holy waters, and returned home. They navigated the grid of roads and bridges in the *nagri*, partook in communal meals, used the water and sanitation facilities, and some lived in the colorful camps, for weeks on end. More than a quarter million visited the health facilities and were all seen and treated free of charge. There were no life-threatening epidemics, and save the stampede at the railway station, no large accidents. Hundreds of thousands of children, women and elderly lost and separated at the *mela* were all successfully reunited with their families. The Kumbh Mela, on all accounts, was a grand success. It was a great religious event, a booming commercial enterprise, and a victorious public health feat. It was also a very lucky affair.

THE KUMBH MELA, STRESSED

A closer look at the healthcare delivery system and the railway station stampede reveal that the *mela*, though a significantly safer and more enjoyable event than ever before, has the potential to quickly unravel under duress.

The healthcare system was completely overwhelmed during busy bathing days, unable to meaningfully provide even routine care. A 1,200% increase in utilization did not see any increase in personnel deployment. Had there been a true emergency, the already flailing system would have, in high likelihood, been incapable of responding efficiently.

The crowd mitigation strategies worked successfully throughout the Kumbh Mela except on the day of the stampede, when they probably mattered the most. Again, the system collapsed under stress. Weighed down by its bureaucracy and inflexibility, the administration was unable to generate the rapid and efficient response the injured warranted.

THE KUMBH MELA, LOOKING AHEAD

The Kumbh Mela has always been a dynamic enterprise—continuously evolving, improving, and adapting to India's changing social, religious, and political contexts. Having now achieved the capability of providing for the safety and enjoyment of hundreds of millions, future *melas* must be better prepared to handle exigencies, which are neither unfamiliar nor infrequent occurrences.

Healthcare delivery may be improved by paying closer attention to matching supply with demand, adopting clinical or public health policies backed by evidence, and taking advantage of the access to the *mela*'s captive population by implementing much needed public health messaging and interventions. Epidemiological surveillance ought to be a necessity at the next Kumbh Mela. Mobile digital surveillance tools can be rapidly and inexpensively deployed at mass gatherings to extract critical real-time data of great public health significance.

Many of the Kumbh Mela's contemporary challenges stem from the difficulty of adjusting supply to the widely fluctuating daily demand. Computational modeling before, during, and after the *mela* will sharpen crowd estimates and flow. The Kumbh Mela administration would benefit from a centralized data collation center that receives daily inputs from car, bus, and train traffic, from surveillance cameras, from food distribution inventory records, and from services utilized (health, sanitation, etc.). Headcounts from anonymized cell phone usage could provide rich data for crowd management, epidemic surveillance, and disaster response.

The Kumbh Mela is an illustrative example of successful public private partnerships where private entities (in this case, the religious orders, contractors, and businesses) express a fair amount of autonomy within parameters mutually agreed upon with the government. An entire township is created and dismantled within months. The ephemeral community demonstrates all the trappings of modern urban cities: roads, electricity, sanitation facilities, and public amenities. Within the compounds of the religious Akharas, communities are given a fair amount of freedom to structure their places of worship, discourse, meals, entertainment, and rest. These self-organizing principles expressed within a larger negotiated framework of multiple actors may find useful applications in other transient communities around the world.

Innovative technology, big data, hard science, and intrepid execution can make the next Kumbh Mela a larger success story than it already is.

1   K. Maclean, *Pilgrimage and Power: The Kumbh Mela in Allahabad 1765–1954* (New York: Oxford University Press), 2008.

2   S. Srivasatava and A. K. Rai, "Socio-Economic Dimensions of Kumbh Mela 2013 and the Organizational Aspect of It: A Study," *International Journal of Management*, vol. 5, no. 5 (May 2014), pp. 25–32.

3   D. Barua, "History of Cholera," D. in Barua and W. B. Greenough, ed. *Cholera* (New York: Plenum Publishing Corp), 1992.

4   K. Khan et al., "Infectious Disease Surveillance and Modeling Across Geographic Frontiers and Scientific Specialties." *Lancet Infect Dis.* 3 (Mar 2012), pp. 222–30.

5   This section is reproduced from Health and South Asia with permission from the South Asia Institute at Harvard University.

6   B. McCloseky et al., "London 2012 Olympic and Paraolympic Games: Public health surveillance and epidemiology." *Lancet* (June 2014), pp. 2083–89.

7   V. Gajalakshmi et al., "Smoking and Mortality from Tuberculosis and Other Diseases in India: Retrospective Study of 43,000 Adult Male Deaths and 35,000 controls." *Lancet* (2003), pp. 507–15.

8   A. Johansson et al., "Crowd and Environmental Management During Mass Gatherings." Lancet Infect Dis. (February 2012), pp.150–56.

9   L. Plaster, "Crowd Control: How the Deadly Stampede Outside the Kumbh Mela Could Have Been Avoided," Quartz, February 11, 2013, online at http://qz.com/52805/how-the-deadly-stampede-outside-the-kumbh-mela-could-have-been-avoided.

10 P. G. Greenough, "The Kumbh Mela Stampede: Disaster Preparedness Must Bridge Jurisdictions." *BMJ* (2013), 3254–55.

11 J. Zhang, "Pedestrian Fundamental Diagrams: Comparative Analysis of Experiments in Different Geometries." *Forschungszentrum Jülich*, IAS Series (2012), p. 103.

12 V. Bignell et al,. *Catastrophic Failures* (Milton Keynes: Open University Press, 1978).

13 A. Bhatti "Disaster Risk Reduction Through Livelihood Concerns and Disaster Policy in South Asia," in P. Sahni P and M. M. Ariyabandu, eds., *Disaster Risk Reduction in South Asia* (Delhi: PHI Learning, 2003), p. 61.

Maximum Load VIGNETTE

CHUAN HAO CHEN

The 2013 Kumbh Mela at Allahabad was estimated to draw 100 million participants to the confluence of the Ganges and the Yamuna rivers. Pictures of the festival testify to the immensity of the gathering, and they beg the question, what does it mean for a temporary city to actually house 100 million people? What strategies are employed, and what are their effects, to move and control that number of crowds? This vignette explores these questions through a parametric analysis of the "pop-up" city.

Extensive infrastructural preparation was necessary to accommodate the influx of thirty million people into the city on any given bathing day. According to the official government numbers (2013), eighteen pontoon bridges were built to supplement the existing permanent bridge, and about 156.2 km of roads were laid. Ninety-nine parking lots were made available, five temporary bus stations were set up, and seven train stations were used to bring people in. 892 regular buses and 3,608 special buses brought in 9 million pilgrims, and 750 trains were in operation. To control the influx of crowds and to fight fires, thirty police stations and thirty fire stations were setup. The state police (numbering 12,461) were supplemented with military forces, and were spread through-

out the festival and stationed at key entrance points to maintain the efficient flow of the population. Eighty-five closed circuit cameras and fifty-six watchtowers (TNN, 2013) were employed at key sites to relay the ground situation to the central station, which then directed the police stationed at various check points. In addition, fourteen hospitals, practicing allopathic, homeopathic, and ayurvedic medicines, with a total of 370 beds were setup to treat the needs of the pilgrims. About 35,000 individual toilets, 7,500 trench toilets, and 1,000 non-conventional toilets (e.g., composting toilets) were set up as well. Over 70,000 people were employed to control the crowds and maintain sanitary condition over the entire area of the festival. Over the fifty-five days of the festival, there were key days that were particularly auspicious. On these days, millions of pilgrims flocked to the Kumbh Mela to take part in the festivities. While the exact numbers of most things at the Kumbh Mela is uncertain—as the influx and flow of people is simply too great and numbers are inflated for various reasons— understanding the implications of these huge numbers may be more productive in exploring this phenomenon than finding an accurate measure. The total number of people in attendance, for example,

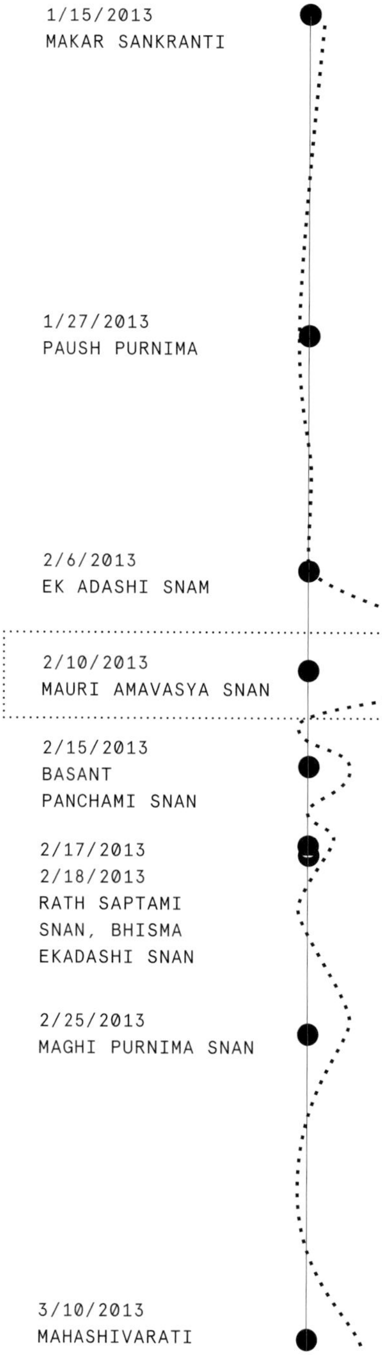

1/15/2013
MAKAR SANKRANTI

1/27/2013
PAUSH PURNIMA

2/6/2013
EK ADASHI SNAM

2/10/2013
MAURI AMAVASYA SNAN

2/15/2013
BASANT
PANCHAMI SNAN

2/17/2013
2/18/2013
RATH SAPTAMI
SNAN, BHISMA
EKADASHI SNAN

2/25/2013
MAGHI PURNIMA SNAN

3/10/2013
MAHASHIVARATI

is most likely exaggerated and the reports are inconsistent. Attendance on Mauni Amavasya Snan, the most auspicious day at the Kumbh, varies from fifteen million (Sugden, 2013) to thirty million (PTI, 2013). Sugden describes how the commissioner of Allahabad, Devesh Chaturvedi, uses headcounters from a series of watchtowers across the Kumbh, with the CCTV installed at key junctions, as well as satellite imagery to estimate the total number who attended. Chaturvedi estimates that eight million people arrived for the opening day of the Kumbh Mela, with fifteen million pilgrims converging during Mauni Amavasya Snan, and a total of 100 million people passing through the entire duration of the festival. Mr. Alok Sharma, the Allahabad police inspector general, estimates 1.5 million on the first day and forty to sixty million people over the entirety of the festival. His calculation is based on counters at Kumbh Mela entry points. Based on the assumption that each pilgrim will take up 1.5 square feet of ground, the maximum road capacity can be calculated. The administration also measures how long it takes for a police officer to move 600 meters. Because the pace of the crowd is dependent upon the density, they can approximate the size of the crowd that has covered that distance. Vehicles at the entry roads are counted manually and trains, which have up to 8,000 passengers each, are added to the total. The official Kumbh Mela website (2013) reports the final number of total attendees as 120 million. To put it into perspective, this is one tenth of the total population of India or the entire population of Japan, the tenth most populous country on Earth (US Census, 2013).

Using CAD tracings of the satellite imagery, this vignette provides an alternate way of imagining the city. It enables a reexamination of the site with various spatial calculations to provide an answer to the question of how over 100 million people fit on fifteen square kilometers? (This number is less than the officially reported twenty-square kilometers, which includes certain administrative regions in the town of Jhusi as well as land in the agricultural region to the south—this independent study considers only the areas that are newly constructed). A key risk management strategy that is employed is the use of corrals at key entry points and along the edges of major roads. Three key junctures are particularly critical. The first bottleneck that exists, by sheer virtue of the size, is the entry to the pontoon bridges. Being smaller in width

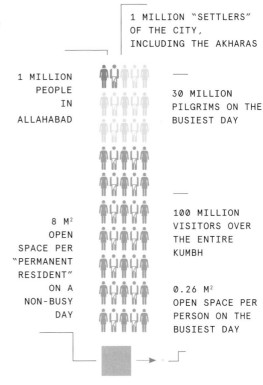

1 MILLION PEOPLE IN ALLAHABAD

1 MILLION "SETTLERS" OF THE CITY, INCLUDING THE AKHARAS

30 MILLION PILGRIMS ON THE BUSIEST DAY

8 M² OPEN SPACE PER "PERMANENT RESIDENT" ON A NON-BUSY DAY

100 MILLION VISITORS OVER THE ENTIRE KUMBH

0.26 M² OPEN SPACE PER PERSON ON THE BUSIEST DAY

than the roads leading up, the pontoon bridges form a bottleneck in crowd flow that requires police control. Indeed, police lines are set up at every pontoon bridge to make sure that the traffic flows smoothly, and that on the busiest day, the traffic moves in only one direction. Another key area is the connection between the main procession route of the Akharas and the various roads and alleys that lead to it. Barricades line the edges of the roads so that pilgrims that try to join the procession do not overwhelm the Akharas. Certain roads are designated to allow traffic to flow in and out, and the barricade and corral can open and close to direct congested traffic to less crowded areas. Some pontoon bridges are also dedicated exclusively to Akhara traffic and visitors (TNN, 2013). Lastly, police efforts are also concentrated at the entrances of the Kumbh Mela and at bus and train stations. Bringing massive influx of transient crowds, these intersections have elaborate corrals and / or heavy police presence to make sure that the sudden appearance of a crowd can be smoothly integrated into the existing traffic flow. The bathing *ghats* themselves are also a critical concern: police barricade them and install signage boards that warn pilgrims not to venture too far into the water (TNN, 2013). Located in sectors three, four, ten, twelve, thirteen, and fourteen, these *ghats* receive intense police scrutiny (IBT, 2013). Security has also been increased in the city. In order to maintain the integrity and safety of the shoreline, sandbags are piled and barricades are set up in the water, anywhere from 2 to 10 meters away from the shore, to prevent people from venturing too far into deep waters and to slow down the currents. Over 700 personnel are stationed at the *ghats* to take care of the pilgrims (TNN, 2013).

For the 60,000 foreign nationals that were expected to attend, a special registration office was set up so that extra security and information could be provided at their tent locations (TNN, 2013). Reflecting on the Kumbh Mela, several conclusions have been drawn by the organizers and the media (Rashid, 2013). Commissioner Chaturvedi pointed out three of the most important lessons from the 2013 Kumbh—the importance of maintaining strict one-way paths, the essentiality of a public address system to keep the public informed, and the benefits of a well-trained police force that can take quick action. Wider roads are part of that initiative as well. Beyond those logistics, it's important to understand the human factors. Commissioner Chaturvedi said that the pilgrims were "Hungry, thirsty, and tired after walking 10 kilometers," and really wanted to go home. They were confused by contradictory announcements and unable to move with the immense crowds, so they instead poured into and occupied the station, making police action very difficult. "There was too much focus on the Sangam area. We ignored the exit points, the crowd management in 2001 was much better." These are considerations to take into the next Kumbh Mela.

Bathing days

On the bathing days, the Akharas march down the
planned major procession routes to the Sangam.
Their order of bathing has been predetermined, but
competition among the sects is fierce. The first group
goes around 5 a.m., with the last group finishing at
around 4 p.m. Each group gets an hour or less at the
Sangam before the next group literally charges to the
river. The main procession routes are barricaded along
its sides to control the crowds of pilgrims. They bathe
along the shore but at areas farther away from the most
auspicious spots. These major roads bring in the daily
influx of short-term visitors. These visitors come on the
holy days, take a dip, then leave. Most pilgrims follow
this pattern. On this most important day, the major
roads are inundated with people and become at risk for
overcrowding. Over 10 million people come on this day.

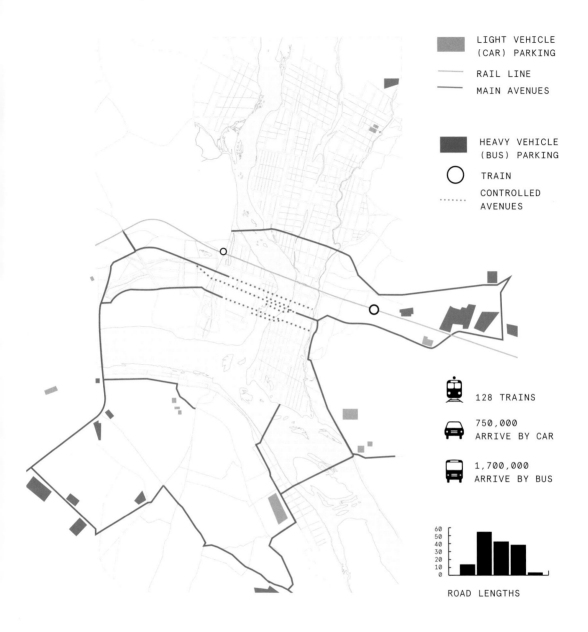

128 TRAINS

750,000
ARRIVE BY CAR

1,700,000
ARRIVE BY BUS

ROAD LENGTHS

Roads system

The major roads funnel people in from the train stations (rail indicated in yellow) and bus parking lots (parking indicated in blue). Pilgrims on buses or in their own vehicles would proceed on foot from the parking lot to the Sangam. While the large majority of pilgrims arrive via mass transit, there are also those who arrive by personal vehicles. Near the end of the festival, so many pilgrims arrive by car that congestion and blockades are caused. The police authorities struggle to manage this influx of personal vehicles (TNN, 2013). To deal with these problems, the administration has set a ban on vehicles entering the Kumbh Mela area. On major bathing days, only police vehicles and ambulances are allowed (PTI, 2013).

3,700 M
LENGTH OF
SANGAM
SHORELINE

~0.5 M
WIDTH OF
HUMAN BODY

7,400
INDIVIDUALS
CAN LINE UP,
SIDE BY SIDE,
ON THE SHORE.

22,200
INDIVIDUALS
IF PEOPLE
STACK UP IN
3 LAYERS

14 HOURS
FROM 5 A.M.
TO 7 P.M.

37 SECONDS
FOR EACH
PERSON IF
30 MILLION
PEOPLE WERE
TO BATHE IN
THESE AREAS

0.075 %
VISITORS
CAN BATHE AT
THE SANGAM AT
ONCE

Purifying spaces

The Sangam is the holy confluence of the Ganges,
Yamuna, and Saraswati rivers. During the Kumbh,
millions of pilgrims are drawn to the site to take
a dip in the holy river. The map illustrates the
collective desire for both holy men who are
seasoned attendees as well as first-time pilgrims
from far away who move toward the holy confluence.

Main procession route

The Akharas lead the procession to the Sangam, or the holy confluence. Starting in the early morning at around 6 a.m., the Akharas march, in a predetermined order based on importance and seniority, to the river shore (Daniel, 2013). They march on two main processional routes that are barricaded along its length. The procession route to the west is the more popular one, having a larger area and hosting the more senior Akharas along its sides. On the bathing days, the Akharas march down this route to the shores.

Most pilgrims want to bathe on this side of the Sangam, but for crowd-control reasons, they are often encouraged or detoured to bathe at *ghats* further to the north, over on the east side, or in the new sectors 13 and 14 to the south. The procession route to the east hosts less senior Akharas and other organizations who don't enjoy the same privileges and relationships with the Kumbh planners. The processional routes widen to accomodate the increasing number of pilgrims at the Sangam.

Main flow and potential overflow routes

At certain checkpoints, the barricades open periodically to allow the pilgrims to join the procession or reach the Sangam via an alternate route. Crowd control is an immense task, and the threat of a human stampede is great. As part of the strategy, the police try to divert people to various *ghats* along the shore.

▶   MAIN ACCESS POINTS

━━   BATHING

‑ ‑ ‑ ‑   ALTERNATE ROUTES

•••• BOUNDARY

→ FLOW OF PEOPLE, LENGTH INDICATES SPEED

Flow at the Sangam

Keeping people moving along is important to maintaining order. Barricades are set up to relieve congestion, forcing people to detour, as well as to ensure the orderly processions of the Akharas to the Sangam. Standing and mounted police keep the pilgrims moving so they can both get to the Sangam and allow more people to come through.

189

0-5 m

5-10 m

10-20 m

20-40 m

Road capacities

Road capacities are a crucial component in the management of the crowd as they dictate, more or less, the number of pilgrims that can be on site at any one time. In a way, they can be seen as holding areas for the pilgrims en route to the Sangam. The roads at the Kumbh span anywhere from tight 3-meter alleys between the tent blocks, to 10-meter-wide pontoon bridges, to 50+-meter-wide processional routes. The pilgrims are brought into the city via 4 entrances. These connect to the unceasing flow of pilgrims coming in every hour via the 200 trains, cars, and buses.

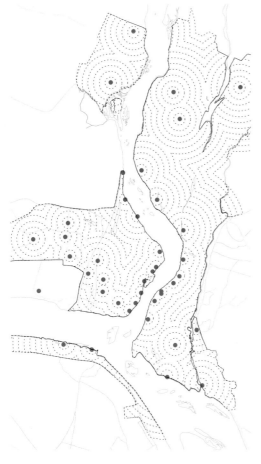

CATCHMENT AREA

STREET POLICE CONTROL GRADIENT

Police and crowd control infrastructure

Policemen are located at intersections where bottlenecks are expected. At these intersections, crowds are directed onto alternate routes away from the Sangam. This way, pilgrims would be directed to different locations along the Sangam, spreading out the crowd so they do not all converge onto the same spot at the same time. The police are also responsible for maintaining order, maintaining the barricades for crowd control, moving bathers along so others can come, looking for suspicious activity, and acting as a resource for lost individuals

Police control grid

The police function in several capacities, one of which
is to provide surveillance for a pre-assigned area. The
Kumbh site is divided into 10 to 20 square meter grids,
with each officer assigned to a block that they round
every 20 minutes. The control grids are densely packed
at the Kumbh. Spatial calculations would give some
30,000+ squares that would require police surveillance,
and there are about 30,000 police officers employed
at the Kumbh, thus ensuring security.

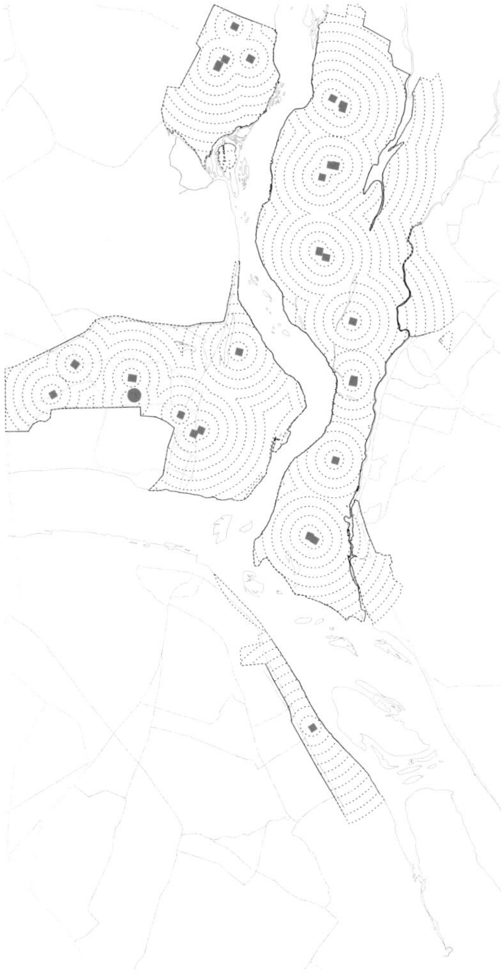

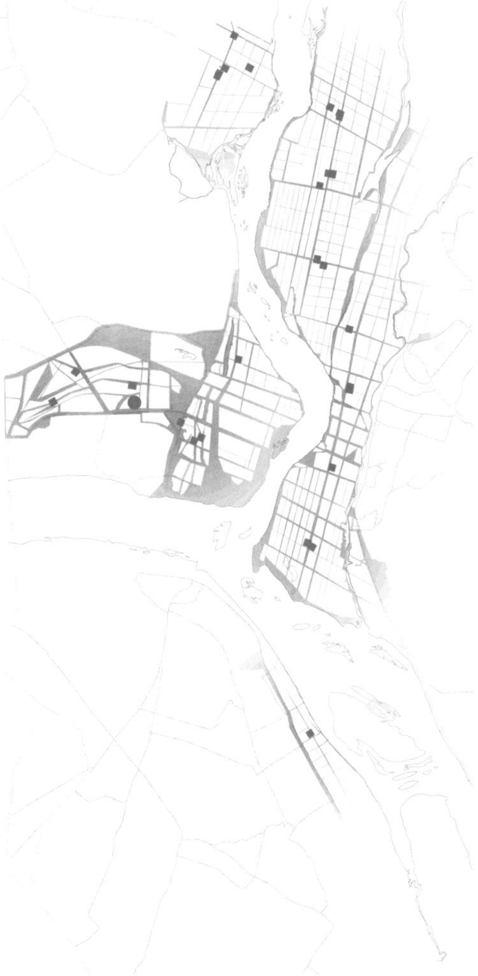

243 DOCTORS

CATCHMENT AREA ZONES

100 PERSON HOSPITAL

MOST ACCESS | LEAST ACCESS

120,000 PILGRIMS PER DOCTOR

Catchment area and street access gradient

The massive number of pilgrims moving through the site poses significant public health challenges, which include possible epidemics, stampedes, and physical injuries. While severe cases are sent to the major hospital in Allahabad, smaller scale tent hospitals and clinics are set up in every sector to take care of the sick and injured. These medical infrastructures are crucial to maintaining the safe management of the Kumbh. The clinics are also tracking centers to manage the spread of disease. On the busiest day, thousands of people go to the clinics for services. The hospitals / clinics are fairly well distributed around the area, as there is at least one, and usually two or three, per sector.

TOILETS

TENTS

SECTOR
BOUNDARY

Sanitation infrastructure

Another key infrastructure to safely manage the number of people is sanitation. More toilets than ever before, including some experimental types, have been installed at the Kumbh. A lot of effort has been put into enforcing the sanitary infrastructure, with thousands of sweepers cleaning the sites at least twice daily. They clean out various alleys that become sites of public defecation and manage the large sewage pits, spraying them with disinfectants and DDT to control insects.

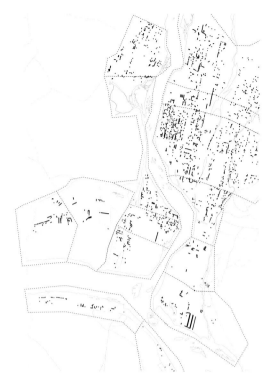

INDIVIDUAL TOILETS

GROUP (SULABH COMPLEX) TOILETS

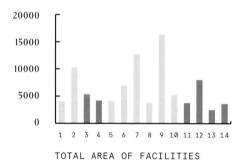

TOTAL AREA OF FACILITIES

GROUP (SULABH COMPLEX) TOILETS

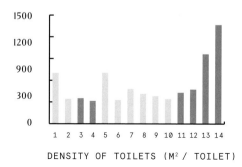

DENSITY OF TOILETS (M² / TOILET)

TRENCH TOILETS

TRENCH TOILETS

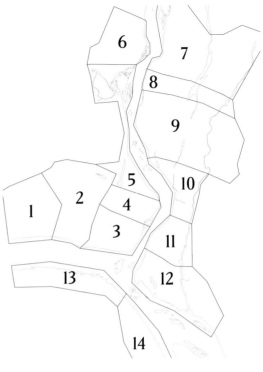

SECTOR KEY

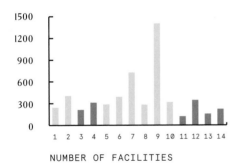

NUMBER OF FACILITIES

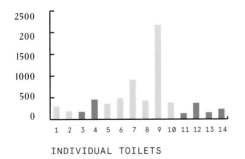

INDIVIDUAL TOILETS

10,976 SANITARY FACILITIES

121,847 TOILET STALLS EQUIVALENT (2M² AREA)

20 MILLION USERS / DAY
CAN USE THE FACILITIES ASSUMING A RATE
OF 5 MINUTES PER USE

0 400 800 1600   3200

Sanitation distribution

The toilets appear to be evenly distributed
throughout the Kumbh and are not placed
at particular sites, with fairly even densities
throughout the sectors. Sangam sectors
appear to have less individual-type toilets.

Investigating Population Dynamics of the KUMBH MELA through the Lens of Cell Phone Data

JUKKA-PEKKA ONNELA & TARUN KHANNA

Introduction

The Kumbh Mela is a religious Hindu festival that has been celebrated for hundreds of years. On the broad sandy flats left behind by the receding waters of the rainy season, a temporary "pop-up" megacity is constructed in a matter of weeks to house the festival. The Kumbh Mela has evoked endless fascination and scrutiny by observers dating back to Chinese and Arab itinerant scholars from centuries past, to contemporary academics, mostly social scientists and humanists of various disciplinary persuasions. Both participants and external observers have documented past Kumbh festivals, and this book brings together various perspectives using different methodologies to the study of the 2013 Kumbh Mela.

In this chapter, we examine the use of cell phone communication metadata to study the 2013 Kumbh Mela. Telecom operators worldwide collect these data routinely for billing and research purposes. At bare minimum, metadata contain information on who calls whom, at what time, and for how long. The metadata studied here, also known as Call Detail Records (CDRs), were made available to us by the Indian telecom operator Bharti Airtel for the period from January 1, 2013 to March 31, 2013. The cohort we introduce here consists of all Bharti Airtel customers who were present at the Kumbh Mela site during this time period and used their cell phone at least once to communicate with someone, whether as senders or receivers of communications. We describe the details of this cohort, consisting of approximately 390 million communication events. To put this number into perspective, if a single individual were to take just one second to examine each record, it would still take twelve years to go through the data (without breaks).

Cell phone metadata in general, and these data in particular, have a longitudinal, spatial, and network component to them, and they describe both calls and text messages. These data characteristics place our work firmly in the "big-data" context and enable us to address questions that would be difficult or impossible to tackle without these data and the requisite data analytic techniques. We hope that our approach could bring the study of this spectacular historic event—purportedly the largest gathering of people in human history—on the intellectual radar of a host of quantitative scientists, such as physicists and statisticians, who may not typically study these types of cultural phenomena. We should note that given their nature, these data could be analyzed using a broad range of sophisticated statistical techniques and mathematical models. In this chapter, our goal is to introduce the idea of using these data to study the 2013 Kumbh Mela, to put forward what may be attained by this approach, to describe the festival's metadata cohort and some salient features of the data, and to report on some of our preliminary findings. We leave more detailed and sophisticated analyses of these data for future work.

Data-Driven STUDY of Human Behavior

Research on human social interactions has traditionally relied on observations reported by humans, and both self-reported data and observer-recorded data, with varying degrees of observer involvement being used to quantify social interactions[1]. Analyzing human behavior based on electronically generated data has recently become popular. One approach is based on actively "instrumenting" study subjects by having them wear electronic devices, such as sociometers (credit card sized devices worn around the neck), to collect detailed data on various dimensions of social interaction, such as talkativeness and physical proximity to others.[2-4]

An alternative approach is to rely on passively generated electronic records of behavior, such as CDRs that are collected by operators for billing and internal research purposes. These data can be analyzed to investigate the structure of social networks,[5,6] human mobility patterns,[7,8] and the role of geography in constraining social ties and social groups.[9,10] They have also been applied to study infectious diseases in epidemiology.[11] Although active instrumentation, such as the use of sociometers, can result in richer behavioral data, it does not scale well to the study of groups larger than perhaps a few hundred subjects. The passive approach relying on CDRs, in contrast, can in principle scale up to any level and has been used to construct, analyze, and model society-wide social networks.[5,12,13]

The Kumbh Mela has always fascinated scholars across different fields, and often these scholars have focused on studying specific aspects of the gathering, such as the nature of gift giving from one participant to the other or the style of clothing worn by participants. These types of studies are fascinating in their own right, but they necessarily involve many subjective decisions to be made by the investigators on issues like which gift-giving event to document or which dress to photograph. This necessarily requires some preconception of what types of behaviors should be captured, naturally leading to some pre-screening on which behaviors are recorded.

Much of the recent scholarship on the Kumbh Mela (e.g., *Pilgrimage and Power*[14] *and the Kumbh Mela Pop-up Megacity Business Case Study*[15]) has the central construct of the value and nature of information flows at the festival. Information was vital through history for several disparate

AN ASCETIC USES A CELLULAR PHONE

reasons. During colonial and pre-colonial times, the Mughals and the British Raj saw Allahabad (or Prayag as it was known at one point) as a logistically important town, and the rush of pilgrims often compromised their ability to control information (and to otherwise mobilize the military). Also during the Raj era, the British were concerned that seditious messages might inadvertently be spread far and wide across India after visitors met at the Kumbh Mela and exchanged ideas with content that was not possible to police. In independent India, in contrast, the Kumbh often features as a way for India's leaders to broadcast nationalist messages, as it does in modern India for those politicians who wish to identify with the predominantly Hindu component of the electorate. Whether monitored in days of lore by *sadhus* (wandering holy men), or more currently by modern transient merchants, or by people in neighboring cities, information flows are vital in controlling commerce. Finally, of course, information is key to the prospect of managing the religious event in real time. Indeed, our use of cell phone metadata to shed light on information flows is perhaps most useful for such management of the event in the years to come. We offer our approach in that preliminary spirit.

Cell phones are now ubiquitous in India, and it is perhaps surprising to some readers how many pilgrims traveled with their cell phones to the Kumbh Mela. This fact enables us to adopt a data-driven approach that makes it possible to investigate not only those phenomena that were deemed interesting a previously, but also to capture unanticipated phenomena. We therefore approach

the Kumbh as an organic, collective event with as few preconceptions as possible. It should be stressed that the type of approach we advocate here is not a panacea by any means and it clearly has its limitations. We do, however, think that the proposed approach is useful for giving us the proverbial 30,000-foot perspective to this magnificent cultural event and it may very well help complement some of the many other ways used to study the Kumbh Mela.

Call Detail RECORDS

Since the data we use to investigate the Kumbh is generated by cell phones and recorded by operators—to understand the potential and limitations of this approach, it is helpful to understand the basics of what happens when a person uses his or her cell phone to call another user. In its most basic form, a cell phone functions like a two-way radio containing a radio receiver and a radio transmitter that transmits the communication data to the nearest cell tower. The cell tower is a steel pole or lattice structure that rises into the air and contains structures to support antennas. Cell towers are accompanied by base stations that contain the needed electronics for handling data transmission. Base station cell sites themselves are connected to the Mobile Telephone Switching Office (MTSO) that monitors traffic and arranges hand-offs between base stations. Each cell phone and nearest base station keep track of the cell phone that happens to be located at a given time. When a cell phone user dials another user, the MTSO searches its database for the target number and transmits the call to the cell tower that is nearest to the person called. The areas of signal coverage from adjacent cell towers overlap slightly near the border of the cells, and if a phone moves to the edge of a cell, the base stations monitor and coordinate with each other through the MTSO and arrange "hand-offs" from one cell tower to another to ensure that the call does not get disrupted.

A CDR is a digital record gathered from an instance of a telecommunications transaction described above. It is automatically generated by the mobile network operator, and contains specific data points about the transaction, but not the content of the transaction, such as voice call and text message data. The types of information included in a CDR may include the following: the phone number of the subscriber originating the call, the phone number receiving the call, the starting time of the call (date / time), the duration of the call, a unique sequence number identifying the record, the identification of the telephone exchange or equipment writing the record, the route by which the call entered the exchange (the nearest cell phone tower of the initiating party), the route by which the call left the exchange (the nearest cell phone tower of the receiving party), and the event type (voice call or SMS).[16] Table 1 illustrates what simple CDR data (artificial, in this case) look like. The first three columns specify the date, the start time of the event, and the type of event. The fourth column indicates call duration (for voice calls only).

MOBILE CELLULAR NETWORK STATIONS

The fifth and sixth columns give anonymized (surrogate) IDs for the caller and recipient, respectively. The last two columns in the table indicate what cell towers were used to transmit and receive the communication event, enabling one to geographically locate individuals at the time of communication. It is this geographical component of the metadata that enables us to define a cohort that is spatially localized at the Kumbh Mela site.

Date	Start time	Event type	Duration (s)	Caller ID	Callee ID	Caller tower ID	Callee tower ID
09/02/2013	14:36	VC	185	9912345678	4412345678	54	42
10/02/2013	14:41	VC	252	9912345678	6612345678	42	73
11/02/2013	14:42	SMS	NA	4412345678	6612345678	73	73

TABLE 1. AN EXAMPLE OF THE METADATA USED IN THE STUDY. HERE *VC* REFERS TO VOICE CALL AND *SMS* TO TEXT MESSAGE

The 2013 KUMBH Cohort

The 2013 Kumbh cohort consists of any Bharti Airtel customer who used his or her cell phone either to make or receive a call, or to send or receive a text message at the Kumbh Mela site between January 1 and March 31, 2013. The Kumbh site comprises 207 unique cell sites, or cell towers, located within the area. This larger than normal density of towers was accomplished by adding several mobile cell towers, situated in fixed locations throughout the festival to meet the expected high service demand. Because a communication event (call or SMS) occurs at the level of pairs of individuals, it is useful to elaborate what is and what is not observed as a consequence of this study design. Any communication event involves two parties—Person A and Person B. Person A may or may not be an Airtel customer, and may or may not be present at the Kumbh Mela site during the period of investigation; the same holds true for Person B. Therefore, each interaction involves zero, one, or two Airtel customers, and either of the two people may or may not be present at the Kumbh site. We observe any communication event that involves at least one Airtel customer who is present at the Kumbh site during the period of investigation. The other party may be a customer of any operator (Airtel or non-Airtel) and may be physically located anywhere in the world (at the Kumbh site or outside of it). Figure 1 shows a schematic of the study design.

We note that one can divide all communication ties into intra-Kumbh communications (both people at the venue) and extra-Kumbh communications (only one person at the venue). We speculate that the intra-Kumbh ties are likely used for local coordination, which will become more important as population density increases and crowds rise, whereas the extra-Kumbh

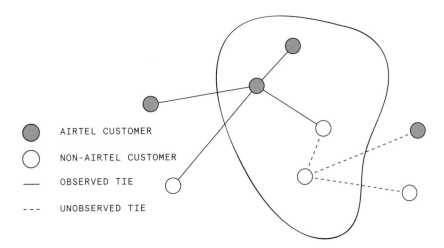

AIRTEL CUSTOMER

NON-AIRTEL CUSTOMER

OBSERVED TIE

UNOBSERVED TIE

FIGURE 1. Schematic of the study design. The large shaded area in the middle represents the Kumbh Mela site. Airtel customers are represented with dark nodes and non-Airtel customers with white nodes. A tie connecting a pair of nodes corresponds to a communication event (call or SMS); observed ties are shown as solid lines and unobserved ties as dashed lines. We observe any communication event that involves at least one Airtel customer who is at the Kumbh site during the investigated time period.

ties are likely driven by other factors. Future research should investigate the differences between these two distinct types of communication events and their consequences for population dynamics.

The following data were available for each communication event for the individuals in the Kumbh Mela cohort:

> NUMBER OF THE CALLER
> IMSI NUMBER
> CDR TYPE (call or SMS)
> NUMBER OF THE CALLEE
> CELL TOWER ID
> DATE
> TIME
> CALL DURATION

The IMSI number corresponds to what is often called the phone's SIM card number; Cell tower IDs are codes used to associate particular cell towers with each communication event.

Privacy of human subjects is always an important concern in any study. In our past work with cell phone metadata[5,6,10] we have relied on anonymized data, which involves mapping the phone numbers and other identifiers to surrogate keys in such a way that this mapping cannot be reversed. The goal of our past and ongoing research efforts is to obtain generalizable knowledge about human behavior, thus an individual identifier is a nuisance parameter of no scientific interest and yet, importantly, it poses an unnecessary threat to subjects because of the potential risk of subject re-identification. Consequently, data anonymization upholds the scientific value of such data, while

NUMBER OF CALLS AND SMS

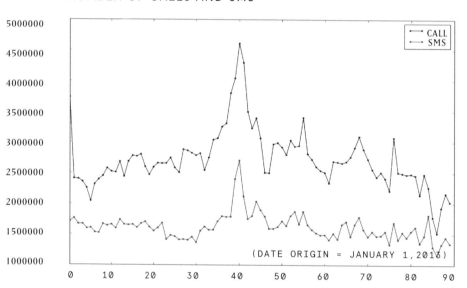

FIGURE 2. The number of calls and text messages as a function of time in the 2013 Kumbh cohort

Date	SMS count	Call count	Total count
7-Feb-13	1,784,464	3,308,496	5,092,960
8-Feb-13	1,788,094	3,803,392	5,591,486
9-Feb-13	2,401,666	4,044,101	6,445,767
10-Feb-13	**2,702,578**	**4,612,422**	**7,315,000**
11-Feb-13	2,118,802	4,296,436	6,415,238
12-Feb-13	1,750,374	3,498,322	5,248,696
13-Feb-13	1,800,575	3,230,284	5,030,859

FIGURE 2. The number of calls and text messages as a function of time in the 2013 Kumbh Cohort

simultaneously providing excellent protection for human subjects. Anonymization is now a routine procedure in this line of work and something that is mandated by most university Institutional Review Board (IRB) regulations. In the present project, the authors did not have direct access to the data. Instead, the data resided at all times on Airtel's computers in Gurgaon, India. The research was carried out by sending computer-programming scripts to an Airtel employee who ran the analyses on a dedicated computer and sent the results, consisting of summary statistics of interest back to the authors.

Preliminary FINDINGS

In the following section, we report on some preliminary findings pertaining to intensity of communication activity, daily fluctuations in cohort size, cumulative cohort size, and length of stay.

Intensity of COMMUNICATION

As a starting point to our analyses, we investigated the total volume of communication in the cohort. The 2013 Kumbh cohort exchanged a total of 146 million (145,736,764) text messages and 245 million (245,252,102) calls, resulting in a total of 390 million (390,988,866) communication events. When plotted as a function of time in Figure 2, where the x-axis gives the index of the day with January 1, 2013 corresponding to day 0, it is clear that the number of calls and text messages are not uniformly distributed in time but instead display one prominent and several smaller peaks.

The main bathing day of the 2013 Kumbh Mela was February 10, 2013, corresponding to day index 40, and this is precisely the location of the most prominent voice call and text messaging peaks. In addition, calling activity was above its baseline value for about a week leading to the main bathing day and then declined over the next several days. The number of text messages also had a clear peak surrounding this event, but it appeared more concentrated around the main bathing day, rising closer to the event than the curve for phone calls and declining faster after it. We report the daily text message and voice call counts surrounding the main bathing day in Table 2.

The ramping up to the peaks on significant bathing days can provide useful information for capacity planning of all sorts, as well as for monitoring (human and vehicular) traffic congestion patterns. These types of regularties in the data could be used for future predictive modeling purposes.

211

Daily FLUCTUATIONS in Cohort Size

Cell phone metadata can be used to investigate the number of people in attendance at the 2013 Kumbh. Here it is useful to distinguish between daily fluctuations in the size of the Kumbh cohort and its aggregate or cumulative size from January 1, 2013 to March 31, 2013. We start with the daily fluctuations by plotting the number of unique daily SIM cards in Figure 3. In this plot, each point represents the number of unique SIM cards that were used to communicate that day, which are re-aggregated each day of the investigation period. If a SIM card is not used on a given day, it does not contribute towards that day's count, and its use on other days is irrelevant for that day's count. One can immediately observe the major bathing days in this plot, with the February 10 bathing day (at time index 40) clearly standing out from the other peaks. On that day, approximately 800,000 unique SIM cards were active.

Using the above numbers for determining the number of Kumbh visitors depends, among other factors; on the fraction of people carrying cell phones and to what extent that fraction may change in time. While estimating the

NUMBER OF DAILY UNIQUE SIMs

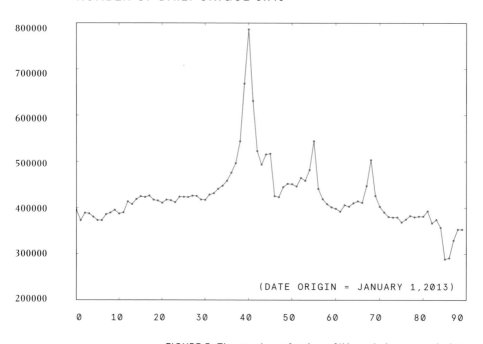

FIGURE 3. The number of unique SIM cards in use each day

CUMULATIVE NUMBER OF SIMs

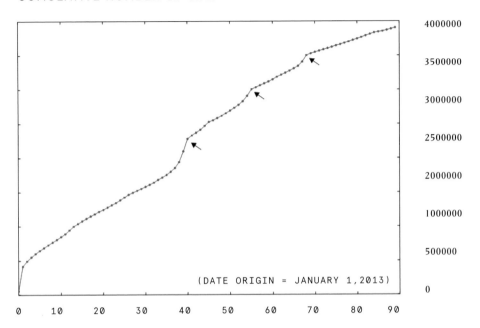

FIGURE 4. The cumulative number of unique SIM cards in the 2013 Kumbh cohort up to the point in time given on the x-axis. The arrows point to "shoulders" in the curve, corresponding to major bathing days

precise numbers is part of our ongoing work, we want to point out that as long as the fraction of people with cell phones and the frequency of cell phone use remain more or less constant, one can use these findings to study day-to-day changes in the size of the Kumbh cohort. For example, from the perspective of infectious disease management, it is important to have accurate estimates of the size of the population and, in particular, of the changes in its size. This is for the simple reason that if the number of cases of a given disease goes up by, say, 50% from one day to the next, if there is an accompanying change of 50% in the size of the underlying population, we likely do not have an epidemic. In contrast, if the population size remains constant, we may have an epidemic at hand. For epidemiological applications, such as detecting an impending epidemic, learning about *relative changes* in cohort size is often sufficient. The present approach may, in fact, be more informative to that end than estimates based on more conventional sources, such as traffic monitoring to and from the site.

JUKKA-PEKKA ONNELA & TARUN KHANNA

Cumulative COHORT Size

We focused above on daily changes in the number of individuals (SIM cards) present at the Kumbh Mela site and argued that cell phone metadata and their statistical analysis can yield important insights into this problem. There are a number of other approaches that can be used to study the number of people present at any given location, such as aerial observation or satellite imaging of the venue. The challenge with these types of approaches is that if the gathering lasts for several weeks like the Kumbh does, it becomes difficult to estimate the aggregate number of people who have passed through the event. For example, we reported above that approximately 800,000 unique SIM cards were active on the main bathing day. However, there is no way to tell from plots like Figure 3 whether we have the same set of visitors across days—or whether there is an inflow and a corresponding outflow of people that keeps the number of daily visitors more or less constant but actually corresponds to an entirely different population dynamic that contributes to an increasing cumulative number of visitors.

To distinguish between the number of daily visitors and the cumulative number of visitors, we examine the cumulative number of unique SIM cards over the time period from January 1st to March 31st. In Figure 4, we plot the number of unique SIM cards that have been active at least once by the time index given on the x-axis. By March 31st, approximately 3.9 million SIM cards had been used by the cohort. In a cumulative plot such as this one, no two adjacent points are independent, which on the one hand leads to a smooth curve, but on the other hand makes it more difficult to detect changes in underlying population dynamics. That said, the three major bathing days are visible as "shoulders" in both the curves, suggesting that large groups of people arrived to the venue specifically to experience these major bathing days.

LENGTH of Stay

There are many different categories of visitors to the Kumbh Mela, ranging from the curious visitor in passing, to the deeply religious *ascetic* staying for the entire duration of the event. To investigate the length of stay of the visitors is therefore an interesting question in its own right, but is also helpful for studying the population churn or for estimating the total number of individual visitors throughout the entire event. Here we focus on the length of stay question by recording for each SIM card the time t_a when it was first used at the venue and the time tb when it was last used. We define length of stay with the formula: $d=t_b-t_a$.

In examining this number, we need to consider the fact that any given SIM card may have been present at the venue before t_a but was not used for the first time until at time t_a. Similarly, a SIM card could have remained at the venue after t_b without being used subsequently. For this reason, the length of stay is estimated as a simple difference between t_b and t_a resulting in an interval-censored estimate. It can be interpreted as a lower bound for the actual (unobserved) duration of stay, leading to conservative estimates. Using this approach, we found the mean length of stay to be 18.1 days, the minimum and maximum being one day and eighty-nine days, respectively. There was also substantial variability in the lengths of stay, with a standard deviation of 29.6 days. Overall, 23.8% of the stays were longer than thirty days and 15.0% of the stays were over sixty days.

We note that while it is possible that the same SIM card is used in multiple handsets, but as long as the SIM card arrives and leaves the site when the person does, there is no systematic bias introduced to our length-of-stay estimates. There are however other scenarios where a bias could be introduced. For example—a person could leave the Kumbh Mela site but give their SIM card to a friend who is staying longer, resulting in an overestimated of length of stay. Considering joint SIM card numbers and unique handset numbers could alleviate this and other potential concerns, more sophisticated statistical approaches could be employed to incorporate SIM card sharing and other behavioral scenarios into the estimation process, leading to more accurate and robust estimates.

Future RESEARCH

In this section, we have reported on a novel approach that may be used to study population dynamics of individuals at the Kumbh Mela and have reported on some of our preliminary results. We would like to conclude this section with two messages. First, from the early results presented here, it is clear that this overall approach can be used in a number of contexts where large numbers of people have gathered together. While the Kumbh Mela is obviously a very carefully planned event, the approach is also suitable to study the population dynamics of misplaced populations such as those resulting from natural disasters like earthquakes or floods. Second, it is clear that the richness of the cell phone metadata lends itself to very sophisticated statistical and mathematical analyses that can incorporate dimensions of the data we have not utilized here, such as the properties of the social network constructed from cell phone call patterns, or the spatial dynamics of individuals at the Kumbh Mela venue obtained from cell tower data. These types of analyses could shed light on large-scale crowd behavior and would be helpful for understanding and predicting crowd movements, thereby helping with crowd control and traffic planning; measures that could help avoid congestion and human stampedes. We leave the investigation of these other topics for future work.

1   J. P. Onnela et al., "Using Sociometers to Quantify Social Interaction Patterns," *Sci. Rep.* 4 (2014).

2   D. Olguin Olguin, et al., "Sensible Organizations: Technology and Methodology for Automatically Measuring Organizational Behavior," *IEEE Trans. Syst. Man. Cybern. B. Cybern.* 39 (2009), pp. 43–55.

3   N. Eagle, "Reality Mining: Sensing Complex Social Systems," *Pers. Ubiquitous Comput.* 10 (2005), pp. 255–68

4   C. Cattuto et al., "Dynamics of Person-to-Person Interactions from Distributed RFID Sensor Networks." *PLOS One* 5 (2010).

5   J. P. Onnela et al., "Structure and Tie Strengths in Mobile Communication Networks," *Proc. Natl. Acad. Sci.* U. S. A. 104 (2007), pp. 7332–36.

6   J. P. Onnela et al., "Analysis of a Large-Scale Weighted Network of One-to-One Human Communication," *New J. Phys.* 9 (2007), p. 179.

7   M. C. González et al., "Understanding Individual Human Mobility Patterns," *Nature* 453 (2008), pp. 779–82.

8   F. Calabrese et al., "Understanding Individual Mobility Patterns from Urban Sensing Data: A Mobile Phone Trace Example," *Transp. Res. Part C Emerg. Technol.* 26 (2013), pp. 301–13.

9   R. Lambiotte et al., "Geographical Dispersal of Mobile Communication Networks," *Phys. A Stat. Mech. its Appl.* 387 (2008), pp. 5317–25.

10 J. P. Onnela et al., "Geographic Constraints on Social Network Groups." *PLOS One* 6 (2011).

11 A. Wesolowski et al., "Quantifying the Impact of Human Mobility on Malaria," *Science* 338 (2012), pp. 267–70.

12 V. D. Blondel et al., "Fast Unfolding of Communities in Large Networks," *J. Stat. Mech. Theory Exp.* (2008).

13 C. Ratti et al., "Redrawing the Map of Great Britain from a Network of Human Interactions," *PLOS One* 5 (2010).

14 K. Maclean. *Pilgrimage and Power: The Kumbh Mela in Allahabad, 1765–1954* (Oxford University Press, 2008).

15 T. Khanna et al., "Kumbh Mela, India's Pop-Up Mega-city," *Harvard Bus. Publ. Case Study* (2013).

16 R. Horak, *Telecommunications and Data Communications Handbook [Hardcover]*, no. 832, 2nd edition (Hoboken: Wiley-Interscience, 2008).

ACKNOWLEDGMENTS

The authors wish to acknowledge the help of Jeanette Lorme. J.P. Onnela is supported by a 2014 Career Incubator Award by the Harvard School of Public Health; T. Khanna is supported by the Harvard Business School.

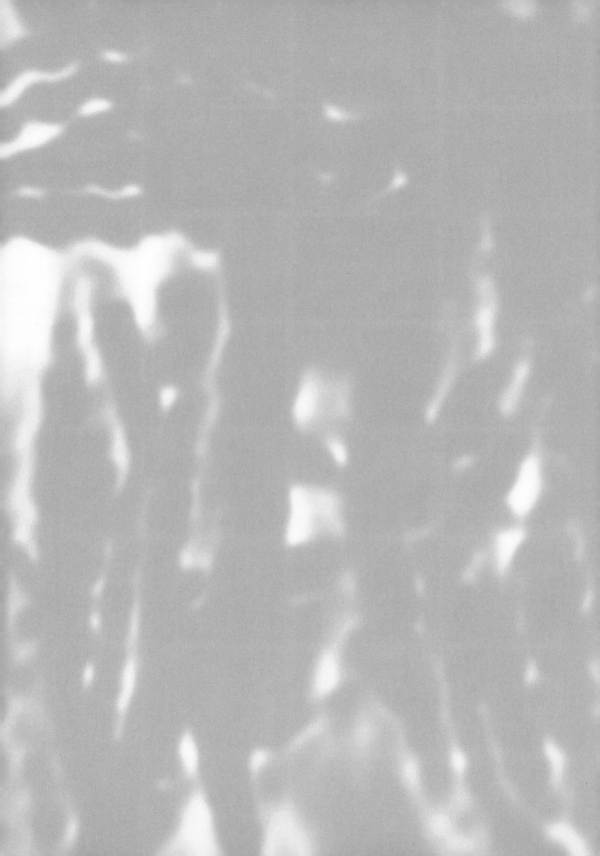

DEPLOYMENT & DECONSTRUCTION

DEPLOYMENT
Photo Essay

DINESH MEHTA

The following photo essay depicts the deployment of the
Kumbh Mela during the month of December. The photogra-
pher Dinesh Mehta used a kite setup to capture the aerial
perspectives. This un-intrusive technology allowed him
to capture highly detailed images of the processes and
assemblies. The images he captured introduce both the
material systems as well as the related labor practices.

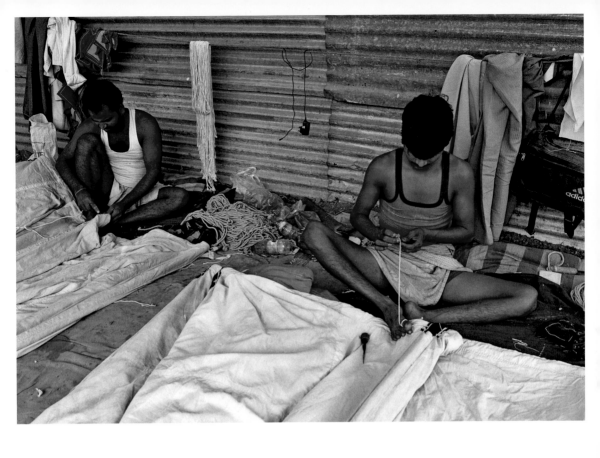

Deployment
MAPS

MICHAEL LEE & JUAN PABLO CORRAL

The following maps show a comparative analysis between satellite images and line tracings to visualize the fluid nature of the riverbed and the deployment of the physical infrastructures, spatially and temporally. The maps investigate the time-based deployment, use, and deconstruction of physical infrastructures at the Kumbh Mela, namely topographic leveling, roads, pontoon bridges, electricity, water supply, sanitation, river edges, land parceling, and the construction of gates and tents within Akharas. The existing surrounding infrastructure is shown in black and the Kumbh-specific elements in red.

MAP 1
MARCH–MAY 2012

AGRICULTURAL
LAND COVERS
MOST OF THE
AREA, INTER-
CONNECTED BY
INFORMAL DIRT
ROADS

MAP OF THE AREA
IN ITS CURRENT
STATE IS SENT
TO THE ARMY

MAJOR ROAD
AXIS DESIGNATED
AND SECURED TO
BEGIN MATERIAL
TRANSPORT

THE CHIEF SECRE-
TARY MEETS WITH
ADMINISTRATION
ON SITE TO AS-
SESS CONDITIONS
AND FUTURE

MAP 2
OCT 15-22, 2012

RIVER RECEDES
AND LEAVES
DAMPENED LAND

MAJOR ROADS
DEMARCATED AND
BULLDOZED IN
PREPARATION FOR
METAL SHEETS

SECTOR BOUND-
ARIES OUTLINED

ELECTRIC POLES
DEPLOYED IN
SOUTHERN SEC-
TORS

INITIAL PON-
TOON DEPLOYMENT
FOR SECONDARY
BRIDGES

MAP 3
DEC 12, 2012

ALL MAJOR ROADS
COMPLETED

SECONDARY ROADS
TRACED

PONTOON DEPLOY-
MENT AND BRIDGE
CONSTRUCTION
75% COMPLETE

RIVER EMBANK-
MENTS 25% COM-
PLETE

INFRASTRUCTURE
DEPLOYMENT FOR
WATER, ELEC-
TRICITY, AND
TELECOMMUNICA-
TIONS

TENT CONSTRUC-
TION AND OC-
CUPATION COM-
MENCES

MAP 4
DEC 21-
JAN 6, 2013

ALL ROAD PRODUC-
TION COMPLETED

CONSTRUCTION
SOUTH OF THE
SANGAM BEGINS

RIVER EMBANK-
MENTS 90% COM-
PLETE

ALL BRIDGE CON-
STRUCTION COM-
PLETED

MAP 5
FEB 7, 2013

KUMBH MELA 100%
GROUND
OCCUPATION

MAP 6
MARCH-APRIL 2013

TENT DISASSEM-
BLY AND SUB-
SEQUENT IN-
FRASTRUCTURE
REMOVAL

SORTING AND
COLLECTION OF
MATERIAL COMPO-
NENTS

STRAW MATS
ALONG THE
EMBANKMENTS
BURNED

SANDBAGS APPRO-
PRIATED BY CITY
RESIDENTS

BRIDGE AND
PONTOON DECON-
STRUCTION

AGRICULTURAL
ACTIVITY RE-
SUMES

SANGAM ACTIV-
ITY WANES TO
SMALLER BATHING
GROUPS

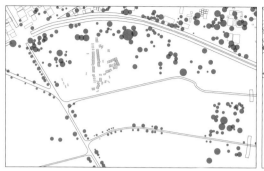

SECTOR 2

SECTOR 4

SECTOR 10   JUNE 10, 2012   NOV 12, 2012

MATERIAL TRANSPORTATION

ASSEMBLED

RAW

| JULY | AUGUST | SEPTEMBER | OCTOBER | NOVEMBER |

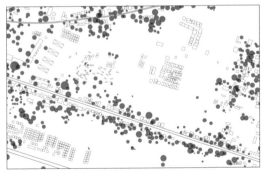
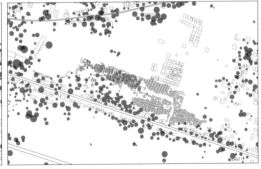

JAN 30, 2013   APRIL 25, 2013

ASSEMBLY   KUMBH MELA   DISASSEMBLY   REABSORPTION

JANUARY   FEBRUARY   MARCH   APRIL   MAY   JUNE

Physical Infrastructure VIGNETTE

JOSE MAYORAL & JOHANNES STAUDT

The 2013 Kumbh Mela took place from January 14 to March 10, 2013. The preparations for this religious gathering started months in advance. Materials were gathered from all over the region and fabrication of specific elements such as the pontoon bridges began close to the site. Once the water re-ceded in September, the ground was leveled and the roads were marked. In November, the basic infrastructure, including the electrical poles, pontoon bridges, and water infrastruc-ture were put into place. As the event grew near in early January, the enclosure systems, which include a wide range of tents, temples, and congrega-tions halls, began to be assem-bled within the framework of the grid.

In March, after the Kumbh Mela was over, the building systems and the infrastructure were disassembled. Some elements, including the reed roads, were left behind to be reabsorbed by the river. Others, like the pon-toon bridges, were transported to new sites in their entirety or reentered the stream of con-struction materials to be used for new construction. Much of the material was stored for use during a future Kumbh Mela or another event.

To understand the spatio-envi-ronmental impact of the Kumbh Mela, one must analyze it as a physical and temporal system. The assembly of the Kumbh Mela is related to natural cycles of the seasons and the river, to the cycles of the different melas, and to the cycles of contraction and expansion that operate on a regional and even national scale. The building systems of the Kumbh Mela are finely calibrated to these spatial and temporal scales. During the festival, the river delta becomes a dense urban space, zoned as a gridded city; during the interim years, it sustains agricultural life. Every year the monsoon floods the land and reverts it to a natural riverbed. Physical infrastructures enable spatial zoning, electricity supply, med-ical facilities, food and water distribution, sanitary services, commerce, and political admin-istration. The lessons learned from the Kumbh Mela can be applied throughout the world to the planning and design of temporary camps and rapid infrastructural deployment as well as to contemporary urbanism in general insofar as it seeks to engage the global metabolism in powerful and meaningful ways.

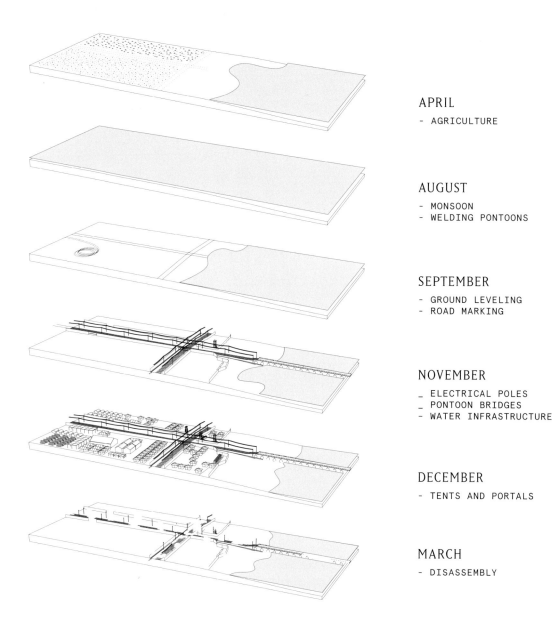

APRIL
- AGRICULTURE

AUGUST
- MONSOON
- WELDING PONTOONS

SEPTEMBER
- GROUND LEVELING
- ROAD MARKING

NOVEMBER
_ ELECTRICAL POLES
_ PONTOON BRIDGES
- WATER INFRASTRUCTURE

DECEMBER
- TENTS AND PORTALS

MARCH
- DISASSEMBLY

Deployment and assembly

The deployment and assembly of the Kumbh Mela is in
tune with the annual cycles determined by the monsoon
season. At the end of the monsoon season, when the fertile
land is no longer being used for agriculture, the phases of
deployment and construction unfold: the ground is leveled;
roads are marked; and infrastructure such as electrical
poles, water supplies, and pontoon bridges are deployed.
After these structures are built, a system of enclosures
is added. When the event ends, all these items are deconstructed, leaving no trace on the site.

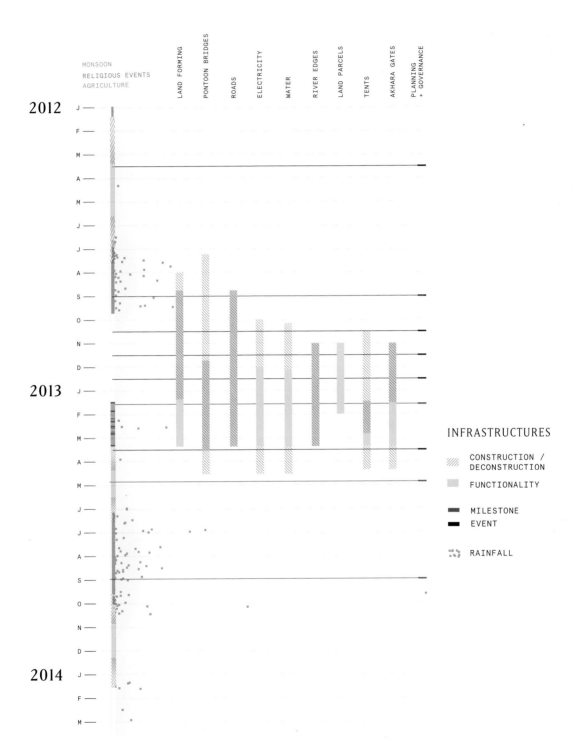

MONSOON
RELIGIOUS EVENTS
AGRICULTURE

LAND FORMING
PONTOON BRIDGES
ROADS
ELECTRICITY
WATER
RIVER EDGES
LAND PARCELS
TENTS
AKHARA GATES
PLANNING + GOVERNANCE

2012

J
F
M
A
M
J
J
A
S
O
N
D

2013

J
F
M
A
M
J
J
A
S
O
N
D

2014

J
F
M

INFRASTRUCTURES

///// CONSTRUCTION /
       DECONSTRUCTION

       FUNCTIONALITY

       MILESTONE
       EVENT

       RAINFALL

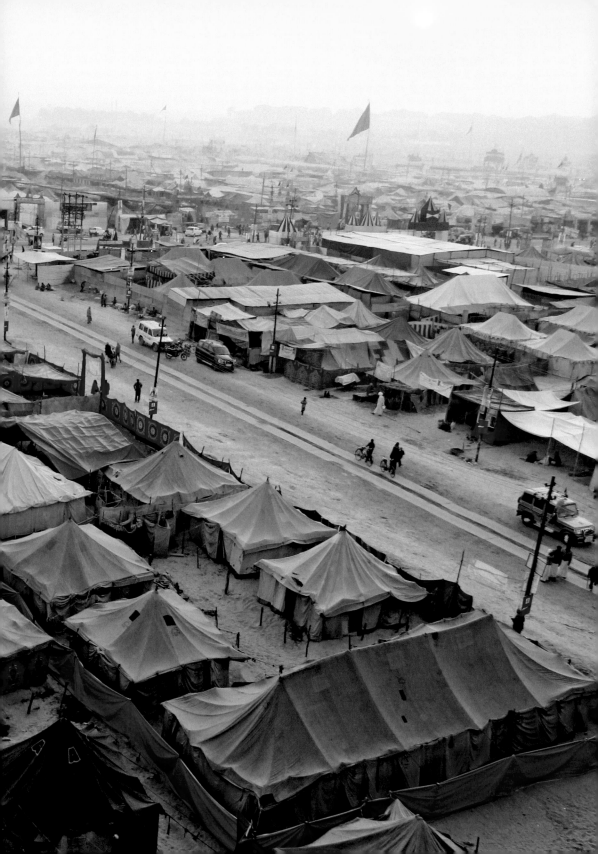

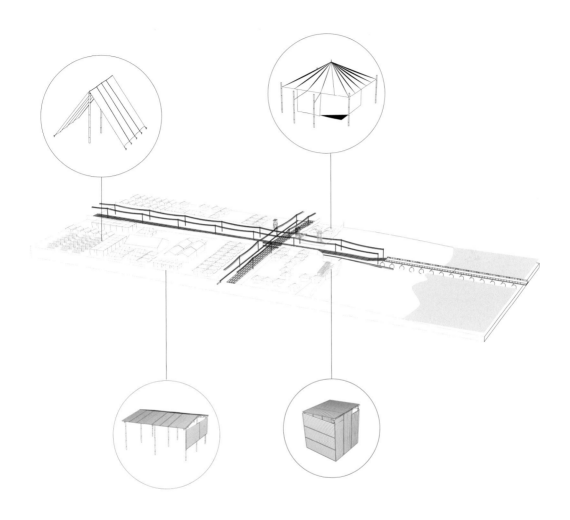

Enclosure systems

The enclosure systems of the Kumbh Mela are based on
simple generic elements. The same basic elements—bamboo
sticks and a surface material such as corrugated metal or
tent fabric—allow for recombinatory assemblies into a wide
range of structures, from small tents to very large congregation halls and temples. The modular enclosure systems
consist of similar basic elements that are aggregated
to generate a multitude of quasi-urban typologies. The
simplicity of these building systems allows for basic logistics and implementation. The elements are small and light
enough for one or two workers to carry and assemble them.

Elements
SURFACE
CONNECTORS
STRUCTURE

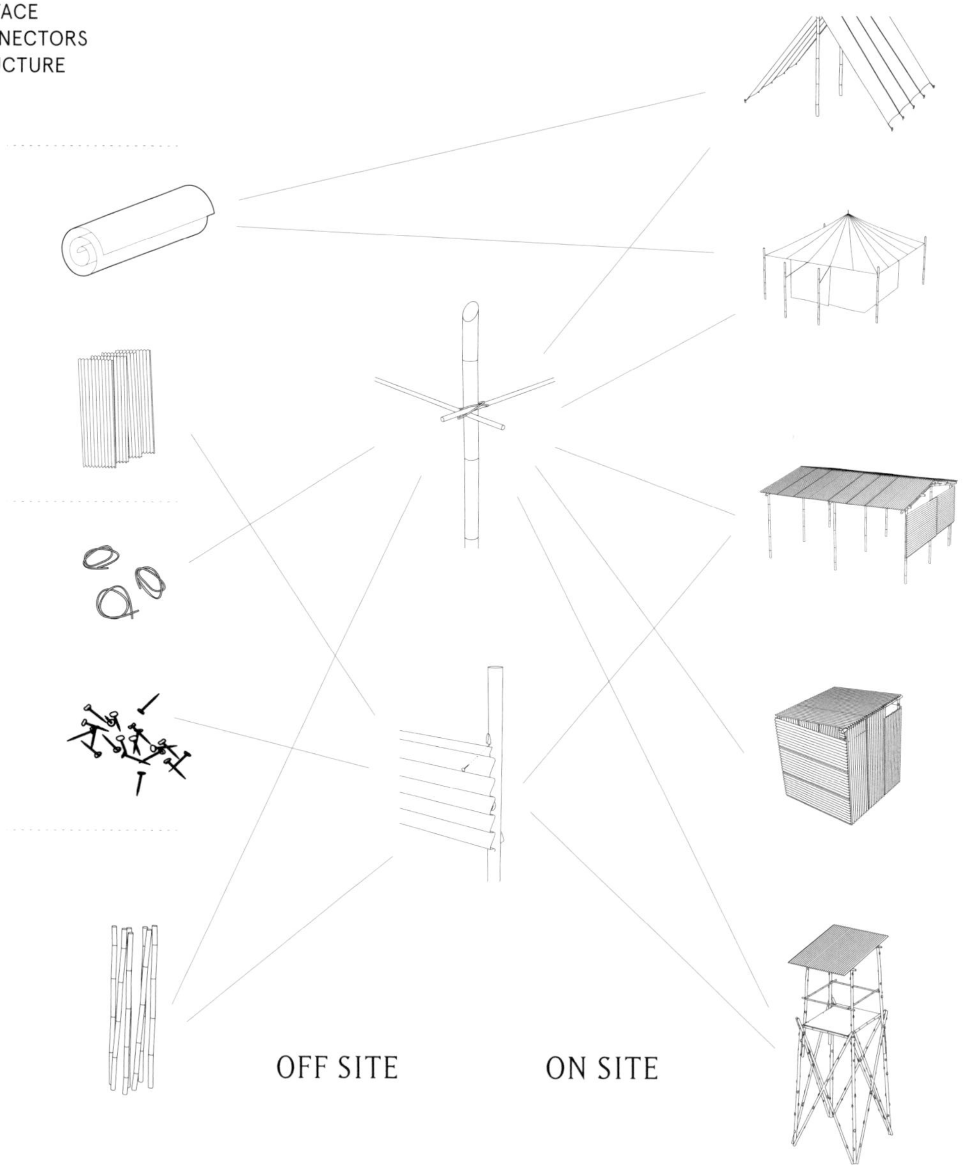

OFF SITE   ON SITE

Recombinatory assembly

Recombinatory assembly reduces the cost of construction
and assembly, while allowing for greater design flexibility. The
generic nature of the sticks and simple connections using
ropes and /or nails ensure the possibility of recombining these
elements in almost infinite ways. After the Kumbh Mela, they
can be reused for other constructions. The assembly of these
systems relies on the availability of cheap manual labor, turn-
ing the Kumbh into a massive labor endeavor.

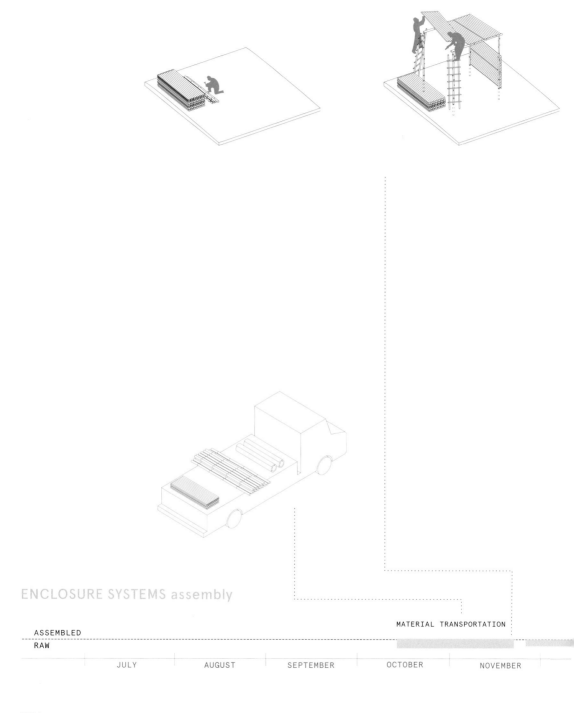

ENCLOSURE SYSTEMS assembly

MATERIAL TRANSPORTATION

ASSEMBLED
RAW

JULY AUGUST SEPTEMBER OCTOBER NOVEMBER

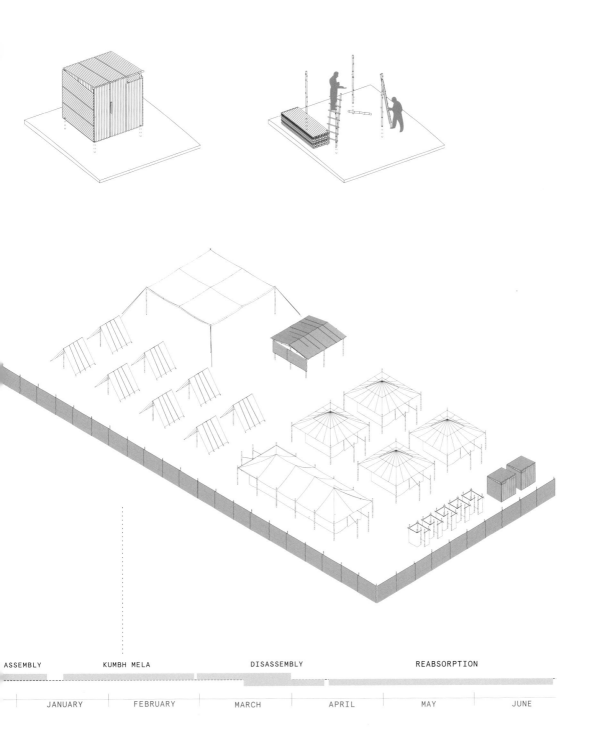

ASSEMBLY   KUMBH MELA   DISASSEMBLY   REABSORPTION

JANUARY   FEBRUARY   MARCH   APRIL   MAY   JUNE

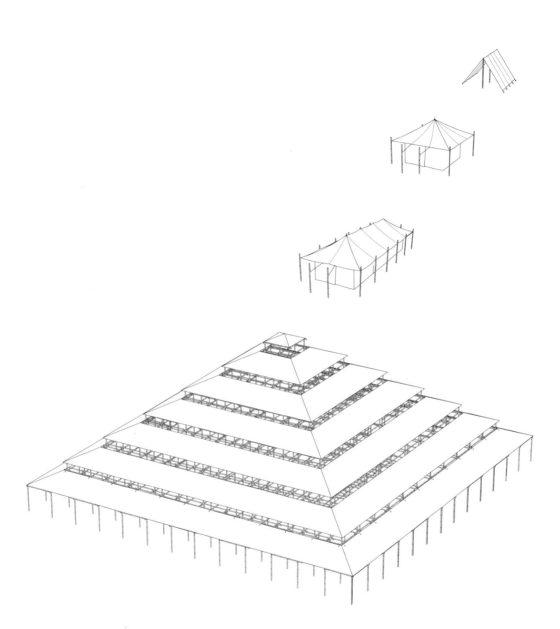

Multi-Scalar Elements

The modular enclosure systems of the Kumbh allow for a wide range of structures, ranging from small tents to very large congregation halls and temples. Similar basic elements are aggregated to generate a multitude of quasi-urban typologies.

Tents

The tents at the Kumbh Mela serve a multitude of uses, from sleeping, socializing, and eating to religious gatherings, entertainment, and healthcare. Accordingly, they vary greatly in size and appearance but are arranged within the basic urban grid. The interstitial spaces define more intimate pathways for walking on foot.

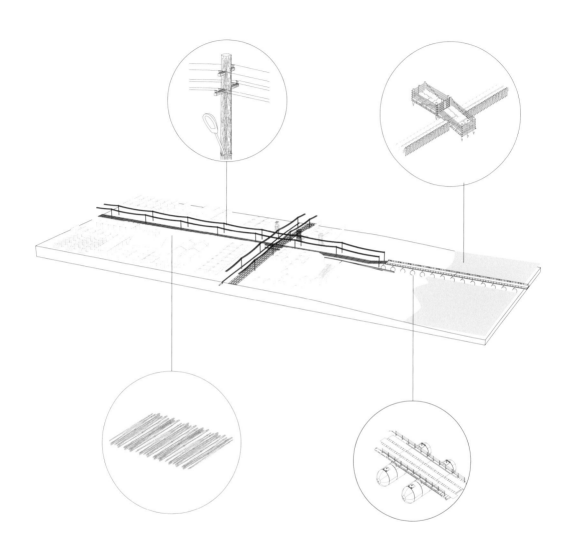

Infrastructural systems

The infrastructural systems range from simple organic ones to more complex aggregations of multiple materials. Wherever possible the systems are assemblies of generic materials that can be reused or recycled to ensure the continuation of their useful life and the minimization of waste.

Steel plates and pontoon bridges

The road infrastructure is laid out according to
historical patterns as well as new conditions created
as a result of receding waters. The main roads are
paved with large steel plates, and steel pontoon
bridges connect the major roads across the river.
These comprise the main traffic network, both for
cars and people on less busy days, and the main access
route by which pedestrian traffic is directed to
the Sangam on the busiest days. Most other roads
are minor and do not receive major pilgrim traffic.

———— STEEL PLATE ROADS

0   200 400   800   1600

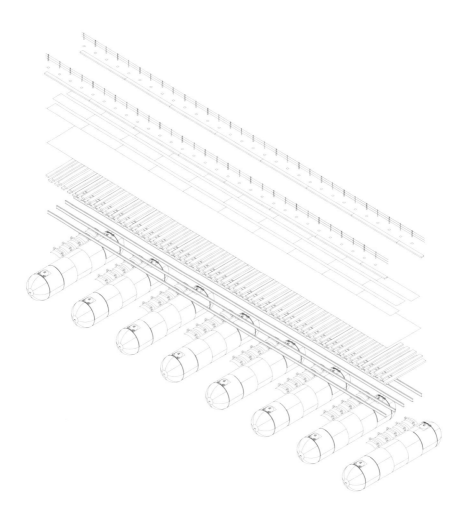

Floating infrastructure

The pontoons are one of the most elaborate components of the Kumbh Mela's infrastructure. They serve as the essential arteries of the site. The labor and time invested into these pontoons is not lost once the Kumbh is over. Other parts of the country and later incarnations of the Kumbh get to benefit from this investment.

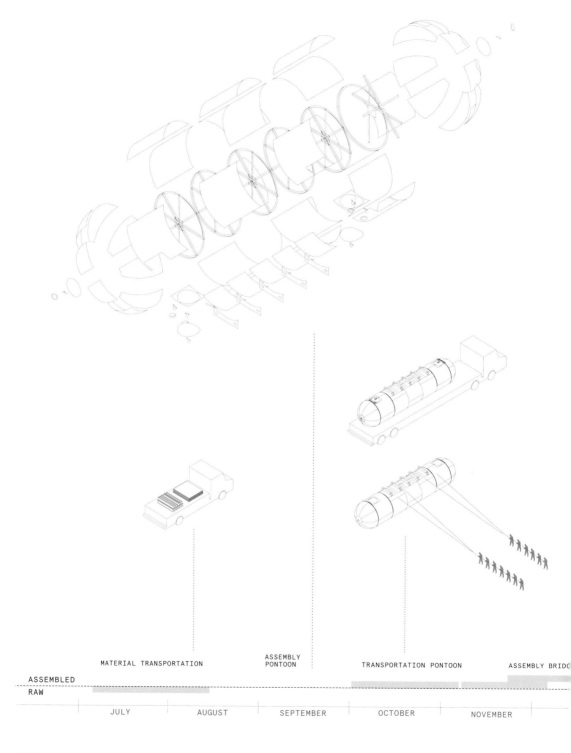

MATERIAL TRANSPORTATION

ASSEMBLY
PONTOON

TRANSPORTATION PONTOON

ASSEMBLY BRID

ASSEMBLED

RAW

| JULY | AUGUST | SEPTEMBER | OCTOBER | NOVEMBER |

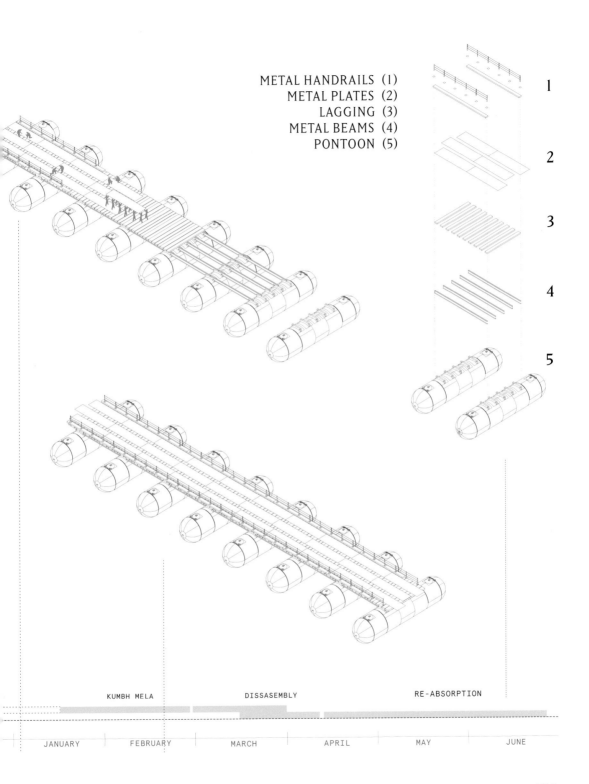

METAL HANDRAILS (1)
METAL PLATES (2)
LAGGING (3)
METAL BEAMS (4)
PONTOON (5)

1

2

3

4

5

KUMBH MELA   DISSASEMBLY   RE-ABSORPTION

JANUARY   FEBRUARY   MARCH   APRIL   MAY   JUNE

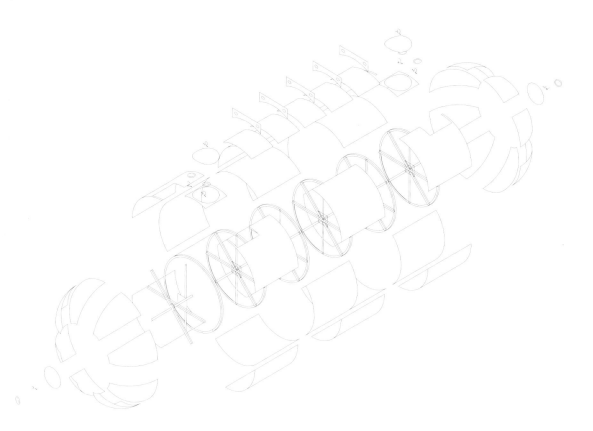

Fabrication and assembly of pontoon bridges

These temporary foot and car bridges join the two sides of the Ganga River. They are brought to the Kumbh from all over the region, with additional pontoons fabricated as necessary close to the site. Workers cut the steel plates and profiles and assemble them into structures of remarkable geometric complexity. Once assembled, they are moved to the river's edge by truck and then pulled and floated into place. One by one they are connected with steel I-beams. The decking consists of wooden lagging covered with the same steel plates of which the roads are made. The pontoons are held in place by simple wooden triangular anchors. The pontoon bridges are built successively outward without the need of additional floats or boats until they finally span the entire river. Once the Kumbh Mela is over, these bridges are dismantled and the pontoons are trucked to various sites where they are stored or used for other events or disaster relief engagements in other parts of the region.

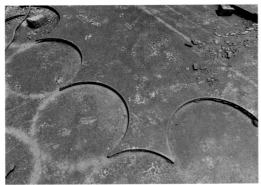

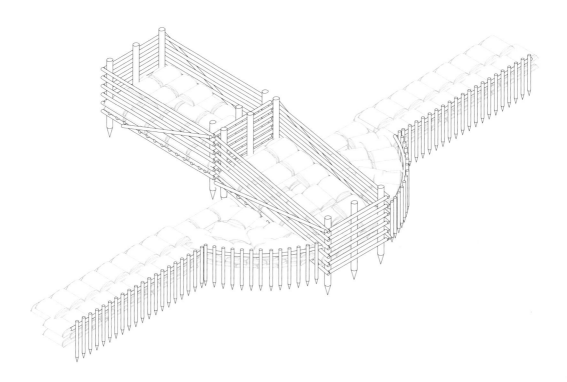

River's edge and adaptive riparian interfaces

The Kumbh as an urban area is structured by the water bodies of the Ganga and Yamuna. Pilgrims come to bathe at the convergence of the rivers. On bathing days, vast numbers of people flock to the river's edge, although many of them do not know how to swim. The river's edge is modified to prevent injuries and fatalities during the bathing process. These infrastructures are adaptive, recombinatory systems that allow for the appropriate modulation of this riparian interface. Made up of sandbags and wooden piles, they can take on whatever form necessary. When the Kumbh Mela is over, the piles are collected and transported to other sites. The sandbags are left in place and many are get collected by locals who find other uses for them.

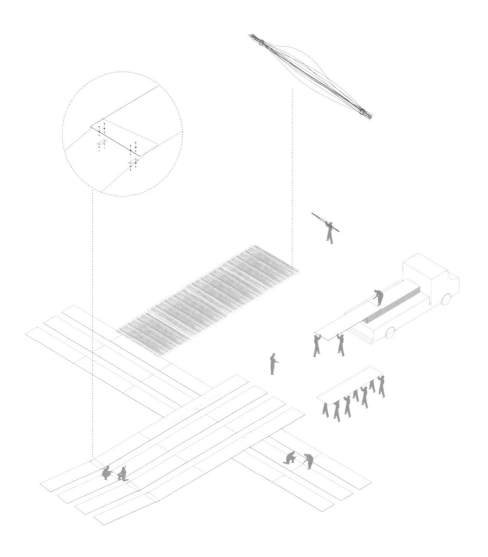

Modular roads system

The roads of the Kumbh Mela form the basic structure of the urban grid, providing the framework for the temporary city. They are an interesting example of the principle of calibration of a material system to the task at hand. Depending on the type of traffic, the roads are either made of steel plates or simply laid out with reed. The steel plates are generic elements that can be reused in multiple ways. To connect them, they are laid in the appro-

priate position, perforated using a blowtorch, and then connected with removable bolts. This allows for maximum adaptability to various radii and slopes without the need of specific connectors or plates. The plates are transported with trucks, each one carried into place by a group of ten workers. The reed roads are renewable organic infrastructures and over the course of the Kumbh Mela, they are replenished as needed.

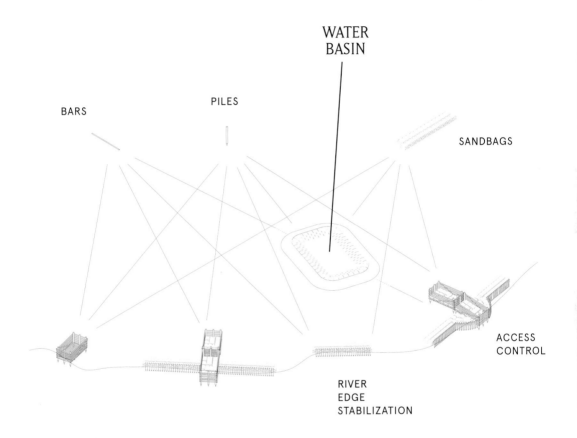

BARS

PILES

WATER
BASIN

SANDBAGS

ACCESS
CONTROL

RIVER
EDGE
STABILIZATION

Recombinatory assembly

Similar to the other construction systems, the riparian edge relies on recombinatory assembly structures. Three basic elements (piles, beams, and sandbags) allow for a great variety of structures that can respond to various edge conditions and serve multiple purposes. These structures stabilize the ground and control access to the water.

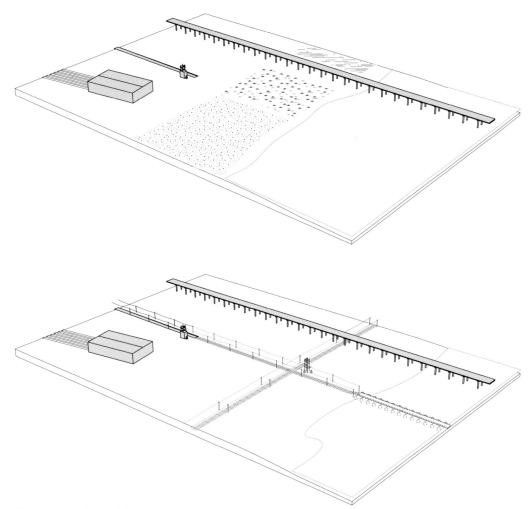

Permanent and temporary infrastructures

The temporary infrastructure of the Kumbh Mela relies on the existing networks of the city of Allahabad and the Uttar Pradesh region. These permanent infrastructures include the electrical grid and the road and rail network. This plug-in approach relies on a temporary reallocation of energy and traffic flows within the state of Uttar Pradesh. The temporary infrastructure is installed simultaneously with the road grid. Electricity lines are run above ground along temporary utility poles, while the water infrastructure is buried underground. These ephemeral infrastructures are constructed and deconstructed without residue within a matter of weeks and leave no trace.

1. ARRAY OF OVERHEAD LIGHTING
2. METAL PLATE ROAD
3. LEVELED GROUND SURFACE
4. CLOTHES CHANGING AREA
5. METAL
6. BATHING AREA FENCING
7. SHORE STABILIZATION
8. CROWD CONTROL FENCING
9. BATHING GHATS AT SANGAM
10. GRASS LANES
11. URINALS
12. WASTEWATER SUMPS
13. FRESHWATER SUPPLY
14. ELECTRICAL SUPPLY
15. WASTEWATER DRAINAGE CHANNEL
16. WATER SUPPLY
17. PIT TOILETS
18. LEVELED GROUND SURFACE
19. MINOR METAL PLATE ROAD
20. ARRAY OF OVERHEAD LIGHTING
21. WATER SUPPLY
22. EDGE-PROTECTING JETTIES
23. BOAT DOCKING AREA
24. PONTOON BRIDGE

DECONSTRUCTION
Photo Essay

DINESH MEHTA

The notion of permanence in our understanding of cities obstructs the fluid metabolism of urban space. In urbanism and architecture, time frames are not correctly anticipated and change is not properly factored. Buildings are generally conceived of as permanent structures while in reality all buildings have limited lifetimes. The afterlife of the things we build once they are not useful anymore is surprisingly absent from the discourse on design and construction. Buildings do not respond smoothly to eventual needs for transformation, they do not thoughtfully incorporate the processes of weathering into their designs, and the options they provide for reconfiguration in cases of obsolescence are not properly factored into the building technology we have at our disposal. In other words, we have developed highly articulated techniques and efficient construction processes to construct and assemble increasingly complex structures. However, very little has been done to develop better ways to disassemble and deconstruct the things we build. The disassembly phase of the Kumbh is thus one of the aspects we can learn from the most. The following photo essay depicts this process.

GOVERNANCE & BUSINESS

Government and the Minimalist Platform:
Business at the
KUMBH MELA

TARUN KHANNA & JOHN MACOMBER

INTRODUCTION:
A Leadership and Organizational Success

The 2013 Kumbh Mela was a leadership and organizational success by almost any measure.

Success was realized in the context of a fast moving and highly dynamic environment that would normally be a ripe breeding ground for confusion. Success was quite visibly achieved in this situation in vivid contrast to many other fast moving urban situations in India, throughout South Asia, and indeed around the world. What was it about the framing and management of the Kumbh Mela that made it successful? Our multidisciplinary Harvard team had a particularly robust view of many elements salient to the Kumbh gathering, including religion, public health, urban planning and design, and of course leadership.

From a business and management point of view, we believe the transferable lessons include an unusual focus by government on providing a solid and limited platform upon which non-government entities and the private sector could effectively deliver many other services to tens of millions of pilgrims. This chapter considers evidence for this assertion; discusses specific aspects of the platform and focus; compares them to other similar situations; and proposes a framework of approaches to a gap in capabilities and ambitions of government and business. We consider several potential opportunities with respect to the sheer number of participants (opportunities that for the most part were foregone but could be enacted in future large gatherings, future ephemeral cities, and future Kumbh Melas). Finally, we develop suggestions for other government and business relationships in fast-growing, resource-constrained cities. The Kumbh Mela situation is more than an interesting story—it is a set of best practices for rapidly growing cities with constrained resources, in South Asia and beyond. The lessons apply to government, for-profit entrepreneurs, and civil society alike.

To some business readers this will feel like the basics of strategic planning and leadership in the private sector: focus and make choices. The successful Allahabad Kumbh Mela shows that governments can focus and make strategic choices—and those choices can help businesses to be better partners with government in providing services.

What We OBSERVED and Did Not OBSERVE

Business leaders might not expect to gain wisdom from the Kumbh Mela, but there are in fact many lessons to be taken from the conception and execution of the gathering, which brings together millions of cold and shivering people to northern India.

ASCETICS AND PILGRIMS GATHER TO BATHE AT A SANGAM

In addition to its fame as a spectacle, the Kumbh Mela was also a big success. It was a spiritual success because the religious aims were fulfilled; there were few major public health issues; and it was delivered cost-effectively and on time. But mostly, the 2013 Kumbh Mela was a success because 100 million pilgrims came to Allahabad and had a good experience. Success was a surprise in the eyes of many who held the impression that it would share the same fate as other big initiatives in India, such as the 2010 Commonwealth Games in Delhi that featured delays, cost overruns, life-safety problems, boycotts by athletes, and spiraling corruption scandals. Others looked at the budget and delivery problems and the nationwide protests that occurred in preparation for the 2014 FIFA World Cup in Brazil. But the 2013 Kumbh Mela did not end up like those other events. Its success asks the question: How did the Kumbh Mela serve millions more people for a duration that was months longer, with less apparent support from the central government?

Several characteristics support the claim of success. We observed millions of people of varying ranks and roles bathing, praying, eating, and shopping together. We did not see religious conflicts, nor any sign of interference by the government on what is taught inside the Akharas. We did not see hunger, uncontrolled fire, significant communicable disease outbreaks, or major stampedes within the grounds. We saw very few informal settlements. These are remarkable characteristics in any large, fast growing city and all the harder to accomplish, one would expect, in this setting.

A large pop-up megacity was built, in short order, to accommodate this surge of humanity. It was then dismantled, in a way that no large city ever experiences. In addition to being an impressive feat of project management and a compelling nexus of spirituality, the bland canvas starting point and temporary nature of the city makes this a useful "pure laboratory" for students of entrepreneurship, urban planning and policy, business in emerging

YEAR	Estimated Attendance (in millions)
1906	2,4
1919	3
1930	4
1942	1,2
1954	6
1966	7
1977	10
1989	15
2001	80
2013	120

TREND IN ATTENDANCE AT THE KUMBH MELAS

BATHING DAY	DATE	Estimated Attendance (in millions)
MAKAR SANKRANTI	JANUARY 14	11
PAUSH PURNIMA	JANUARY 27	5.5
MAUNI AMAVASYA	FEBRUARY 2	30.5
BASANT PANCHAMI	FEBRUARY 15	19.3
MAGHI PURNIMA	FEBRUARY 25	16.5
MAHA SHIVRATRI	MARCH 10	5.5

MAIN BATHING DAYS DURING THE 2013 KUMBH MELA

markets, and design. These lessons can be applied to companies working in complex and fluid urban situations, and can be applied to leaders in public / private interactions as many Tier II and Tier III emerging market cities experience very large influxes of people migrating from the countryside.

The main players are the Government of India, the Government of Uttar Pradesh, the Government of Allahabad, the Head Adhikari (administrator), seventeen Akharas (the main religious sects and the principal non-government deliverers of the experience), twenty or so other prominent religious organizations, many private players, 200,000 monks, priests, and ascetics, and 100,000,000 pilgrims.

ASPIRATIONS, CAPABILITY, and CHOICES: The Government Provides a Minimal Platform

Our team of religion, public health, urban planning, and business researchers believes that the success is attributable to constrained and selective government involvement, as compared to ubiquitous interventions. We use our observations from experts in religious studies, urban planning and infrastructure, and public health to illustrate this argument. We maintain that the success is due to matching ambition with capabilities, amplifying the impact of non-government entities, and creating a platform for those entities to succeed. The Kumbh Mela happens once every twelve years as a pop-up megacity. This makes it an ideal pure laboratory for a "natural experiment" with respect to effective state involvement in urbanization and growth.

We observed that the administration focused on a handful of initiatives, rather than trying to promise everything. Some of these were in pre-planning, others were in order, and still others helped to establish context where non-government actors—Akharas and other religious entities, NGOs, and the private sector—could effectively provide other services.

Advance Purchasing of the Components of INFRASTRUCTURE

The organizers plan two years ahead for the semi-permanent infrastructure—the gross quantity plan for pontoons, pipes, and plates is set so those items can be procured before the exact location of the grid is known. In the field, private companies are hired to install these state-owned components—a simple, effective, and well-understood form of partial public-private partnership. The state funds a low-yield asset (e.g., road plates, which

HIGH-LABOR ACTIVITY AND LOW-YIELD ASSETS, SUCH AS METAL PLATES, PRODUCE MOBILITY INFRASTRUCTURE

few private firms want to have on their balance sheet) and outsources a high-labor short-term activity (e.g., install and remove the plates with labor that the state would rather not have on its permanent payroll).

Land ALLOCATION

Land allocation is tightly controlled at the macro level, although the content of activities within each parcel is not overseen. "Our policy is to support every religion," according to Devesh Chaturvedi; this embraces many Akharas and many different interpretations of Hinduism. According to *mela* organizers and consistent with the open ethos in India—Muslim, Christian, and Buddhist pilgrims and their leaders are welcome, although the writers did not observe these groups in large congregations.

Land is allocated by thinking first about the pilgrims: "The main rule is: everyone wants a dip," according to Alok Sharma. The team starts when the rivers recede by identifying where the main bathing areas will be. That leads to establishment of circulation: how will the pilgrims walk to and from the bathing ghats on the peak days? In turn, this dictates the number and location of bridges, and this leads to the location of camping areas off of the Kumbh Mela grounds (often across the rivers).

After the determination of bridge and road locations, the relative placement of the Akharas becomes a major and extended negotiation. In historic times, the Akharas would arrive with warriors and fight to the death to be nearest the Sangam. In modern times, the priority of the Akharas is determined by the previous size of their facilities (square feet and membership); by current membership; by historic precedent; and by other factors. The Kumbh Mela administration oversees and facilitates the negotiation but the wisdom of the years, and of decades of Akhara leadership holds certain influences. It would be a deep blow to the organizers if an Akhara were to become so incensed with the process that it stayed away.

Although there are many legitimate claims for space, there are also many that are clearly spurious. Sometimes, others try to claim ground informally during various proceedings that occur in advance of the Kumbh Mela. The *mela* leadership has the information and the authority to deal with these situations quickly, in contrast to the circumstance in many other informal or temporary cities in South Asia.

POWER and LIGHT

Some Westerners travel to the Kumbh Mela expecting a tone of serenity and sanctuary befitting a religious event, they also often assume to see a setting of chaos and disorder similar to any informal settlement or slum elsewhere in India. Neophyte observers arrive with headlamps, compasses, and an expectation of stepping over huts and tents and cooking areas. Quite in contrast, the Kumbh Mela is totally electrified with 22,000 temporary power poles, 24 x 7 bright light from each, and a cacophony of sounds broadcast all hours of day and night ranging from prayers, to speeches, to call-and-respond sermons, to lost child announcements. Our understanding is that power is neither metered nor charged; usage is controlled by the simple distribution of outlets and bulbs. A temporary thirty-megawatt, diesel-fueled substation is installed nearby. This is one example of the government providing a basic good, and letting the non-government religious, for-profit entities deliver added services from that platform. With respect to illumination, there is a public safety benefit as well. This resource was not used particularly efficiently as power was effectively not measured at all; future Kumbh Melas will most likely take place in a context of more attention to generation of electricity (notably the fuel cost and greenhouse gas aspects).

Avoiding DISASTER

Disaster planning is a main concern of the administrators. One leader observed that the biggest risk is fire; everything is flammable including the frames and fabric of the Akhara's tents and of course almost everyone's clothing. Among fuel sources, LPG is particularly flammable and not well regulated; the organizers did substantial proactive education on fire prevention and on what to do if fire breaks out. Similarly, the bathing ghats are potentially treacherous—people are bathing and they are wet, and the mud and straw used becomes slippery. If there is a tragedy on a ghat, there is a chain reaction and people slip in. The organizers continually replace straw and move sandbags, and the protective barriers and boatmen in the river are keys to disaster prevention. It can be difficult, if not impossible, to move ambulances in a crowd of several millions; so the emphasis is on disaster prevention, not response.

Stampede avoidance and mitigation is a key concern for the leaders of the *mela*. Stampedes happen at bottlenecks. This is controlled by use of holding areas, notably where the input end is much smaller than the output end. Barrier handling and barriers are effective for holding people; it's when they are released that unfortunate crowd surges can occur. There is not a best practice for crowd control at this scale; rather, there are rules of thumb—one of the best is to keep people moving.

Bridges can oscillate and become turbulent due to crowd rhythms, water movement, or both. The psychology is to have numerous bridge monitors with the goal to pick up the fallen in three seconds.

Land and ghat allocation is ongoing, as the river continues to meander throughout the duration of the *mela*. Since the safe zone changes, "There needs to be dynamic planning every day as erosion points and water level changes," according to Chaturvedi. Sandbags and safety barricades are moved every day, making the system a prime example of highly variable hydrodynamics.

A Clear PLATFORM

The platform is basic: 1) road and bridge layout and installation (to move millions of pilgrims and to delineate the Akhara boundaries); 2) rigorous, methodological, and enforced land-use allocation; 3) ubiquitous electric power and light, less ubiquitous but ambitious water and sanitation; and 4) public safety with a focus on disaster prevention (fire, stampede, drowning, as well as reactive public health and personal security infrastructure).

CROWD FLOWS ARE GUIDED THROUGH THE SETTLEMENT AS PART OF A BASIC
MANAGEMENT PLATFORM

Civil SOCIETY and the Private SECTOR
Building on the Platform

The Kumbh Mela platform enthusiastically supports the Akharas, the entrepreneurs, and the NGOs in providing services within its grid of land and
roads. This encouragement for other actors to provide services raises the
experience of the pilgrims above what the state seems able to do on its
own—above what the Kumbh Mela administration tries to do on its own.
Counter-intuitively, the end experience for the pilgrims is observably closer
to "high ambition," with this minimalist approach than it would have been
if the government had tried to do everything on its own. This quality of experience is beyond what would have been expected from a position on the
capability / ambition effectiveness curve. Please see Table 2 for more expansion on this concept.

Larger BUSINESS:
PPP for Roads and Bridges

There is little evidence of big business at the Kumbh Mela. The government
contracts with private vendors to accomplish tasks like building roads and
pontoon bridges, although the government owns most of the materials. This
is a simple form of public-private partnership where there is no financing
or revenue risk, nor any ownership of assets, taken on by the private firm.

There is virtually no commercial advertising, although Unilever cleverly branded soap promotions onto bread (Indian *chappatis* or *rotis*) and Co-ca-Cola managed to hang a large sign from a railroad bridge (not part of the Kumbh Mela grounds). There is, however, substantial promotion for visiting or resident religious leaders at the Kumbh Mela by their followers. There is no commercial lodging within the Kumbh grounds, although adjacent permanent hotels and temporary camps (ranging from luxury to subsistence) do a thriving business.

The AMBITION / Capability GAP

The experience of the Kumbh Mela shows how limited government, intentionally working to provide a platform for other actors to provide services, can accomplish a substantially better outcome than a resource-constrained government trying to do everything itself. The paragraphs above have recounted many observations of what the government does and what it does not do.

What is the generalizable lesson that made the Kumbh Mela so successful compared to other large events in India and South Asia? What are the action steps for both the government and the private sector?

A LIMITED GOVERNMENT FACILITATES THE SUPPLY OF SERVICES WITH NON-GOVERNMENTAL ACTORS

We propose that this can be explained by an "ambition / capability gap." Consider these three different contexts, each from the perspective of a common person in three different locations: an average Norwegian in Norway, an Indian worker in a slum, and a pilgrim at the Kumbh Mela.

NORWAY: High Ambition, High Capability

In a country like Norway, where it has recently been announced that the government will deploy incremental oil revenues into both infrastructure improvement and public pensions, the state has high ambition and high capability to provide services. For example, the existence of well-established financial intermediaries in the country ensures that the money "pumped into" society will be allocated reasonably and efficiently. That financial intermediation is one example of a high level of capability that is missing in the countries on the less capable parts of the spectrum. The capability of the state is robust in both a financial sense and an institutional sense. The common person lives well and this experience is delivered effectively.

INDIA (as Commonly Perceived): High Ambition, Low Capability

Consider India as perceived and understood by most observers. The state has high ambition to provide for everyone from farmers to migrants to factory workers to corporate leaders; the state seems to attempt everything from railroads to farm subsidies to education to food supply as well as taking on major responsibilities like the Commonwealth Games. Yet as documented over and over, the ambitions of the state are far greater than its capabilities. This results in low effectiveness, which typically leads to disappointment and bad experiences for slum dwellers and businesses alike. The extent of the operative governing strategy for change seems to be to move from low to high and reach the effectiveness curve based on hope— but hope is not a strategy.

KUMBH MELA and the State: Matching Ambition with Capability

Consider in contrast the Kumbh Mela state actions. The Kumbh administration and the governments of Allahabad and of Uttar Pradesh focused on just a few elements in the pop-up megacity. They did these very well by intentionally matching ambitions to capabilities. They ensured that the pilgrims would be safe (and well electrified) based on what the government provided. However, the experience for a pilgrim at the Kumbh Mela was better than an experience at a different, fast-growing informal settlement in India.

How Was the Minimalist BALANCE Struck?

In this situation the wisdom of centuries applies (compressed into a timespan of weeks). The government administrators are smart enough to let the senior people in the religious organizations get all the exposure and credit—while carefully constraining a few aspects like land allotment and promotion / advertising / proselytizing outside their allotment (the allotments are many acres). Institutional memory is honored, even in an era of satellite imagery and dynamic mapping. The security head was a veteran of four Kumbhs, an individual who knows the traditional tools of administration and also possesses the connections to the influential players.

There is an inevitable political calculus underlying why the state was especially keen to make this event work. After all, one hundred million votes is a lot, even in a democracy as large as India's. The Kumbh Mela is important. It is a once in twelve-year event, very visible, in an electorally important state. The political penalty of a disaster would be very high, so there is every incentive to get it right. While India can be a notoriously slow bureaucracy, the Kumbh Mela leaders enjoy significant leeway so that the event can be delivered. One manager pointed out that approvals can be hastened, and sometimes requirements for clearances can be ignored. The Kumbh Mela supersedes most other claimants on the state's time. Some unforeseen thing always happens. This near monopoly on the state's attention is a clear contributor to the success of the Kumbh Mela compared to other events in India, but as we discuss later, this does not come without its own costs.

DISCUSSION: Takeaways

While the ephemeral pop-up city is in many ways unique and hard to replicate, in many other ways its lack of constraints make it an uncluttered, "pure laboratory," for observing best practices in aspects of city building and leadership. Our observations include the following: If the state clearly is not intending to provide a service (like the food and shelter provided by the Akharas) then others step in to fill the need. But, if the state is attempting to provide services in addition to the ones we describe above, other actors back off.

SADHUS WAIT TO EAT FOOD PREPARED BY THEIR AKHARA

The old is the key to the new. In this situation, older and very robust social relationships—as represented by the Akharas—help the new event. The organizers are smart enough to let these senior people get all the exposure and credit, while carefully regulating land allotment and the promotion / advertising / proselytizing outside their allotment.

Institutional Memory. The security head is a veteran of four Kumbh Melas. Memory here is not stored in a technology but in people.

NGO and BUSINESS Contribution

The Akharas and the businesses were explicitly drawn in for help with the guidelines and the boundaries. What can be learned from this is that businesses can then apply in other locations. Even in a greenfield location like this, such collaboration and negotiation stands in stark contrast to more formal, more "sophisticated" city planners and government interfering with established cultural relationships to impose supposed "best practices" taken from other cultures.

A Single OBJECTIVE

There was one objective for everyone: "Facilitate a good experience for the pilgrims." This seems like a trivial point, but it is very hard to find, articulate, and agree on a single objective for a city. Singapore, for example, is more successful than most cities at articulating a common objective—namely, to survive as a trading nation on a tiny island with no resources. A city like Lagos, with many competing agendas, more resources, and far less shared purpose between day-to-day people, businesses, and government is much less able to come upon an agreed objective for its investments and affairs.

An Idiosyncratic SITUATION

The Kumbh Mela is clearly an unusual circumstance. Many factors make this an idiosyncratic situation. Some of these factors can be recognized and their implications borrowed in a replicable way, others must be changed due to their diminishing usefulness. Some of these factors include the following:

> The Kumbh Mela was a one time, short, temporary event on a set of dates that were widely anticipated. This meant that the best administrators and managers could be identified, assigned to the project, and then reassigned. This is not true in most cities—although it could be possible in the instance of fast growing informal sections.

THE KUMBH MELA IS A UNIQUE CIRCUMSTANCE WITH SPECIALLY-APPOINTED ADMINISTRATORS, A CLEAR PURPOSE, AND A CLEAN SLATE FROM WHICH TO PLAN

The local government had the formal and informal authority and resources to play a strong central role. They also had the motivation towards the sole big goal of a good experience for the pilgrims. This is not the same in refugee camps or in newer, informal settlements within existing cities.

The Kumbh Mela site was not encumbered with any existing hard infrastructure, buildings, or unmanageable property rights. This allowed the organizers to build from scratch, rather than work around prior structures and claims.
The planning period was able to step logically through an additive sequence of bridges, roads, power, Akharas, and public safety. This is a luxury that most cities don't have—they perceive the need to do everything at once. The process might be well utilized in other situations, including people flow, power facilitation, and then safety, in that order, and let civil society and business fill in the rest.

This city only exists in twelve-year increments (albeit with smaller melas in interim years). This means there is not a continuum of history, population, investment, personality, or trust and mistrust. The leaders do not have an in-place population to slowly move; the population will arrive and depart on its own, following a known timetable.

In contrast to a refugee camp, but consistent with slums and shantytowns in many parts of the world, individual identity was preserved at the Kumbh Mela. Pilgrims had free choice of Akharas with whom to associate.

The Kumbh Mela is not a real city in one other major category: it does not require an economic purpose for being, it does not need to host industry, and it does not need to create jobs. In this sense the economic model is much more like a gigantic US state fair or even a huge trade show. This difference means that the people movement, land use, and public safety emphases are still valid; but the "reason to be" is not replicable and a real city would have further resource allocation, land use policy, and revenue considerations.

Missed OPPORTUNITIES

No discussion of the Kumbh Mela—the largest gathering of humanity in one place for one purpose—would be complete without mentioning missed opportunities for teaching and learning in a community of that size. The overarching thought we hear most is if you had real-time numbers about location, personal profiles, and individual health, what would you do with the knowledge? India could use the information from the largest group of people ever assembled. This was christened the "Big Data Kumbh," in that the authorities were awash in data, although data management seems to have played a minimal role in orchestrating the event.

Some of our students have asked, "Why are we not capitalizing on having this giant group of people in one place at one time? Shouldn't we instruct about hygiene, hand washing, and tooth brushing? And couldn't we have a vaccination program?"

The Kumbh Mela does not have a concept of an admissions fee, ticket price, or fee for services. On the one hand, this is because the purpose is religious, and for centuries the riverbank has been free. On the other hand, a nominal ticket price could help to count attendance and defray state cost or further improve the experience. In theory, charging different prices for different days would spread the bathing load across more than the five key dates. Of course a policy like this would be highly discriminatory around wealth, highly antithetical to the idea of individual equality in the Kumbh Mela grounds, a threat to Akharas interested in growing the size of their memberships, and generally objectionable on many other grounds. But if the Kumbh Mela is to last and thrive in Allahabad for twelve, twenty-four, forty-eight, or 1,200 more years, as India grows and as the rivers get more and more stressed, something like this may be implemented.

The 2013 Kumbh Mela was also coined the "Green Kumbh." Indeed, there was much to commend and much to learn about low-impact urbanism. But there was also much physical waste revealed ex post, and much room for improvement, as the numerous activists made vociferously clear. The extensive electrical power and the universal use of pit toilets, plus the millions of humans bathing in the two rivers, were not particularly sustainable. Future Kumbh Melas will be challenged in this regard.

There were disasters including drowning, fires, and stampedes both on and off the premises; but their scale was small relative to the size of the event and the existing context of Indian railways. There were not any terror incidents or any major public health incidents (cholera, dysentery, flu, SARS / MERS, norovirus, floods, riots, building or bridge collapses, or serious hunger).

Business observers are interested in the accuracy of metrics like attendance. Since there is no ticketing scheme, it's not clear how many attend. The organizers count people passing thru waiting areas, they look at the circulation through the bathing area, and they consider area density, and average time per section. Crucially, it's not known when people come and go multiple times. Almost everyone comes multiple times. The organizers recounted subsequently that about 200 million "visits" occurred.

Conclusion

Every twelve years, this pop-up megacity arises, is sustained, and is destroyed. The fact of its success—even in the context of much more typical government and administrative shortcomings—is a very clear illustration of the benefits of matching capabilities to ambitions, proving focused excellent services and saying no to others, and establishing a platform from which many other organizations can deliver services, save souls, and run businesses.

We observed five overarching lessons both for future *melas* and for the establishment and growth of new cities in much of the emerging world. These lessons apply primarily to local governments and providers of the platform and secondarily to private businesses and civil society who add services and material to bridge the ambition / capability gap for the benefit of citizens. The first lesson is to uncover and promote a single goal that is plausibly shared by all. At the 2013 Allahabad Kumbh Mela, this goal was basic—provide a good experience for pilgrims. The second lesson focuses on the roles of government in achieving the primary goal, in the case of the Kumbh Mela, providing a good experience). It aims to organize ground transportation avenues, allocate land, provide some level of power and water, and provide a high level of security, as well as disaster avoidance and mitigation. The third lesson is to retain legitimate authority through careful engagement of the main actors, including in this case both the Akharas as an order and the organizational memory residing in Akhara elders, police, public health, and prior *mela* administrators. The fourth lesson is to embrace what non-government actors can contribute—and to give them a lot of leeway inside the clear boundaries listed above. The fifth and final lesson is to determine what is a success and repeat (in this situation, the experience of pilgrims, the absence of mass disasters, and the evident competence of the administration). These are useful guidelines for future Kumbh Melas and other religious gatherings as well as for other temporal, ephemeral cities such as refugee camps and other areas of otherwise informal settlement in the many rapidly growing cities of South Asia and the world

RESEARCH COMPONENT	WHAT GOVERNMENT DID DO	WHAT GOVERNMENT DID not DO
RELIGION (HARVARD DIVINITY SCHOOL RESEARCH) Faith is the only reason why the Kumbh Mela exists. Our team consisted of global experts in both pilgrimage and in Indian rivers. They brought the background and wisdom to help our team cut to the main issues; they brought relationships and credibility that led to "the real story," and they interpreted for us what is important and what's not.	Recognize the pull of the Ganga, the power of faith, and the rhythm of centuries (attempt to direct it, not to constrain it). Defer to the religious leaders for the primary content of the Kumbh Mela. Order relationships among the Akharas, a delicate dance to preserve sense of status hierarchy that has been preserved for centuries (don't mess with success!)	Zero meddling inside each Akhara, so that each of these communities of tens of thousands acted of their own volition, and "added their own color" to the Kumbh. This is a safety valve of sorts for religious emotion and religious expression. Government did not have to create a purpose or reason for being, as is the case with so many new attempts at urbanization. The religious awareness emphasized that the pilgrimage, the sacred dip, and the interaction with sadhus and Akharas and priests IS the common purpose.

RESEARCH COMPONENT	WHAT GOVERNMENT DID DO	WHAT GOVERNMENT DID not DO
URBAN PLANNING AND INFRASTRUCTURE	Land allocation, draconian but sensitive to religious sentiment and hierarchy (even kowtowing to angry shankaracharyas of religious orders to buy peace).	Minimal sanitation, as witnessed by environmental pollution and waste (What they did not do on security).
Recording, mapping, and cataloguing the site for this year and for posterity was a major task. There are few records of planning or land use, and the team set out to make that record. At the same time, expertise in traffic design, infrastructure implementation, and architecture helped the group to understand the layout. The urban planning team focused on the metabolism of the Kumbh Mela—the flows of people and goods, so that the divinity team could explain the "why" and the business team could understand the "how."	Roads, minimalist functionality; pontoon bridges (reusable) Security, lots of personnel, sheer presence in force, but minimalist and "soft" training only, eschewing brute force. Public safety at ghats, and sharpshooters to ward against terrorist threats. Upstream water management (prevent flooding, keep water flowing). Electricity (too much, completely free, excessively used), over subsidized. (FAILING IN OUR VIEW)	"We encourage [police officers] to be more empathetic [than in conventional urban settings] . . . we focus on teaching them just three things—crowd psychology, security, and traffic management." This seems more appropriate to a religious setting and likelier to work well.

RESEARCH COMPONENT	WHAT GOVERNMENT DID DO	WHAT GOVERNMENT DID not DO
PUBLIC HEALTH The public health team used its experience in infectious disease control, in first responder setups in war zones and refugee camps, and its knowledge of basic care that can be provided at a venue like this that is not provided in pilgrims' home cities.	Dispersed clinics and hospitals, though some evidence that efficiency could have been improved quite a bit. State provided for 44,000 toilets for sanitation. (cleanliness outsourced though, see adjacent column; and then state cleaned up daily solid waste).	NGOs providing healthcare services or transport services to ferry those needing medical care to hospitals nearby (check the scale); Food for pilgrims mostly outsourced to the Akharas, who in turn relied on donors and well wishers.
Empirical measurement of public health and sanitation criteria like coliform bacteria counts, spread of cold and flu, and cataloguing of complaints at clinics provided comprehensive tracking that had never been done before. Accompanying clinic physicians to note the rate and types of complaints and the nature of treatment.	Some ordering of platforms from which individual entrepreneurs could vend food. Some orchestration of peripheral wholesale markets.	Cleanliness of the toilets outsourced to private contractors (presumably with some sort of incentive payments. Sadly, no action on pollution despite rhetoric that this was the "Green Kumbh." Massive debris left over after Kumbh ended. (FAILING IN OUR VIEW) Space given to NGOs who agitate for cleaning the Ganga.

COMPONENT	HIGH STATE CAPABILITY	LOW STATE CAPABILITY	MINIMALIST
		HIGH AMBITION	
	Norway, Sweden, Singapore	*Understood India*	*Kumbh Mela*
Land Allocation and Enforcement	Robust systems of property rights, land registry, zoning.	Chaotic land ownership, little zoning, poor property registration.	Very strict allotment of space to the Akharas based on history and membership.
INFRA-STRUCTURE: Roads, Electricity, Water	Public sector has high capacity to finance and fund.	Poorly planned and maintained, both traffic jams and pedestrian stampedes are legend.	Second commitment of Kumbh leadership including pedestrian projections.
PUBLIC HEALTH: Security, Communicable Diseases, Clinics	Single payer care at individual level, robust public health at collective level.	(Pandemonium . . .)	Focus on pedestrian and bather control and safety, water borne pathogens, safety.
Food, Education, Housing, Employment	Substantial state support of well-funded programs with capable and experienced delivery.	State attempts to do all, does most of them poorly according to most observers.	Left to Akharas and NGOs and entrepreneurs working on the platform.
IMPLICATIONS FOR ENTRE-PRENEURS AND CIVIL SOCIETY	Entrepreneurs to serve as vendors and concession-aires more than as main organizers.	Select opportunities with filters around institutional maturity and segment selection following "Winning in Emerging Markets."	BUILD SERVICES ON THE PLATFORM: Religious Food Education Lodging Entertainment Employment Ritual

Governance & Organizational STRUCTURES

BENJAMIN SCHEERBARTH, ALYKHAN MOHAMED & VINEET DIWADKAR

In many ways, the Kumbh Mela is a masterpiece of urban organization and governance. The organizational apparatus behind it spans scales of institutional hierarchies and geographies. During the event, the site, also called Kumbh Nagri, is operated as a city and involved central, state, and district governmental agencies operate temporary offices onsite. Each department subdivides the Kumbh Nagri into sectors, and representatives report both to their state-level home departments and to the district magistrate also known as the Mela Adhikari.

The Magh Mela administration, or, Kumbh Mela administration, is the institutional body administering the Kumbh. However, describing the administration as a static organizational space does not capture the reality of its operations. Rather, much like its physical counterpart, the institutional composition transforms over time as it serves different stages of material maturity. As the Kumbh Mela progresses through four successive stages—planning, implementation, monitoring, and deconstruction—the institutional space concurrently changes in leadership style, de-gree of authority, and decision-making routines. In many ways, organizational thinking is guided by the tasks it needs to perform. Between planning and operating the Kumbh, every layer of authority is involved from the central government to the local sanitation worker. During the planning stage alone, the host state of Uttar Pradesh engages twenty-eight of their own departments as well as seven central departments.

It is clear that the structural organization behind the Kumbh Mela can provide lessons not only for India's rapid urbanization, but also for other ephemeral sites of urban character. To be sure, the most critical or success-bearing factors are, in fact, the hardest to transfer. In addition to the herculean effort to plan and fund the Kumbh, the government is also responsible for the leveling of the ground, the deployment of the metal-plate roads, the pontoon bridges, and the provision of sewerage, water, and electricity. However, once the Kumbh is gridded, the closed government space transforms into a space that is both inviting and dependent upon collaborative governance. Allowing for governance, in this context, shall be defined as the willingness and ability to engage in partnerships and delegate tasks to non-governmental actors stemming from both the private and nonprofit sectors. Hence, in analogy to the metal-plate roads, the administrational framework first sets clear parameters and borders and then allows for informal networks of kinship within its confinements. Indeed, the remarkable speed and efficiency displayed during both set up and operation is a result of shared codes and implicit understandings enacted through generational knowledge and expertise. This experience-derived confidence is often reason for contractors to move materials before official orders. The ephemeral spaces, in between more permanent governmental infrastructures, are leased and programmed by non-governmental actors, first and foremost to the twelve Akharas. This programming includes the spatial layout of the living spaces within the grid, subcontracting tent construction, food supply, lost and found, and other functions. Further, various kinds of shops, both formal and informal set up and draw on their own local supply networks.

To respond to ever-changing situations emanating from the ground in a timely manner, the routines and media by which decisions are made take on different emphases in each stage. Oftentimes, the monitoring and reviewing stage of the Kumbh, as headed by the Mela Adhikari, reverses the routines of the planning stage to achieve greater flexibility. Beginning in 2001, the mobile phone in conjunction with motorcycles and horses was widely used to flexibly and speedily communicate and respond. Without doubt, the 2024 Kumbh Mela will see further advances in availability and utilization of digital technologies. It is clear that the structural organization behind the Kumbh can provide lessons not only for India's rapid urbanization, but also for other ephemeral sites of urban character. Indeed, it is against the background that India's handling of its rapid urbanization is a far cry from the effectiveness displayed at the Kumbh Mela, and that development and disaster relief practices are critiqued as being behind the time, and an exploration and a mapping of governance structures might be insightful. To be sure, the most critical or success-bearing factors are, in fact, the hardest to transfer. The Kumbh at its heart, the holy act of bathing, is deeply rooted in the Indian psyche, both symbolically as well as materially in terms of generational knowledge. Bathing in the Sangam is not only seen as a religious duty but also as great accomplishment. This sense of pride and privilege has little role in disaster and conflict sites of ephemeral urbanism. Furthermore, the budgetary generosity to employ the best and highest standing officials for whom the Kumbh is a prestigious assignment, is a luxury not all sites of ephemerality enjoy. There are, however, normative lessons to be learned. All actors involved in the organization of the Kumbh Mela are expected to have—and indeed do show, the greatest respect for the pilgrims. Dignity and cultural tolerance are pursued over individual ego and identity. This strong sense of a shared purpose allows the government to engage in partnerships, delegate power, and foster a form of collaboration with non-governmental actors that is agile, flexible, and responsive.

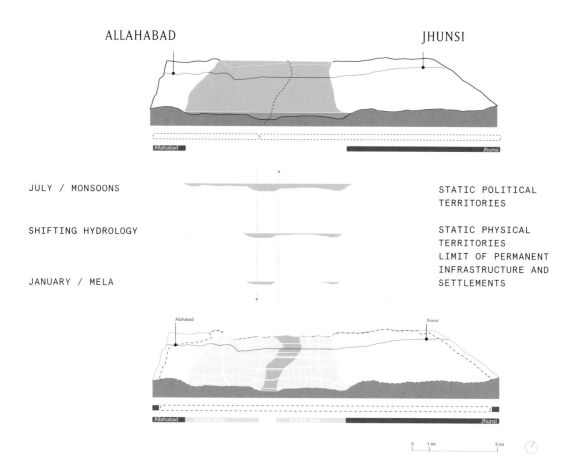

ALLAHABAD   JHUNSI

JULY / MONSOONS   STATIC POLITICAL
                                                            TERRITORIES

SHIFTING HYDROLOGY   STATIC PHYSICAL
                                                            TERRITORIES
                                                            LIMIT OF PERMANENT
                                                            INFRASTRUCTURE AND
JANUARY / MELA   SETTLEMENTS

0   1 mi   5 mi

KINETIC POLITICAL
TERRITORIES

KINETIC PHYSICAL
TERRITORIES

Kinetic physical territory and
elastic political boundaries

Driven by the shifting hydrology of the monsoon cycle
and anchored by the need to allocate land, the Mela
Act provides legal and decision-making capacity for
administrators to build and manage the Kumbh Mela.

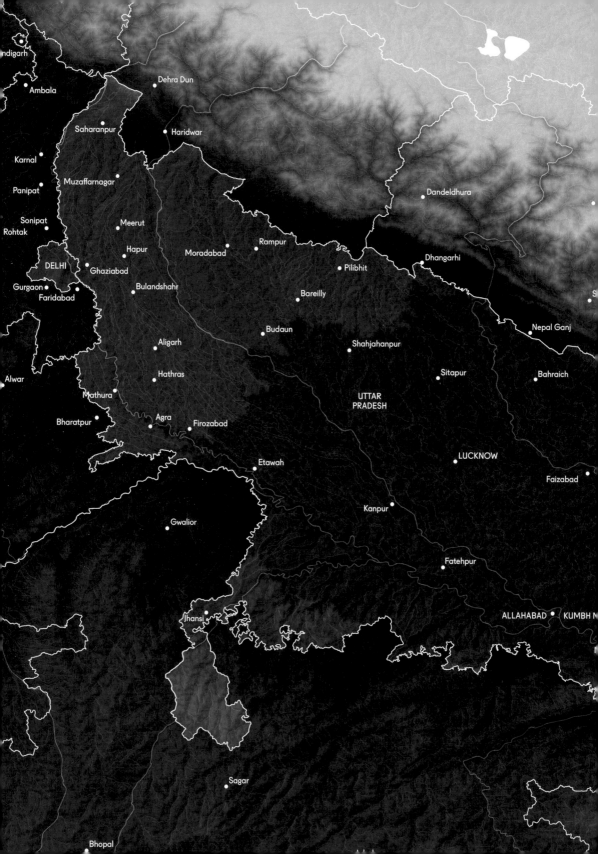

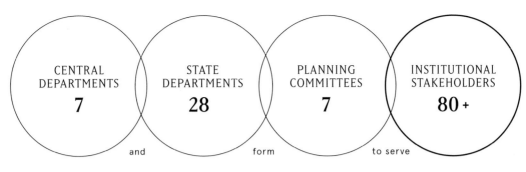

| CENTRAL DEPARTMENTS 7 | STATE DEPARTMENTS 28 | PLANNING COMMITTEES 7 | INSTITUTIONAL STAKEHOLDERS 80+ |

and   form   to serve

GOVERNANCE ACTORS

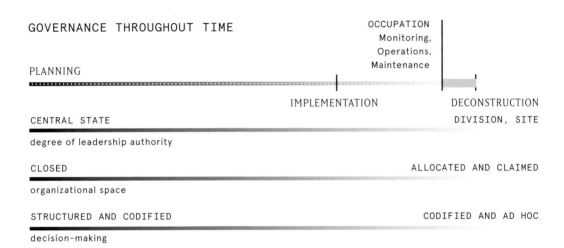

GOVERNANCE THROUGHOUT TIME

OCCUPATION
Monitoring,
Operations,
Maintenance

PLANNING

IMPLEMENTATION   DECONSTRUCTION

CENTRAL STATE   DIVISION, SITE

degree of leadership authority

CLOSED   ALLOCATED AND CLAIMED

organizational space

STRUCTURED AND CODIFIED   CODIFIED AND AD HOC

decision-making

Governance and territory

The seven planning committees of the Kumbh each
differ in time of initiation prior to the Kumbh,
frequency of meeting, and level of governmental
authority. Roughly corresponding to the progression
from the planning to the implementation stage, one can
begin to see a shift in authoritative level toward a more
agile network that is, in all senses, closer to the site and
pilgrims. Albeit, many institutional actors are involved
in the planning process, four of them—the state
departments of Administration and Urban Development,
the Divisional Commissioner and the Police Inspector
General Allahabad Range—together account for 60% of
all formal links among actors that each have a minimum
of 3 links. Moreover, these nodal actors are involved
in 100% of all planning decisions, i.e. extend a node
to all spheres and places of decision making. The Mela
Adhikari, arguably the person displaying the highest
levels of link density once the Kumbh is in operation,
has limited input in the planning stages.

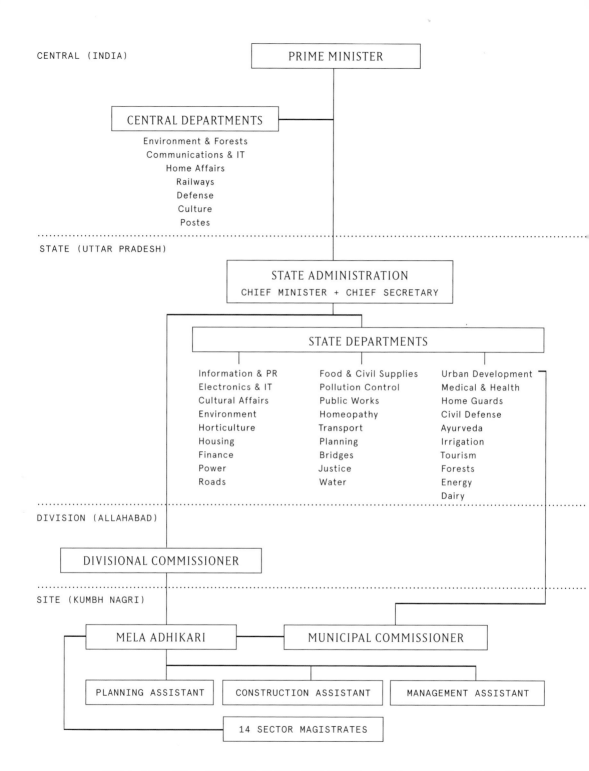

CENTRAL (INDIA)

PRIME MINISTER

CENTRAL DEPARTMENTS

Environment & Forests
Communications & IT
Home Affairs
Railways
Defense
Culture
Postes

STATE (UTTAR PRADESH)

STATE ADMINISTRATION
CHIEF MINISTER + CHIEF SECRETARY

STATE DEPARTMENTS

Information & PR   Food & Civil Supplies   Urban Development
Electronics & IT   Pollution Control   Medical & Health
Cultural Affairs   Public Works   Home Guards
Environment   Homeopathy   Civil Defense
Horticulture   Transport   Ayurveda
Housing   Planning   Irrigation
Finance   Bridges   Tourism
Power   Justice   Forests
Roads   Water   Energy
                                                Dairy

DIVISION (ALLAHABAD)

DIVISIONAL COMMISSIONER

SITE (KUMBH NAGRI)

MELA ADHIKARI   MUNICIPAL COMMISSIONER

PLANNING ASSISTANT   CONSTRUCTION ASSISTANT   MANAGEMENT ASSISTANT

14 SECTOR MAGISTRATES

*MELA ADHIKARI = DISTRICT MAGISTRATE KUMBH = MELA OFFICER = FAIR OFFICER
THERE IS ALSO A DISTRICT MAGISTRATE (NOT DISTRICT MAGISTRATE KUMBH)

364

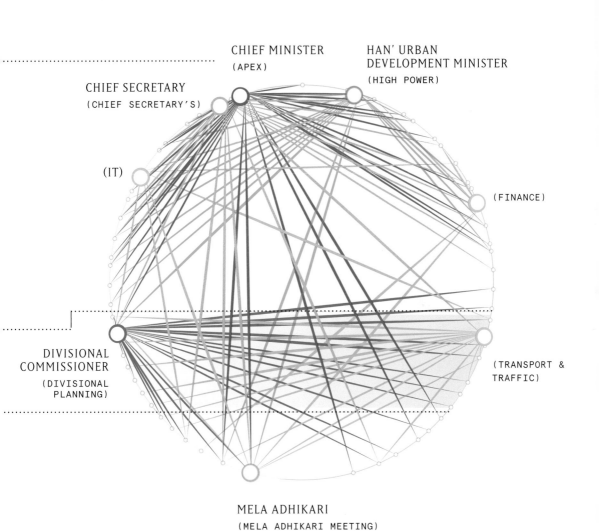

CHIEF MINISTER
(APEX)

HAN' URBAN
DEVELOPMENT MINISTER
(HIGH POWER)

CHIEF SECRETARY
(CHIEF SECRETARY'S)

(IT)

(FINANCE)

DIVISIONAL
COMMISSIONER
(DIVISIONAL
PLANNING)

(TRANSPORT &
TRAFFIC)

MELA ADHIKARI
(MELA ADHIKARI MEETING)

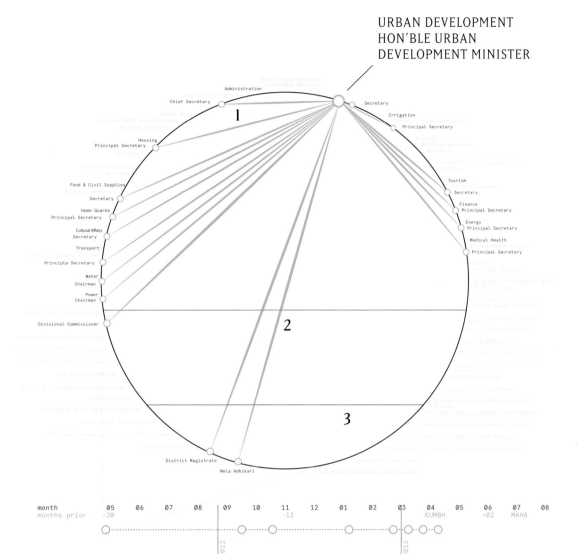

URBAN DEVELOPMENT
HON'BLE URBAN
DEVELOPMENT MINISTER

Administration
Chief Secretary

Secretary

Irrigation
Principal Secretary

1

Housing
Principal Secretary

Food & Civil Supplies
Secretary

Tourism
Secretary

Home Guards
Principal Secretary

Finance
Principal Secretary

Cultural Affairs
Secretary

Energy
Principal Secretary

Transport

Medical Health
Principal Secretary

Principle Secretary

Water
Chairman

Power
Chairman

Divisional Commissioner

2

3

District Magistrate

Mela Adhikari

| month months prior | 05 -20 | 06 | 07 | 08 | 09 | 10 | 11 -12 | 12 | 01 | 02 | 03 | 04 KUMBH | 05 | 06 +02 | 07 MAHA | 08 |

2012

2013

Preparing the master plan and budget

The High Power Committee (HPC) prepares and
recommends amendments to the Kumbh's master plan
and budget; it oversees departmental preparations as
well as approves and curtails departmental proposals.
Under the chairmanship of the Honorable Urban
Development Minister, the HPC meets almost two years
in advance of the Kumbh and continues to guide its
planning throughout. The participating line departments
begin to prepare their individual proposals as early
as October 2010, i.e. 27 months before the Kumbh.

HIGH POWER COMMITTEE

STATE (1)
DIVISION (2)
SITE (3)

ADMINISTRATION
HON'BLE CHIEF MINISTER

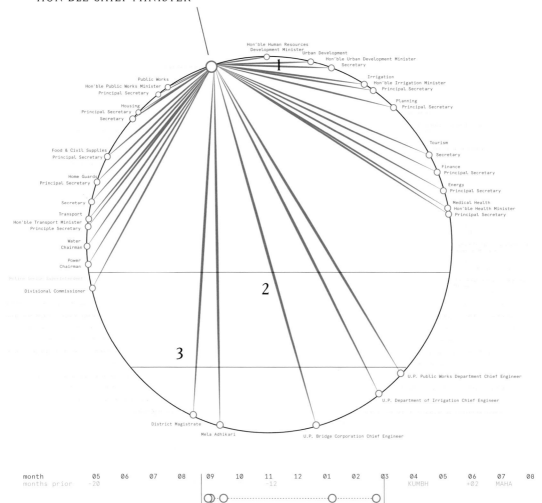

Hon'ble Human Resources
Development Minister
Urban Development
Hon'ble Urban Development Minister
Secretary

1

Public Works
Hon'ble Public Works Minister
Principal Secretary

Housing
Principal Secretary
Secretary

Food & Civil Supplies
Principal Secretary

Home Guards
Principal Secretary

Secretary
Transport
Hon'ble Transport Minister
Principle Secretary

Water
Chairman

Power
Chairman

Police Senior Superintendent
Divisional Commissioner

Irrigation
Hon'ble Irrigation Minister
Principal Secretary

Planning
Principal Secretary

Tourism
Secretary

Finance
Principal Secretary

Energy
Principal Secretary

Medical Health
Hon'ble Health Minister
Principal Secretary

2

3

U.P. Public Works Department Chief Engineer

U.P. Department of Irrigation Chief Engineer

District Magistrate

Mela Adhikari

U.P. Bridge Corporation Chief Engineer

| month | 05 | 06 | 07 | 08 | 09 | 10 | 11 | 12 | 01 | 02 | 03 | 04 | 05 | 06 | 07 | 08 |
| months prior | -20 | | | | | | -12 | | | | | KUMBH | | +02 | MAHA | |

2012   2013

Sanctioning the master
plan and budget

APEX COMMITTEE

STATE (1)
DIVISION (2)
SITE (3)

The apex committee sanctions the master plan and
budget. It starts to meet approximately a year in
advance and continues to monitor the developments
at site level. In contrast to the HPC, apex also invites
the voices of key positions on the ground such as the
chief engineers from various departments.

ADMINISTRATION
CHIEF
SECRETARY

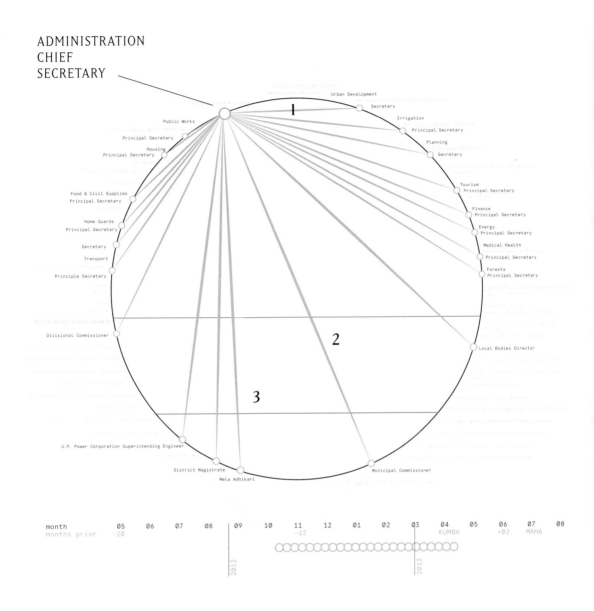

Urban Development
  Secretary
Irrigation
  Principal Secretary
Planning
  Secretary
Tourism
  Principal Secretary
Finance
  Principal Secretary
Energy
  Principal Secretary
Medical Health
  Principal Secretary
Forests
  Principal Secretary

Local Bodies Director

Public Works
Principal Secretary
Housing
Principal Secretary
Food & Civil Supplies
Principal Secretary
Home Guards
Principal Secretary
Secretary
Transport
Principle Secretary

Divisional Commissioner

U.P. Power Corporation Superintending Engineer

District Magistrate
Mela Adhikari

Municipal Commissioner

1

2

3

month	05	06	07	08	09	10	11	12	01	02	03	04	05	06	07	08
months prior	-20						-12					KUMBH		+02	MAHA	

2012   2013

Reviewing planning and ensuring coordination

The chief secretary's committee meets biweekly to
review the planning process and ensure coordination
between the numerous executing line departments. It
draws its members from largely the same departments
as the apex committee does.

CHIEF SECRETARY'S
COMMITTEE

STATE (1)
DIVISION (2)
SITE (3)

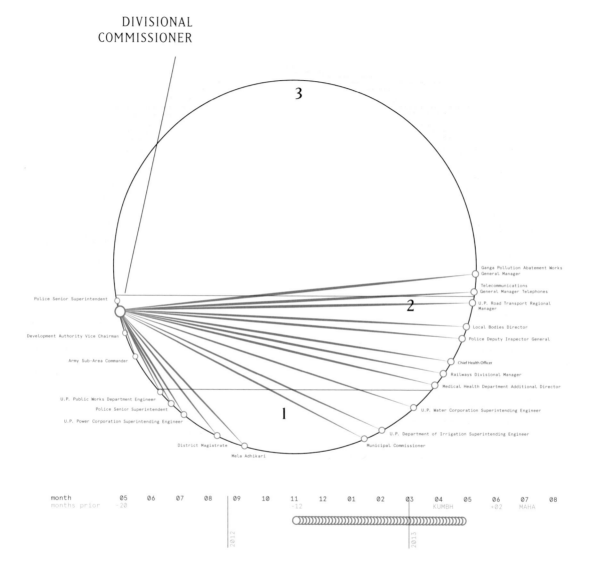

DIVISIONAL
COMMISSIONER

3

Ganga Pollution Abatement Works
General Manager

Telecommunications
General Manager Telephones

2

U.P. Road Transport Regional
Manager

Police Senior Superintendent

Local Bodies Director

Police Deputy Inspector General

Development Authority Vice Chairman

Chief Health Officer

Army Sub-Area Commander

Railways Divisional Manager

Medical Health Department Additional Director

U.P. Public Works Department Engineer

Police Senior Superintendent

U.P. Water Corporation Superintending Engineer

U.P. Power Corporation Superintending Engineer

1

U.P. Department of Irrigation Superintending Engineer

District Magistrate

Municipal Commissioner

Mela Adhikari

| month | 05 | 06 | 07 | 08 | 09 | 10 | 11 | 12 | 01 | 02 | 03 | 04 | 05 | 06 | 07 | 08 |
| months prior | -20 | | | | | | -12 | | | | | KUMBH | | +02 | MAHA | |

2012

2013

Implementing on the ground

The divisional planning committee implements the
plans and decisons made by higher committees. It
also suggests plans and solutions at the local level.
To effectively and responsively oversee day-to-day
activities, the committee maintains a flat structure.
In his role of the committee chair, the Divisional
Commissioner invites mostly people from the divisional
or site level to meet every week.

DIVISIONAL PLANNING

STATE (1)
DIVISION (2)
SITE (3)

MELA ADHIKARI

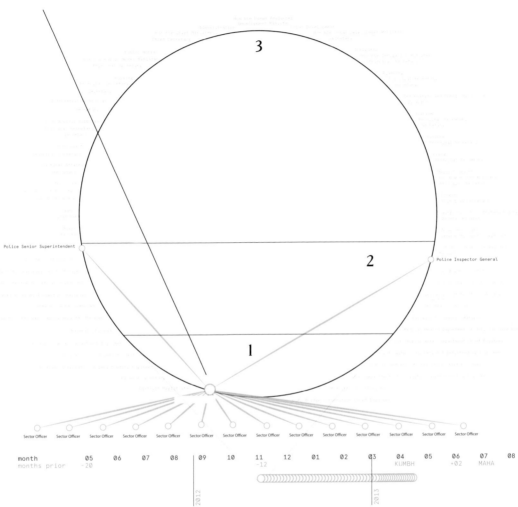

3

2

Police Inspector General

Police Senior Superintendent

1

Sector Officer Sector Officer Sector Officer Sector Officer Sector Officer Sector Officer Sector Officer Sector Officer Sector Officer Sector Officer Sector Officer Sector Officer Sector Officer Sector Officer

month		05	06	07	08	09	10	11	12	01	02	03	04	05	06	07	08
months prior		-20						-12					KUMBH		+02	MAHA	

2012

2015

Reviewing implementation and executing

The Mela Adhikari is arguably the most important role on the ground. His role is posted in December of the preceding year, i.e. just over a year in advance of the Kumbh. The Mela Officer then joins the team during mid May. From thereon, his team, which consists of representatives of the police as well as 14 sector magistrates, meets weekly (and daily for the 4 days preceeding a bathing day) to discuss implementation issues and all other matters.

MELA ADHIKARI'S
MEETING

STATE (1)
DIVISION (2)
SITE (3)

In addition to the herculean effort to plan and fund the Kumbh, the government is also responsible for the leveling of the ground, the deployment of the metal-plate roads, the pontoon bridges, and the provision of sewerage, water, and electricity. However, once the Kumbh is gridded, the closed government space transforms into a space that is both inviting and dependent upon collaborative governance. Allowing for governance, in this context, shall be defined as the willingness and ability to engage in partnerships with and delegate tasks to non-governmental actors stemming from both the private profit and the non-profit sectors. Hence, and in analogy to the metal plate roads, the administrational framework, too, sets clear parameters and borders first and allows for informal networks of kinship within its confinements thereafter. Indeed, the remarkable speed and efficiency displayed during both set-up and operation is a result of shared codes and implicit understandings enacted through generational knowledge and expertise. This experience-derived confidence is often reason for contractors to move materials before official orders.

The ephemeral spaces, in between more permanent governmental infrastructures, are leased to and programmed by non-governmental actors, first and foremost the twelve Akhadas. This programming includes the spatial layout of the living spaces within the grid, outcontracting tent construction, food supply, lost and found, and other functions. Further, various kinds of shops, both formal and informal set up and draw on their own local supply networks.

To respond to ever-changing situations emanating from the ground in a timely manner, the routines and media by which decisions are made take on different emphases in each stage. Oftentimes, the monitoring and reviewing stage of the Kumbh, as headed by the Mela Adhikari, reverses the routines of the planning stage to achieve greater flexibility. Beginning in 2001, the mobile phone in conjunction with motorcycles and horses, was widely used to flexibly and speedily communicate and respond. Without doubt, the Kumbh in year 2025 will see further advances in availability and utilization of digital technologies.

It is clear that the structural organization behind the Kumbh can provide lessons not only for

India's rapid urbanization, but also for other ephemeral sites of urban character. Indeed, it is against the background that India's handling of its rapid urbanization is a far cry from the effectiveness displayed at the Kumbh, and that development and disaster relief practices are critiqued for being behind-the-time (or some might say "rural"), that an exploration and a mapping of governance structures might be insightful. To be sure, the most critical or success-bearing factors are, in fact, the hardest to transfer. The Kumbh and its heart, the holy act of bathing, are deeply rooted in the Indian psyche, both symbolically as well as materially in terms of generational knowledge. Bathing in the Sangam is not only seen as a religious duty but also a great accomplishment. This sense of pride and privilege has little role in disaster and conflict sites of ephemeral urbanism. Furthermore, the budgetary generosity to employ the best and highest standing officials for whom the Kumbh is a prestigious assignment is a luxury not all sites of ephemerality enjoy.

There are, however, normative lessons to be learned. All actors involved in the organization of the Kumbh are expected to have, and indeed do show, the greatest respect for the pilgrims. Dignity and cultural tolerance are pursued over individual ego and identity. This strong sense of a shared purpose allows the government to engage in partnerships, delegate power, and foster a form of collaboration with non-governmental actors that is agile, flexible, and responsive.

3 · · · · · ·
2 · · · · · ·
Administration

Public Works
Hon'ble Public Works Minister
Principal Secretary

Housing
Principal Secretary
Secretary

Information Technology
Secretary

Food & Civil Supplies
Principal Secretary
Secretary

Home Guards
Principal Secretary

Cultural Affairs
Secretary

Transport
Hon'ble Transport Minister
Principle Secretary

Water
Chairman

Power
Chairman

4 · · · · · · Police Senior Superintendent

Northern Railways Deputy Regional Manager
Development Authority Vice Chairman
Police Deputy Inspector General (Railways)
Army Sub-Area Commander
Eastern Railways Deputy Regional Manager
Baumruli Airport
U.P. Public Works Department Superintending Engineer
Police Senior Superintendent
U.P. Power Corporation Superintending Engineer
Finance Secretary
District Magistrate

5 · · · · · ·

05   06   07   08   09   10
-20

HON'BLE URBAN DEVELOPMENT MINISTER (1)
HON'BLE CHIEF MINISTER (2)
CHIEF SECRETARY (3)
DIVISIONAL COMMISSIONER (4)
MELA ADHIKARI (5)

month
months prior

374

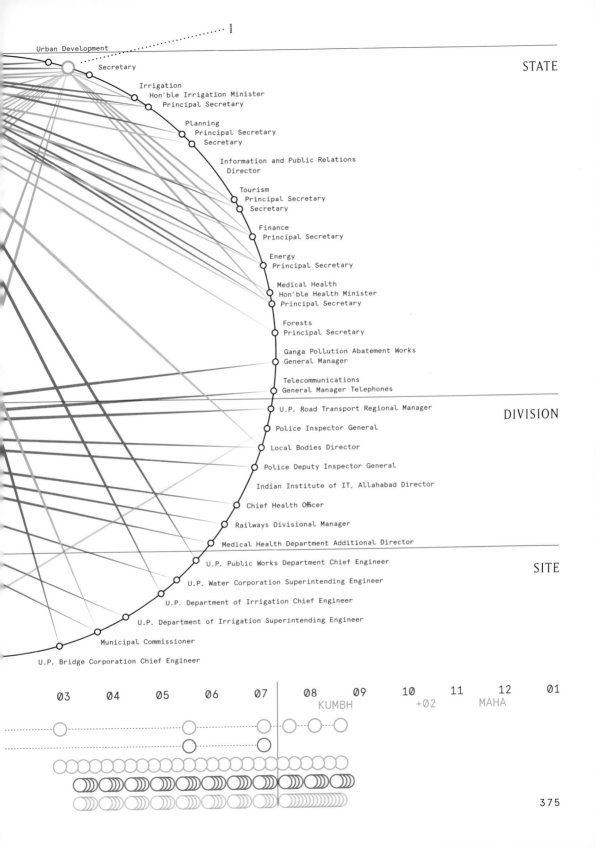

1

Urban Development
Secretary

STATE

Irrigation
Hon'ble Irrigation Minister
Principal Secretary

Planning
Principal Secretary
Secretary

Information and Public Relations
Director

Tourism
Principal Secretary
Secretary

Finance
Principal Secretary

Energy
Principal Secretary

Medical Health
Hon'ble Health Minister
Principal Secretary

Forests
Principal Secretary

Ganga Pollution Abatement Works
General Manager

Telecommunications
General Manager Telephones

U.P. Road Transport Regional Manager

DIVISION

Police Inspector General

Local Bodies Director

Police Deputy Inspector General

Indian Institute of IT, Allahabad Director

Chief Health Officer

Railways Divisional Manager

Medical Health Department Additional Director

U.P. Public Works Department Chief Engineer

SITE

U.P. Water Corporation Superintending Engineer

U.P. Department of Irrigation Chief Engineer

U.P. Department of Irrigation Superintending Engineer

Municipal Commissioner

U.P. Bridge Corporation Chief Engineer

| 03 | 04 | 05 | 06 | 07 | 08 | 09 | 10 | 11 | 12 | 01 |

KUMBH   +02   MAHA

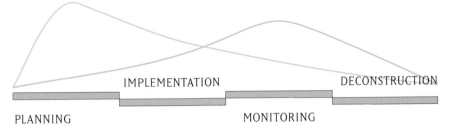

SCHEDULED MEETINGS UNSCHEDULED MEETINGS

IMPLEMENTATION   DECONSTRUCTION

PLANNING   MONITORING

Scheduled meetings, i.e. meetings that have been agreed to take place at a specific time, give way to spontaneous meetings to accommodate unforeseen issues that require leadership attention.

TELEPHONE CONFERENCE MOBILE PHONE

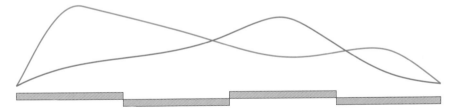

Most meetings take place in person. Paradoxically though, when the actors are physically in closest proximity, distant meetings are commonplace due to the widespread use of mobile phone technology.

FACE-TIME MEETINGS DISTANT MEETINGS

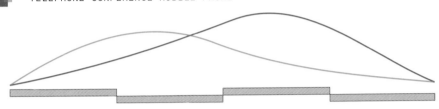

The use of mobile phones and the speed of communicating increases as the Kumbh progresses. A prerequisite for this is the decreasing need to consult higher authorities for low-impact decisions.

DIRECT CONVERSATION ROUTED THROUGH FILE

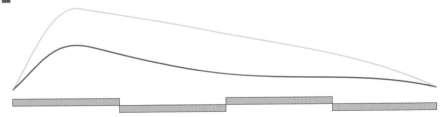

As the number of contractual decisions decreases over time, so does the need to route requests through files. This increases the responsiveness and flexibility of decision-making immensely.

377

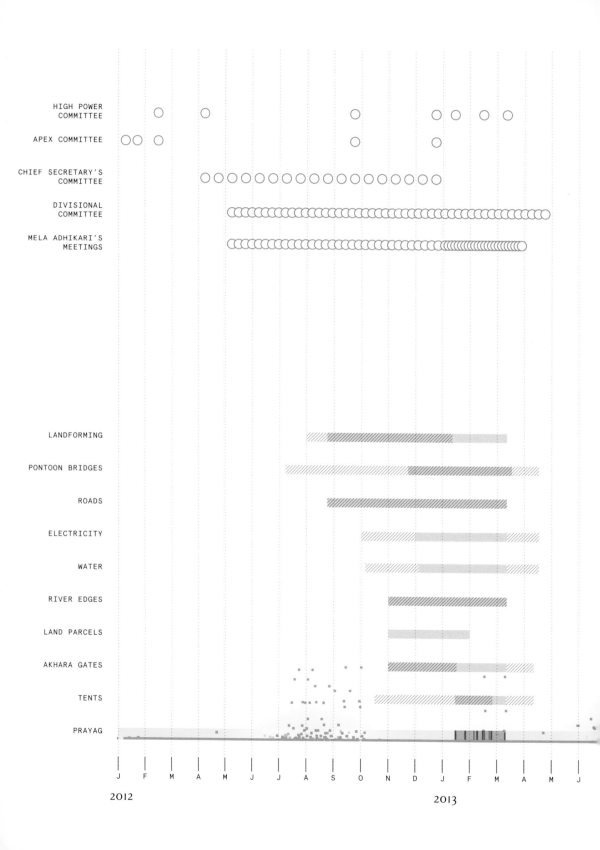

HIGH POWER
COMMITTEE

APEX COMMITTEE

CHIEF SECRETARY'S
COMMITTEE

DIVISIONAL
COMMITTEE

MELA ADHIKARI'S
MEETINGS

LANDFORMING

PONTOON BRIDGES

ROADS

ELECTRICITY

WATER

RIVER EDGES

LAND PARCELS

AKHARA GATES

TENTS

PRAYAG

J F M A M J J A S O N D J F M A M J

2012   2013

HEALTH State and Central governments create a budget and provide funding. State governments and the Mela administration create a plan. Government engineers and sector magistrates enforce the plan in each sector. Contractors build clinics and hospitals. Doctors and paramedics are recruited from hospitals and health programs across UP. Over 9,000 laborers are hired to sweep streets, clean toilets, and sanitize cesspools.

ALLOCATION Akharas negotiate with the Adhikari to finalize the plan. Planners and surveyors work in parallel to create a map. Akharas hire contractors to build camps. Expenses are paid for by the administration.

ROADS & PONTOON BRIDGES State and Federal governments provide funding. The government and Mela administration together create a plan. Government engineers and sector magistrates enforce the plan in each sector. Contractors hire laborers and buy materials to build roads and pontoon bridges.

ELECTRICITY The Federal government provides 30% of the funding, and government engineers and sector magistrates enforce the plan in each sector. Often they need to track down the contractors, hire laborers, and buy materials for the electricity grid and substations.

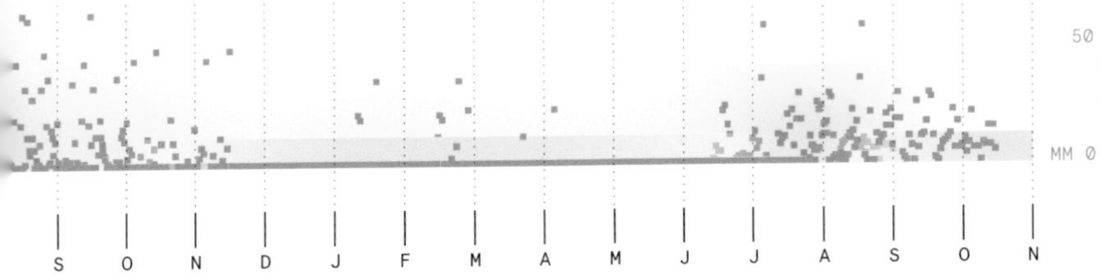

HARVARD UNIVERSITY

FV	FIELD VISIT
W	WORKSHOP
■	MILESTONE
■	EVENT
■	RESEARCH SEMINAR
■	RESEARCH LAB

PLANNING + GOVERNANCE

|||| COMMITTEE MEETINGS

450

400

350

INFRASTRUCTURES

300 //// CONSTRUCTION / DECONSTRUCTION

FUNCTIONALITY

250

200

150

100

AT PRAYAG

50

■ RELIGIOUS EVENTS

AGRICULTURE

MM 0 RAINFALL

S   O   N   D   J   F   M   A   M   J   J   A   S   O   N

2014

STATE LEVEL
INSTITUTIONS

TOURISM DEPT

Estimates population size based on
past Kumbhs +20% population
growth. Makes recommendations for
amending sectors

UP POWER CORPORATION

DIVISIONAL & SITE LEVEL
INSTITUTIONS

KUMBH ADMINISTRATION

ALLAHABAD COMMISIONER
In charge of police and laws
Appoints the Mela Adhikari

MELA ADHIKARI

Responsible for planning and construction

3 assistants support   14 sector magistrates are responsible
the Mela Adhikari   for enforcing land use and overseeing
                            construction in each sector

PLANNERS

Lay out space and infrastructure
for Kumbh Mela per the Amin's plan

PUBLIC

PRIVATE   DIVISIONAL & SITE
           LEVEL PRIVATE ACTORS

AMIN

Marks out the city, including
the electrical grid, roads,
and land allotments

External

AKHARAS

12 person leadership council

- Decides who and how many
people will live in camp
- Lobby for land allocation
- Decide layout for camps
- Submit elictricty demands

GENERAL CONTRACTORS

Build camps at a discount for Akharas

Lalooji, the dominant contractor,
is organized through 13 different subsidiaries.
It is said that they build the Kumbh,
including hospitals and shelter.
Local firms employ specific communication
techniques to mark camp typologies with
which they are familiar. They "often turn
up right as you are about to call a contractor"

Local Assets

PANDA CAMPS

Other Religious Groups

- Space alloted afterwards
- Electricity demands
- Lobby for land allocation
- Decide layout for camps

FORESTRY DEPT

Supplies wood needed for
construction

UP JAL NIGAM

Department is headed
by a chief engineer
and is split into
three main departments

PUBLIC WORKS DEPARTMENT

Responsible for building
pontoon bridges and street signage

HEALTH & SANITATION

Department is headed by a chief engineer
and is split into three main departments:

DRINKING WATER
DRAINAGE WATERING

3 executuve engineers
16 assitant engineers
23 junior engineers

Chief engineer is appointed by
the state PWD department and
manages the work of assistant
engineers on site

Public Health, Clinics, and Vector Diseases.
Doctors, nurses, and paramedics are
recruited from hospitals throughout
Uttar Pradesh

NEHRU INSTITURE
OF TECHNOLOGY

Responsible for 3rd
party checks

LOCAL LABOR POOL

9,000 day laborers are hired to sweep and sanitize
latrines
Unskilled laborers are paid for 250 Rs per day

SELF
ORGANIZED

LESSONS

Learning from the POP-UP Megacity: Reflections on Reversibility and Openness

RAHUL MEHROTRA & FELIPE VERA

The physical structure of cities around the globe is evolving, morphing, mutating, and becoming more malleable, more fluid, and more open to change than the technology and social institutions that generate them. Today, urban environments face ever-increasing flows of human movement, acceleration in the frequency of natural disasters, and iterative economic crises that modify streams of capital and their allocation as physical components of cities. As a consequence, urban settings are required to be more flexible in order to be better able to respond to, organize, and resist internal and external pressures. In a time that change and the unexpected are the new normal, urban attributes like reversibility and openness seem to be critical elements for thinking about the articulation of a more sustainable form of urban development. The lessons we can extract from the Kumbh Mela are clearly aligned with these attributes. This massive gathering, resulting in the biggest ephemeral megacity in the world, generates an extreme case that forces us to reflect deeply on the way we think of cities more broadly. This essay reflects upon two key attributes of the ephemeral city of the Kumbh Mela and the lessons we can extrapolate from it for architecture, urban design, and planning in the contemporary world.

Reversibility

The city of the Kumbh Mela challenges the idea of sustainability, by engaging us to think about urban design as a reversible operation. Upon examining the stunning images of the ephemeral city, we tend to fix the eye onto the incommensurable expansion the city has when it is in operation. However, what is most remarkable about the Kumbh Mela is not that it is only constructed in such a short period of time, but also that it has the ability to be disassembled as quickly. The Kumbh Mela raises a nuanced set of questions about how "reversibility" can be better imagined in the assembly of future cities. In a matter of weeks, the biggest public gathering in the world deploys its own roads, pontoon bridges, cotton tents that serve as residences and venues for spiritual meetings, and a spectrum of social infrastructure— all replicating the functions of an actual city. This pop-up megacity serves approximately five to seven million people who gather for fifty-five days and an additional flux of ten to ten million people who come for twenty-four-hour cycles on the five main bathing dates. Once the festival is over, the whole city is disassembled as rapidly as it was deployed, reversing the constructive operation, disaggregating the settlement to its basic components, and recycling a majority of the materials that were used.

Without seeing images of the Kumbh Mela, one could hardly believe that a complex megacity of such extensive scale could be deployed in such a short and compressed time span, even with all the technological instruments and disciplinary knowledge that we currently possess. However, it is precisely this lack of technological specificity and reversibility—previously considered a constraint for deployment—where its true robustness lies. Therefore, one of the most valuable lessons offered by the Kumbh Mela is in the implementation of tactics that allow for the deployment of a whole city as a holding strategy for temporary urban processes that do not aspire to be permanent. It is in the non-permanent solution for a non-permanent problem that is the city's raison être. This alignment between the temporary nature of the problem—in this case, to host millions of people for fifty-five days—and that of the solution is something we could and perhaps should incorporate as a basic protocol for the cities we reshape and create in the future.

Reversibility can be examined in two contrasting dimensions—material and immaterial. Its material aspects translate into a physical reversibility of the constructed armature that supports the existence of the Kumbh Mela. On the other hand, the immaterial aspects frame a reversible political and institutional structure that supports the construction and organization of the ephemeral city.

In the context of more permanent settlements, institutions associated with urban processes take time to form and are not often created as malleable and flexible structures. However, in the case of the Kumbh Mela, a flexible temporary governance system is created to act as a surrogate for what might have been more permanent. This system of governance plugs into a pre-existing urban management organization at the state level and draws its expertise from existing institutions—often pulling together (for a short period of twelve months), the best administrators in the state. During the festival, the institutional framework of the Kumbh Mela becomes an autonomous city managed by several temporary governmental agencies that have jurisdiction over the site. The institutional structure that manages the city evolves depending of the stage in which they operate. The deployment of the city is then divided in four main stages that affect the nature of its governance. The first phase is used for the initial phase of planning, which is held outside the physical space of the Kumbh, and involves government authorities that range from the local to the national level. The second stage is for implementation that happens both in the peripheries of the site while the river is still high and onsite when the river Ganges and Yamuna recede. Management is the third stage of the deployment, which corresponds to the period in which the city is in operation, which not only includes the challenge of handling the massive crowds of people, but also the oversight of a river that might fluctuate or shift in its trajectory by thirty feet per day. And finally, the deconstruction stage starts after the last bathing day of the Kumbh Mela, which launches that reprograms the space into agricultural fields for a few weeks before the Ganges floods again in the monsoon to reclaim the site of the city.

The administration of the city is implemented by an organizational structure that is not only impermanent—something one could expect given the temporal condition of the city, but also flexible, allowing the progressive appearance of transversal links of communication across diverse hierarchies. This is clear when one examines the nature of the meetings and the authority each member has during different moments of the city's deployment. Relations of power and connections vary depending on the stage of the deployment. During the planning stage, interactions are framed in departmental meetings that are small in scale with the authority mostly residing among representatives of the state. During this process, the state of Uttar Pradesh engaged twenty-eight departments as well as seven different central departments from the national government.

Over time, once the implementation stage begins, the governance system gets more dynamic, articulating constituencies at different levels that are represented onsite. During this stage, diverse mechanisms of feedback among different levels within the hierarchies get set up in order to deal with the need for quick decisions of adjustment in the materialization of the plan. The dynamism of the structure reaches its climax while the city is in operation. At this time, authority shifts from the high levels of the pyramid that operate at the state and regional levels into the grounded administration of the Kumbh. Crucial is the fact that the Kumbh administration meets on the ground each evening during the festival in a dynamic that connects with every single level of the otherwise hierarchical administrative structure. This gives the administrator for the event the capacity to react to any unpredicted incident or requirement of the city quickly and effectively, bypassing inefficient clearance processes when necessary. Once the whole process is over, administrators are often promoted or reappointed in the pre-existing governmental structure. The institutional frameworks that supported such an enormous operation vanishes like the traces of the city once the river washes over the terrain due to the flooding from the seasonal monsoon rains.

Reversibility is also the main attribute that supports the physical deployment of the city. The implementation strategy, which is generic, and employs low-tech construction techniques, facilitates the shaping of the most amazing buildings and morphologies, leaving open the possibility of reversing such operations once the festival is finished. This also allows the materials to be recycled by their reincorporation into regional economies and local industries. The few building techniques implemented at the Kumbh are based in the repetition and recombination of a basic module with simple inter-connections. This is usually a stick (approximately six to eight feet long) that by aggregation, generates diverse enclosures in a wide range of forms from small tents into complex building paraphernalia—providing expression to various social institutions such as theaters, monuments, temples, hospitals, etc. All of them are constructed out of the same elements; with bamboo sticks used as the framework and laminar materials such as corrugated metal and fabric. The simplicity of the building systems not only facilitates the attributes for assembly, reconfiguration, and disassembly on-site, but also facilitates the logistics and channels of distribution for each component and piece. One person or groups of people provide the modulation of every material in a way that can be carried and handled in absence of heavy machinery. Material components are small and light enough to be easily transported and distributed to every corner of the settlement in a rapid and efficient manner facilitating both construction and reconstruction, as well as formation and reabsorption into the various ecologies and geographies of the region. Everything is constructed—and afterwards, deconstructed with equal ease.

The entire Kumbh *nagri* starts to get dismantled after the last major bathing day, which was on February 17, 2013 during the last cycle. Since it rained heavily during this time period—over a period of three days, some of the Akharas, Ashrams, and Kalpavasis decided that it was better to leave earlier than other years. The rain also caused flooding in sector seven and eight, drenching tents. However, most of the people left the site between February 20 and 26. By March 10, which is the last bathing day, only a few private groups of dwellers were still at the Kumbh and participated in the bathing. The emptiness of what was before a full functioning city was by early March, largely unoccupied, except for the government structures that were still in place. However, several visitors still came in for a day or two. By March 16, 2013, only half of the governmental structures were still standing, most of which were electricity board structures.

The disassembly of Akhara's camps and Ashrams started with the devotees taking their things by different means—cars, trucks, or tractors—while chief organizers of each religious order and their *chelas* (followers) stayed until the last day. When a religious order is ready to leave the Kumbh, they get in touch with the contactor that constructed their camp. They do this either directly, if they paid for the camp themselves, or through the sector magistrate, if the camp was constructed with funding from the Kumbh Mela administrator. Days are arranged when trucks and workers arrive to remove all the material—the tents, the plywood, and the steel sheets that formed fences, and every other component of the camp. Once disassembled, the material is taken to the compounds to be stored, counted, and sorted for damaged pieces. After that, different elements are sent to tents suppliers all over India in trucks, with each one carrying one specific type of material. A large part of the common infrastructure is also disassembled once the Kumbh is over. For instance, by digging up wastewater and water supply pipes, Jal Nigam Contractors removed all of the tap connections. In the same way that tents are deconstructed and separated by materials to be returned to their original supplier—tap connections, motors, and pipes are returned to the Jal Nigam store from which they were originally ordered. Once disaggregated, the material is reused in different locations of Uttar Pradesh in other Jal Nigam projects. A meter-long pipe is then welded as an attachment to the tube wells, in order to extend their height and prevent the river from filling them up.

Part of the common infrastructure remains on site. Sewerage pits, for instance, are uncovered from their bamboo structures, treated with chemicals and covered with sand— the same is done with water reservoirs. Other kinds of infrastructure, like sandbags and toilets, get removed. Toilets are one of the most dispersed infrastructures built by the Kumbh Mela administration. The sweeper community oversees toilet removal; they take the ceramic seats to the main health store while the rest of the brick and bamboo is sold to different contractors to be reused in other locations. The same happens with electricity infrastructure. Wires are taken down and wound, poles are disassembled into concrete parts, and metal pieces are taken back to storage. Special electricity boards keep a digital inventory of every registered item.

Roads and pontoons are taken apart sector by sector and brought to three main storage locations in the area—one in the parade ground, the second near the railway yard, and the largest in Jhusi, next to the bus stand. Bridges are broken up in parts, first the railing, then the plates, and finally the joist and pontoons. Once all the material is disassembled, the state government decides where to apportion the bridges and road. This depends on the different district needs—for instance, villages with mud roads that are prone to flooding. Once these decisions are made, the infrastructure is distributed and reconstructed in diverse locations of Uttar Pradesh.

Not only does the construction material get reused after the Mela ends, but even waste becomes a resource to be taken off site. A large number of scavengers from areas in and around Allahabad arrive at the site. They dig up waste coal dumped by community kitchens to use as fuel; they empty the sand bags from which the *ghats* were constructed to make ropes. They take any discarded wood or bamboo to burn on their fires. Scavengers take almost everything, cleaning up the site completely.

After all the material is removed, the flood plain of the river is still a landscape full of patterns, dots, and traces of the city. It is possible to see a big range of elements, from bricks and toilets that are unusable, to altars that remain as a fleeting trace. Big statues are taken away but their brick plinth remains on site with some small sacred statues like *shiva lingams* and other minor statues that were not taken away. Organic material that is left behind, such as sandbags and bamboo poles, gradually disintegrate with time.

Once the deconstruction activity is over, the site reestablishes its natural, annual patterns. People from nearby villages prepare beds for planting seasonal vegetables, like cucumber and gourds. Thick grass or thatch that served as the matting for the tent floors is usually burned, making the soil more fertile. Small wells are also built near creating a bountiful agricultural site. The cremation ground on Sector Five is eventually overtaken with vegetation and the river's edge is recolonized.

Reflecting on the processes described above, one is reminded that the most revolutionary opportunities for redefining the ways we produce the built environment, lie in much simpler, low-tech tactics. What is most remarkable about the Kumbh is not that it is constructed in such a short period of time but also that it has the ability to get disassembled as quickly and efficiently. Multiple, highly heterogeneous structures are organized around combinatory system that relies on minimal building strategies. Their construction techniques allow greater degrees of flexibility. The generic condition of basic elements—sticks connected by rope, or simple nails in both orthogonal and diagonal relationships—offer infinite possibilities of recombination. The strength is in the capacity of achieving specific and determinate forms with a couple of indeterminate solutions that are applicable in different contexts and adjustable at any moment. On account of this kit-of-parts approach, the material used for erecting tents, gathering spaces, and constructing monuments that are several meters high, is after the fact reused in other constructions.

In a way, this reversible condition becomes a counterpoint to our contemporary building culture; to the one aspect that has been notoriously absent from the current debate over what to do with the afterlife of the built-things we perceive as not useful anymore. Today buildings are constructed to last as long as possible. The usually do not consider the eventual need for transformation, meaning that the provision of options for reconfiguration, in cases of obsolescence, are not appropriately factored in the designs. We have developed a highly articulated technique for constructing and assembling all sorts of structures, which allow us to handle more complex and efficient construction processes. However, very little has been imagined in relation to advancing in the development of more efficient ways to disassemble and deconstruct the things we build. Paradoxically, what we can learn from the Kumbh Mela is that the most unsustainable practices do not rely on the construction of the built environment, but rather how inefficient we are with reconfigurations of the space that is already built. Unfortunately, in more permanent settings, demolition has been the generalized answer for opening up space that the city requires for growth and adapting to new needs. In short, the lack of incorporation of disassembly strategies as an inherent part of the design imagination—to go along with construction protocols—obstructs the fluid and sustainable metabolism of contemporary urban space.

In a context in which the introduction of digital tools in the production of the built environment undoubtedly has become an unstoppable force behind innovation in the disciplines associated with the construction of the built environment, perhaps the most revolutionary opportunities for redefining the ways we produce the constructed space can be found in low-tech tactics. Downscaling into the more technical elements allow the deployment of the ephemeral city, we can see how looking closely into the technology implemented at the Kumbh there are several lessons to learn as well as several assumptions of current design practices that could be challenged.

Openness

The city of the Kumbh Mela challenges the idea of design as a linear, top down, over-determinate, equilibrated, integrated, and contextual effort. Charles Waldheim, in his 2010 essay "On Landscape, Ecology and Other Modifiers to Urbanism," has argued for incompletion and spatial-temporal openness as becoming central when addressing urban questions in contemporary cities. It is in this context, where temporary urban intensity is considered simultaneously with permanent and accomplished density, that the focus in urbanism will shift from discreet and closed solutions to a more encompassing, open-ended system. Hence, today we are forced us to rethink what we consider to be a desirable urban design outcome across multiple scales and extreme conditions.

Over the past decades, technology has empowered designers with the ability to control form and matter in ways that we had previously never imagined. We provide a greater capacity to anticipate by using mapping techniques, representing complex dynamics that inform modeling natural and artificial design operations. The emergence of a complete new world of possibilities, especially in digital design and fabrication, enables a more effective capacity to imagine forms of growth and performance in the city. Fueled by the ambition of being able to make almost everything, new techniques present the opportunity for restructuring design and planning processes around immaterial or "paperless" fictions, rendering the project of design increasingly a much more specific while speculate endeavor.

Several aspects of the Kumbh Mela reminds us of how important and powerful it is to understand design as an incomplete, circular, and intentionally unbalanced operation. The process by which the city of the Kumbh Mela is assembled, managed, and deconstructed presents an opportunity for learning about scenarios in which cities, as unfinished open systems, accommodate diverse temporalities as part of their own material discourse.

For Richard Sennett, "open" in a city means incomplete, errant, antagonistic, and non-linear. The pop-up settlement presents us with an project that is not just made for people, but one in which the guidelines of the city are given to people as an open template to be developed, transformed, and materialized. In this regard it is interesting to see how the city of the Kumbh Mela as a project is not defined in detail as a fixed plan, it is neither a close definition of buildings and plots but something more abstract, in between an idea and a map. It is thought more as a set of relationships between components that get organized and progressively specified, after the city—as a conceptual drawing—lands in the shifting geography of the floodplains. The stage of physical materialization is also informed by several negotiations, happening on the ground, between Akharas, dwellers, and other visitors, that last until a spatial agreement is reached. Both the adaptation to dynamic geographical processes and the dialogue between diverse agents, progressively complete the form of the city.

Once the project of the city gets grounded and completed, several limits start to appear within the *nagri*, designating spaces, all diverse in nature and function, generating all sorts of forms and morphological expressions. When comparing what is considered "opened" or "closed" at the urban scale,

Sennett distinguishes that, "The closed city is full of boundaries and walls" while "the open city possesses more borders and membranes." In this case, the almost complete absence of massive walls, replaced by thin sheets or membranes of different kind, and nuances much more subtle divide between spaces. Every limit is in a way almost completely permeable and at the same time function as separation. Even though the border condition is still recognized as a divider and contributes to create diversity in size, permeability is omnipresent in the character of the space. At the Kumbh Mela, divisions are not just separations but actually vertical limits with porous layers that mediate connection and relationships, while creating ephemeral but powerful, spatial narratives. These porous borders at the Kumbh Mela manifest the physical and planning structure of the city while forming interesting patterns of space occupation and internal organization, motivated by a deep sense of communality.

In the ephemeral city, public, private, and sacred spaces are at the same time blended and distinguished. For instance, how food was arranged throughout the festival helped form patterns of space occupation generated. Very few shops, stalls, and street vendors were seen along the temporal roads of the Kumbh Mela. While there was some interesting commerce on the streets comprised of a few small tea stalls and vendors selling shampoo, religious items and trinkets clustered at major intersections, and big stores for food trading were completely absent. Contrary to what one might think, the Kumbh Mela does not have an established system of trading inside its boundaries. Religious orders, pilgrims, and visitors bring food and a great part of it is distributed for free in large tents that provide free spaces for people to sit in rows and receive food together. Outside the limits of the settlement, at the border with the permanent city, markets are set up for trading very different things, ranging from food to clothes. Talking with vendors, we realized that some stalls are rented for several years and the same people run small businesses in different *melas*. Most of them come from cities nearby, within the state of Uttar Pradesh. Many goods are brought from Jhusi market, and the vegetables provided help covering the gap between what is needed and what religious orders can bring with them for feeding their people. In addition some of the vending and transactions occur through small stalls that are spontaneously set up along some avenues. Interestingly, this form of market is not as omnipresent as one might expect. It occurs on only on a few streets, which house the large Akharas or are part of major thoroughfares of the temporary city. Perhaps the frugal nature of most people's existence at the Kumbh Mela diminishes the pressure to buy while in retreat or religious pilgrimage.

The three million people that dwell at the Kumbh Mela get their food at the *langar* (a massive communal meal hosted by each Akhara three times a day). According to some of our interviews, these simple meals feed over 100,000 pilgrims, during the busiest days of the Mela. Each Akhara and Ashram has its own corps of volunteers who help organize these gatherings, cook the food, and take care of supplies. They draw upon regional resources, sending representatives several times a week to wholesale markets on the outskirts of Allahabad, Jhunsi, and Naini to purchase fresh vegetables from local farms. They also aggregate the small amounts of fresh vegetables, rice, and flour that many pilgrims bring as contributions. Finally, although the Mela administration organizes shops for grain, rice, and oil, Akharas and Ashrams bring their own stocks of rice, flour, and firewood from their Ashrams in Punjab, Kashmir, and other parts of India. Each Akhara is in a sense a self-contained managerial shelter that provides services for its members and guests.

The porous limits of the Kumbh Mela are not only physical, they are also constructed with vertical elements such as flags that designate the Akhara's sacred spaces, defining a completely different set of rules structured by immaterial demarcations. In accordance with tradition, the area for each sect is organized around an identifying flag, which stands in the center of the space, clearly visible from the street. The flag shows the identity of the Akhara and a larger flag indicates the older, Juna Akhara. Areas for the tents of the gurus and their followers are distributed around it, with the most prominent gurus located along the path from the main entrance to the flag. The importance of each guru is connected with the number of devotees he attracts, which is manifested spatially in the organization of space at the Kumbh Mela. Locations with prime exposure are given to more prominent gurus, allowing them to gather more potential followers, and when one teacher's followers become too numerous for the allotted space, a new "suburban" Akhara is created with its own space and flag.

The Akharas themselves are also arranged within the sector according to their prominence, with Juna Akhara, the biggest and oldest of the sects, occupying a privileged spot while next to it there were Mahanirvani and Niranjan (along with the Juna, other major sects of the Akhara). One of the most interesting and complex spatial textures of the Kumbh Mela is found walking across these religious orders. It is interesting to see that while virtually everything changes from one version of the Kumbh Mela to the next, the spatial configuration of the Akhara remains the same, keeping the same structures and strictly preserving spatial relationships and internal configurations. Continuing with Sennet's ideas, the Kumbh Mela could act as a refined example of growth in an open city as a matter of evolution rather than erasure.

At the Kumbh Mela, openness manifests at different scales and stages from the constructive detail to the measure of the master plan, as well as from the planning stages on through to the deconstruction. However, perhaps the most powerful moments in which openness gets expressed in the deployment of the city is when one recognizes that such a mega operation received its robustness and resilience exactly, from being conceived as an open work, as text that is written in dialogue with users, complementing the pragmatism of the officials with the appropriation of devotes, *kalpavasis*, and saints. Such a fluid openness is based on an implicit contract of confidence, sealed with the common religious purpose. Again, in Sennet's words the ephemeral city of the Kumbh Mela is unlike the closed city and is resilient exactly because it "is a bottom-up place; it belongs to the people." The Kumbh Mela challenges current design and planning trends by demonstrating how improvisation and incompleteness can become fundamental parts in construction.

Openness also displays how the city gets materialized. The power of constructive methods is actually an extreme generic solution, which is always open to combination. For instance, the modularity of steel plates that can be carried by four men is what allows them to be deployed wherever needed. The simplicity of hand-stitched cotton tents stretched over lightweight bamboo frames enables them to be incorporated into the skeleton of a megacity, whatever shape it may need to take, and in whatever colors and patterns may be desired. Heavy machinery and advanced technology are, for the most part, not required—nor are highly trained specialists. Highly heterogeneous structures are organized around combinatory systems that rely in few building strategies. The construction techniques employed grant greater degrees of flexibility. The strength comes from the capacity of achieving specific and determinate forms with a couple of indeterminate solutions that are applicable in different contexts and adjustable at any moment. Therefore the material used for erecting tents, gathering spaces and even monuments that are several meters in height can be reused afterwards in other constructions. Each of the few building techniques implemented at the Kumbh Mela are based on the repetition and recombination of a basic module with a simple connection. This is usually a stick that by aggregation allows generating diverse enclosures in a wide range of forms that go from small tents into complex paraphernalia. This gives expression to diverse social institutions such as theaters, monuments, temples, and hospitals (to list a few). All of them are constructed out of the same elements, bamboo sticks used as framework to laminar materials such as corrugated metal and fabric.

The simplicity of the building systems not only shows the attributes to the assembly, reconfiguration, and disassembly on site but also facilitates the logistics and channels of distribution for each component and piece. The modulation of every material is provided in a way that it can be carried and handled by one person or several groups of people in absence of heavy machinery. Materials are small and light enough to be easily transported and distributed to every corner of the *nagri* in rapid and efficient manner, facilitating both construction and deconstruction as well as the formation and reabsorption into the various ecologies and geographies of the region. Therefore, it is a strategy that serves not only the Kumbh Mela, but the whole regional economy as well.

After the festival ends, the city is dismantled and its components are quickly and effectively recycled or repurposed, with metal and plastic items finding their ways to either storage or to other festivals and construction projects. Biodegradable materials such as thatch and bamboo are left to reintegrate with the site, which, nurtured by the floodwaters, serves as valuable agricultural land for the eleven monsoon cycles between festivals. This open condition of planning, urban design, space occupation, and constructability could also be applied to other non-permanent settlements such as refugee camps or disaster relief efforts, as well as for future urban design and redesign projects.

Recently, we have witnessed some anxiety about embracing new ways to use incremental design as a strategy. At the urban scale this operation needs greater exploration. The aspiration for almost absolute control, brought by the empowerment of new technologies, has been challenged by some practical and conceptual efforts that placed incompletion and incremental design as more effective strategies for dealing with the natural entropy. Therefore, in the same way that we have learned from experiences of incremental social housing, the city of the Kumbh Mela we could certainly extract some applicable lessons in openness that could work in more permanent cities at the urban scale.

Toward a More Nuanced TEMPORALITY

After studying the Kumbh Mela, one could suggest that it is time for urbanism and design to find new ways for effectively factoring in temporalities as critical components of institutional and technological orthodox. For engaging in this discussion, the exploration of temporal landscapes opens a potent avenue to explore by questioning permanence as a univocal solution for the urban conditions. Instead one could argue that the future of cities depends less on the rearrangement of buildings and infrastructure, and more on the ability for us to openly imagine more malleable technological, material, social, and economic landscapes. This is to say that we should design cities (or at least parts of cities) as holding strategies, which grow out of a close alignment with the temporal scale and solutions we conceptualize in our urban imaginary.

The form of urbanism that emerges after the construction and occupancy of the Kumbh Mela, in a way provides what Kaliski describes as a deficiency in the temporal dimension of contemporary permanent cities. The Kumbh Mela offers a flexible model of spatial construction that is temporal, cyclic, in constant advancement, ready to spring into motion as the environment changes and to make way for the needs of pilgrims seeking the connection with a sacred geography. As we have seen, the Kumbh Mela's design anticipates elasticity, building robustness through the capacity to articulate diametrically opposed indices of population, velocities, and concentrations, without having to erase the spatial manifestations of the religious practice or restrict them. The city is constantly designed to frame the human experience, making its religious component a core determinant of its form.

An inspiring thought that comes after having examined the construction and disassembly of the city is that perhaps design must incorporate the anticipation of diverse temporalities into it's imagination. In single buildings as it is in master plans, the embracing of change, as an active dimension in spatial production is something that architects and planners need to consider. Change is everywhere and the intellectual wealth that one can gain from the close analysis of this cases, relies in understanding that every city in some way or another, goes through a constant processes of internal reformulation; they are constantly in a state of disassembly. Whether perceptibly or imperceptibly, different materials fade at different paces and geographies change at different speeds. The modulation of change through design allows for the production of flexible, elastic, and weak structures at any scale.

From this city, we can learn how to move towards an urbanism that recognizes and better handles the ephemeral nature of the built environment with a more intelligent management of change as an essential element. In this case, several layers of change have been managed and negotiated. It should inspire flexible designs that are generally taught to design for static or stable situations.

Aside from the technical refinement that has already been highlighted through this study, one cannot avoid giving a glimpse at how the experience is lived and perceived from within. It all coalesced on a hilltop overlooking a great view of the Kumbh Mela—this great temporary megacity that literally spread outward below our feet. From afar, it was impossible to guess the city was ephemeral, a prowess of planning, engineering, and construction, built in a couple of months and just as quickly disassembled. We stood there silently observing, gauging how to best map and understand this ephemeral city, completely focused on tents, streets, and infrastructure. We were impressed with the fluidity with which the most elementary components could duplicate an everyday city. Then someone put a question to the owner of the camp, a *sadhvi* who worked closely with the Akharas: "So . . . the whole plain in which the city is constructed is actually flooded by the river? Are the banks inaccessible during the monsoon?" we asked. "Yes," she responded sharply. "We feel blessed that during the Kumbh Mela, the mother goddess—the Ganga—retreats, and lets you sit on her lap."

Individual
PORTRAITS

GILES PRICE

APPENDIX

Close-Ups

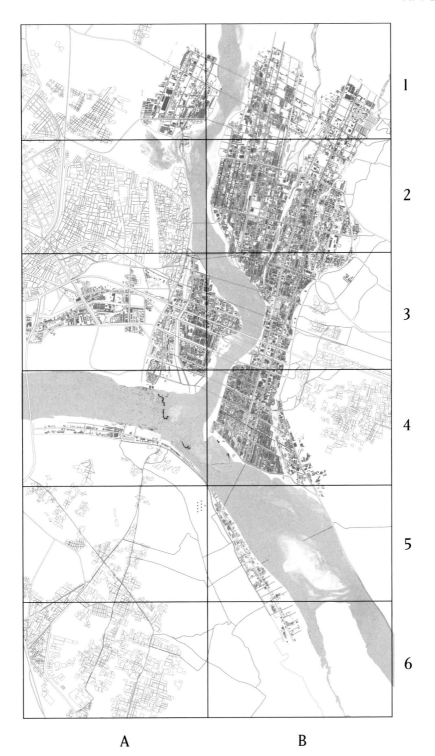

1

2

3

4

5

6

A   B

A2

NAG VASUKI MARG

HARISHCHANDRA SETU MARG

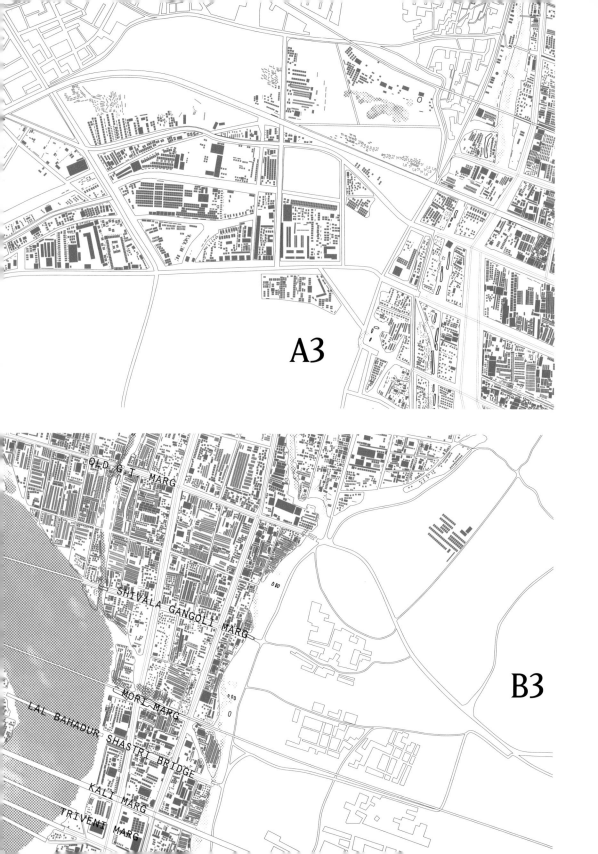

A3

B3

OLD G.I. MARG

SHIVALA GANGOLI MARG

MORI MARG

LAL BAHADUR SHASTRI BRIDGE

KALI MARG

TRIVENI MARG

A4

B4

JAGADISH MARG

MAHAVEER MARG

AKSHAYVAT MARG

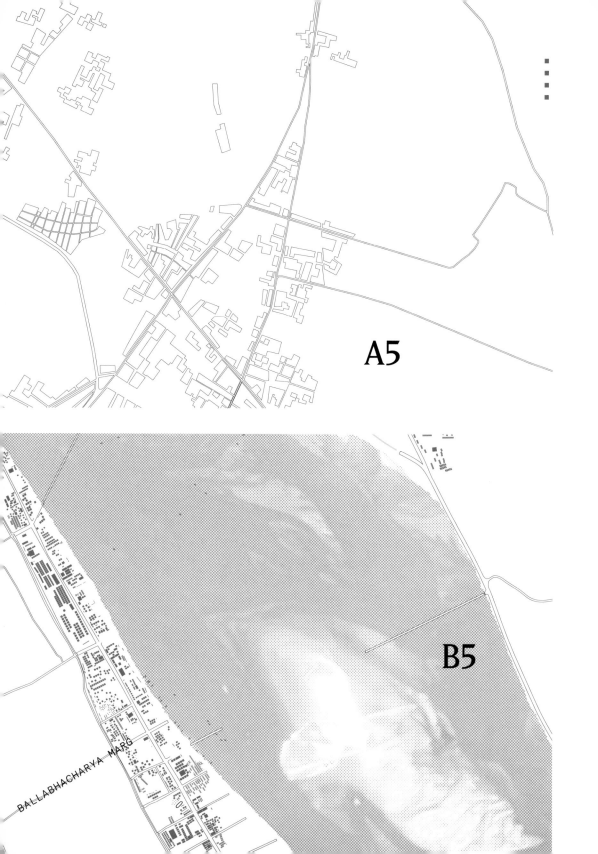

A5

B5

BALLABHACHARYA MARG

STATISTICS

AREA
1,936.56
HECTARES

SECTORS
14

PARKING LOTS
99

POLICE STATIONS
30

STATE POLICE PERSONNEL
12,461

CENTRAL PARAMILITARY
PERSONNEL
40

CCTV CAMERAS
85

VARIABLE SIGNBOARDS
30

FIRE STATIONS
30

LENGTH OF ROADS LAID
156
KILOMETERS

PONTOON BRIDGES
18

LENGTH OF PIPELINES
FOR WATER
550
KILOMETERS

WATER TAP CONNECTIONS
20,000

ACTIVE WATER TUBE WELLS
40

KILOWATT HOURS
OF POWER CONSUMED
30
MEGAVOLT AMPERES

LENGTH OF ELECTRICITY LINES
770
KILOMETERS

STREETLIGHTS
22,000

PRIVATE ELECTRICAL
CONNECTIONS
130,000

ELECTRICAL SUBSTATIONS
73

ALLOPATHIC HOSPITALS
14

HOMEOPATHIC HOSPITALS
12

AYURVEDIC HOSPITALS
12

HOSPITAL BEDS
370

INDIVIDUAL TOILETS
35,000

PUBLIC TOILETS
340

TRENCH PATTERNS
7,500

NON-CONVENTIONAL TOILETS
1,000

TEMPORARY BUS STATIONS
5

REGIONAL BUSES IN OPERATION
892

LOCAL BUSES IN OPERATION
3,608

PILGRIMS (estimated)
120,000,000

PILGRIMS IN RESIDENCE
FOR FIFTY-FIVE DAYS
(estimated)
5,000,000

TRAIN STATIONS IN OPERATION
7

TRAINS IN OPERATION
750

PEOPLE LOST DURING
FESTIVAL (estimated)
200,000

SOURCE:
http://kumbhmelaallahabad.gov.in

BIBLIOGRAPHY

Abubakar, Ibrahim et al. "Global Perspectives for Prevention of Infectious Diseases Associated with Mass Gatherings." *The Lancet Infectious Diseases* 12.1 (2012): 66–74.

Agamben, Giorgio, and Daniel Heller-Roazen. *Homo Sacer: Sovereign Power and Bare Life*. Stanford: Stanford University Press, 1998.

Agier, Michel, and David Fernbach. *Managing the Undesirables: Refugee Camps and Humanitarian Government*. Cambridge: Polity, 2011.

Alagh, Yoginder K. "Water and Food Security in South Asia." *International Journal of Water Resources Development* 17.1 (2001): 23–36.

Ayyagari, A., et al. "Use of Telemedicine in Evading Cholera Outbreak in Mahakumbh Mela, Prayag, UP, India: An Encouraging Experience." *Telemedicine Journal and E-Health: The Official Journal of the American Telemedicine Association* 9.1 (2003): 89–94.

Babb, Lawrence A. "Glancing: Visual Interaction in Hinduism." *Journal of Anthropological Research* 37.4 (1981): 387–401. Print.

Bagchi, C., and S. C. Banerjee. "The Kumbh Fair (1966): Aspects of Environmental Sanitation and Other Related Measures." *Indian Journal of Public Health* 11, no. 4 (1967): 180–84.

Balarajan, Y. S. Selvaraj, and S. V. Subramanian. "Health Care and Equity in India." *The Lancet* 377.9764 (2011): 505–15.

Banks, A. Leslie. "Religious Fairs and Festivals in India." *The Lancet* 277.7169 (1961): 162–63.

Belinchón, Sergio. "Ciudades Efímeras." *Quaderns d'arquitectura i urbanisme* 234 (2002): 12ff.

Bettencourt, Luís M. A., et al. "Growth, Innovation, Scaling, and the Pace of Life in Cities." *Proceedings of the National Academy of Sciences* 104.17 (2007): 7301–06.

Bhardwaj, Sinder Mohan. "Prayaga and Its Kumbha Mela." *Purana* 19.1 (1977): 81–179.

—. *Hindu Places of Pilgrimage in India: A Study in Cultural Geography*. Berkeley: University of California Press, 1973.

Bharne, Vinayak. "Anointed Cities." *The Emerging Asian City: Concomitant Urbanities and Urbanisms* (2013): 17.

Bishop, Peter, and Lesley Williams. *The Temporary City*. New York: Routledge, 2012. Print.

Bonazzoli, Giorgio. "Prayaga and Its Kumbha Mela." *Purana* 19 (1977): 81–159.

Brick, Greg A. *Subterranean Twin Cities*. Minneapolis: University of Minnesota Press, 2009.

Brown, Rodger Lyle. *Ghost Dancing on the Cracker Circuit: The Culture of Festivals in the American South*. Jackson: University Press of Mississippi, 1997.

Bryceson, A. D. "Cholera, the Flickering Flame." *Proceedings of the Royal Society of Medicine* 70.5 (1977): 363–65.

Burkle Jr., Frederick M., and Edbert B. Hsu. "Ram Janki Temple: Understanding Human Stampedes." *The Lancet* 377.9760 (2011): 106–07.

Burris, Scott, et al. "Emerging Strategies for Healthy Urban Governance." *Journal of Urban Health: Bulletin of the New York Academy of Medicine* 84, suppl. 1 (2007): 154–63.

Chandola, T. "Spatial and Social Determinants of Urban Health in Low-, Middle- and High-Income Countries." *Public Health* 126.3 (2012): 259–61.

Chatterjee, Suranjan. "New Reflections on the Sannyasi, Fakir and Peasants War." *Economic and Political Weekly* 19.4 (1984): 2–13.

Chauhan, Anjali. "Indian Corporate Women and Worklife Balance." *International Journal of Interdisciplinary Social Sciences* 5.4 (2010): 183–96.

—. "The Descent of Gods: Creating Cultural History in the Kumbh Mela." *The International Journal of Religion and Spirituality in Society* 1.3 (2011): 37–46.

Chauhan, Muktirajsinh-ji. "Vastu Shastra: Sacred Architecture of India." *Archaeology Online,* 2005, http://archaeologyonline. net/artifacts/vastu-shas-tra (last accessed February 10, 2015).

Chhachhi, Sheba. "The Householder, the Ascetic and the Politician: Women Sadhus at the Kumbh Mela." *India International Centre Quarterly* 29.3 / 4 (2002): 224–34.

Chiu, Rebecca L. H. "Urban Housing Policy Issues in Re-Surging Asia." *Urban Policy and Research* 26.3 (2008): 245–47.

Chui, Ernest. "Doomed Elderly People in a Booming City: Urban Redevelopment and Housing Problems of Elderly People in Hong Kong." *Housing, Theory and Society* 18.3–4 (2001): 158–66.

Crawford, Margaret, Michael Speaks, and Rahul Mehrotra. *Everyday Urbanism: Margaret Crawford vs. Michael Speaks.* Vol. 1 Mich-igan Debates on Urbanism. Ann Arbor: University of Michigan, A. Alfred Taub-man College of Architec-ture; New York: Distributed Arts Press, 2005.

Darian, Steven G. *The Ganges in Myth and History.* Delhi: Motilal Banarsidass, 2001.

Desmet, Klaus, et al. "The Spatial Development of India." *Journal of Regional Science* (2013): n. p.

Devi, Indira, and Dilip Ku-mar Roy. *Kumbha: India's Ageless Festival* (1955). Mumbai: Bharatiya Vidya Bhavan, 2009.

Doron, Assa. "Encounter-ing the 'Other': Pilgrims, Tourists and Boatmen in the City of Varanasi." *The Australian Journal of Anthropology* 16.2 (2005): 157–78.

Dubey, D. P. *Prayūga, The Site of Kumbha Mela: In Temporal and Traditional Space.* New Delhi: Aryan Books International, 2001.

—. "Kumbha Mela: Origin and Historicity of India's Greatest Pilgrimage Fair." *National Geographical Journal of India* 33.4 (1987): 469–92.

—. "Maghamela at Prayaga." *Purana* 30.1 (1988): 60–68.

Duka, Theodore, et al. "An Address on Tropical Medi-cine." *The Lancet* 144.3706 (1894): 561–64.

Ebrahim, Shahul H., et al. "Pandemic H1N1 and the 2009 Hajj." *Science* 326.5955 (2009): 938–40.

Echavarria, Pilar. *Portable Architecture and Unpre-dictable Surroundings.* Barcelona: Links Interna-cional, 2004.

Eck, Diana L. *India: A Sa-cred Geography.* New York: Harmony Books, 2012.

—. "India's 'Tūrthas': 'Crossings' in Sacred Geog-raphy." *History of Religions* 20.4 (1981): 323–44.

Fâ-Hien. *A Record of Buddhistic Kingdoms: Being an Account by the Chinese Monk Fâ-Hien of His Travels in India and Ceylon.* Translated and annotated by James Legge. Oxford: Clarendon Press, 1886.

Fischer, Julie E., and Rebecca Katz. "The Inter-national Flow of Risk: The Governance of Health in an Urbanizing World." *Global Health* 4.2 (2011): n. p.

Frank, Georgia. *The Mem-ory of the Eyes: Pilgrims to Living Saints in Christian Late Antiquity.* Berkeley: University of California Press, 2000.

Fruin, John J. "The Causes and Prevention of Crowd Disasters." *Engineering for Crowd Safety* (1993): 99–108.

Gold, Ann Grodzins. *Fruit-ful Journeys: The Ways of Rajasthani Pilgrims*. Berkeley: University of California Press, 1990.

Gupta, Sudheer, and Joseph W. Elder. *Allaha-bad's Mela: The People and Their Great Fair*. Madison: Center for South Asia, University of Wisconsin-Madison, 2009.

Haberman, David L. *River of Love in an Age of Pollution: The Yamuna River of Northern India*. Berkeley: University of California Press, 2006.

Halbwachs, Maurice. *On Collective Memory*. Chicago: University of Chicago Press, 1992.

Hausner, Sondra L. *Wandering with Sādhus: Ascetics in the Hindu Himalayas*. Bloomington: Indiana University Press, 2007.

Hebner, Jack, and David Osborn. *Kumbha Mela: The World's Largest Act of Faith*. La Jolla: Ganesh Editions, 1990.

Helbing, Dirk, Anders Johansson, and Habib Zein Al-Abideen. "Dynamics of Crowd Disasters: An Empirical Study." *Physical Review E* 75.4, April 18, 2007.

Herbert, H. "The Natural History of Hardwar Fair Cholera Outbreaks." *The Lancet* 146.3752 (1895): 201–02.

Herz, Manuel, and ETH-Studio Basel. *From Camp to City: Refugee Camps of the Western Sahara*. Zurich: Lars Müller, 2013.

Hollick, Julian Crandall. *Ganga: A Journey down the Ganges River*. Washington: Shearwater Books, 2008.

"How the Media Covered the Mela: Did Journalists and Photographers Have a Narrow Depth of Field?" *Hinduism Today* June 30, 2001: 31.

Howitt, Peter, et al. "Technologies for Global Health." *The Lancet* 380.9840 (2012): 507–35.

Husain, Iqbal. "Hindu Shrines and Practices as Described by a Central Asian Traveller in the First Half of the 17th Century." *Medieval India* 1 (1992): 141–53.

India Central Pollution Control Board, ed. *Environmental Study During Kumbh-2001 at Prayag (Allahabad)*. Ministry of Environment and Forests, Government of India, 2003.

Jacobsen, Knut A. *South Asian Religions on Display: Religious Processions in South Asia and in the Diaspora*. South Asian Religion Series. New York: Routledge, 2008.

Jalacic, M., and D. Gans. "The Refugee Camp: Ecological Disaster of Today, Metropolis of Tomorrow."

Architectural design 2 (2004): 82–86.

John, T. Jacob, et al. "Continuing Challenge of Infectious Diseases in India." *The Lancet* 377.9761 (2011): 252–69.

Kaushik, Sudhanshu, and Bishambhar Datt Joshi. "A Comparative Study of Solid Waste Generation at Mansa Devi and Chandi Devi Temples in the Shiwalik Foothills, during the Kumbh Mela 2010." *Green Pages* (April 2001), http://www.eco-web.com/edi/110408.html (last accessed February 10, 2015).

Kam Ng, Mee. "From Government to Governance? Politics of Planning in the First Decade of the Hong Kong Special Administrative Region." *Planning Theory & Practice* 9.2 (2008): 165–85.

Kane, Pandurang Vaman. *History of Dharmaśāstra: Ancient and Mediaeval Religious and Civil Law in India*. Vol. 6. Poona: Bhandarkar Oriental Research Institute, 1930.

Keller, Mikaela, et al. "Use of Unstructured Event-Based Reports for Global Infectious Disease Surveillance." *Emerging Infectious Diseases* 15.5 (2009): 689–95.

Keller, Mikaela, Clark C. Freifeld, and John S. Brownstein. "Automated Vocabulary Discovery for

Geo-Parsing Online Epidemic Intelligence." *BMC Bioinformatics* 10 (2009): 385.

Khan, Kamran, Ziad A. Memish, et al. "Global Public Health Implications of a Mass Gathering in Mecca, Saudi Arabia During the Midst of an Influenza Pandemic." *Journal of Travel Medicine* 17.2 (2010): 75–81.

Khan, Kamran, Clark C. Freifeld, et al. "Preparing for Infectious Disease Threats at Mass Gatherings: The Case of the Vancouver 2010 Olympic Winter Games." *Canadian Medical Association Journal* 182.6 (2010): 579–583.

King, Anna S., and Spalding Symposium on Indian Religions. *Indian Religions: Renaissance and Renewal: The Spalding Papers on Indic Studies.* London: Equinox Publications, 2006.

Klüpfel, H. "The Simulation of Crowd Dynamics at Very Large Events—Calibration, Empirical Data, and Validation." *Pedestrian and Evacuation Dynamics 2005.* Nathalie Waldau, et al., eds. Berlin: Springer, 2007: 285–96.

Koch, Katie. "Among Millions, a Blank Slate." *Harvard Gazette,* February 22, 2013, http://news.harvard.edu/gazette/story/2013/02/among-millions-a-blank-slate (last accessed February 10, 2015).

—. "Inside India's Pop-up City." *Harvard Gazette,* January 21, 2013, http://news.harvard.edu/gazette/story/2013/01/inside-indias-pop-up-city (last accessed February 10, 2015).

—. "Mapping a Megacity's Metabolism." *Harvard Gazette,* February 5, 2013, http://news.harvard.edu/gazette/story/2013/02/mapping-a-megacitys-metabolism (last accessed February 10, 2015).

—. "Saving the Mother River." *Harvard Gazette,* February 14, 2013, http://news.harvard.edu/gazette/story/2013/02/saving-the-mother-river (last accessed February 10, 2015).

—. "Tracking Disease in a Tent City." *Harvard Gazette,* March 1, 2013, http://news.harvard.edu/gazette/story/2013/03/tracking-disease (last accessed February 10, 2015).

Kolff, D. H. A. "Sannyasi Trader–Soldiers." *Indian Economic & Social History Review* 8.2 (1971): 213–18.

Koolhaas, Rem. "Preservation Is Overtaking Us." *Future Anterior* 1.2 (2004): 1–3.

Kumar, A. K. Shiva, et al. "Financing Health Care for All: Challenges and Opportunities." *The Lancet* 377.9766 (2011): 668–79.

Lennard, Suzanne H. Crowhurst, Henry L. Lennard, and Paul Bert. *Livable Cities: People and Places: Social and Design Principles for the Future of the City.* New York: Gondolier Press, 1987.

Lin, Yanliu, and Bruno De Meulder. "The Role of Key Stakeholders in the Bottom-up Planning Processes of Guangzhou, China." *Journal of Urbanism: International Research on Placemaking and Urban Sustainability* 4.2 (2011): 175–90.

Lochtefeld, James G. *God's Gateway: Identity and Meaning in a Hindu Pilgrimage Place.* Oxford: Oxford University Press, 2010.

—. "The Construction of the Kumbha Mela." *South Asian Popular Culture* 2.2 (2004): 103–26.

Lynch, Kevin. *What Time Is This Place?* Cambridge: MIT Press, 1972.

Maclean, Kama. *Pilgrimage and Power: The Kumbh Mela in Allahabad, 1765–1954.* Oxford: Oxford University Press, 2008.

—. "Conflicting Spaces: The Kumbh Mela and the Fort of Allahabad." *South Asia: Journal of South Asian Studies* 24.2 (2001): 135–59.

—. "Seeing, Being Seen, and Not Being Seen: Pilgrimage, Tourism, and Layers of Looking at the Kumbh Mela." *CrossCurrents* 59.3 (2009): 319–41.

MacLean, Kama. "Making the Colonial State Work for You: The Modern Beginnings of the Ancient Kumbh Mela in Allahabad." *The Journal of Asian Studies* 62.3 (2003): 873–905.

Maheshwari, Saurabh, and Purnima Singh. "Psychological Well-Being and Pilgrimage: Religiosity, Happiness and Life Satisfaction of Ardh-Kumbh Mela Pilgrims (Kalpvasis) at Prayag, India." *Asian Journal of Social Psychology* 12.4 (2009): 285–92.

McConnell, John. "Mass Gatherings Health Series." *The Lancet Infectious Diseases* 12.1 (2012): 8–9.

McConnell, John, and Ziad Memish. "The Lancet Conference on Mass Gatherings Medicine." *The Lancet Infectious Diseases* 10.12 (2010): 818–19.

McMullen, R. "Understanding Hinduism: The Kumbh Mela." *Bulletin of the Christian Institute of Religious Studies* 28.1 (1999): 24–32.

Mehrotra, Rahul. "Negotiating the Static and Kinetic Cities: The Emergent Urbanism of Mumbai." *Other Cities, Other Worlds: Urban Imaginaries in a Globalizing Age* (2008): 113–40.

Mehta, Ved. *Portrait of India*. New York: Farrar, Straus and Giroux, 1970.

Melis, Liesbeth. *Parasite Paradise: A Manifesto for Temporary Architecture and Flexible Urbanism*. Nai Uitgevers Pub, 2003.

Memish, Ziad A., et al. "Emergence of Medicine for Mass Gatherings: Lessons from the Hajj." *The Lancet Infectious Diseases* 12.1 (2012): 56–65.

—. "The Hajj: Communicable and Non-Communicable Health Hazards and Current Guidance for Pilgrims," http://www.eurosurveillance.eu/images/dynamic/EE/V15N39/art19671.pdf (last accessed February 10, 2015).

Mines, Mattison. *Public Faces, Private Voices: Community and Individuality in South India*. Berkeley: University of California Press, 1994.

Mishra, J. S. *Mahakumbh: The Greatest Show on Earth*. New Delhi: Haranand Publications, 2004.

Morris, William. "Manifesto of the Society for the Protection of Ancient Buildings." *Historical and Philosophical Issues in the Conservation of Cultural Heritage* (1877): n. p.

Morrison, Dan. "A River Runs through It." The Opinions Pages. *International New York Times*, May 21, 2012, http://latitude.blogs.nytimes.com/2012/05/21/ganges-cleanup-will-cost-tens-of-billions-of-dollars-but-is-a-great-idea (last accessed February 10, 2015).

—. "India Stems Tide of Pollution Into Ganges River." *National Geographic*, November 23, 2011, http://news.nationalgeographic.com/news/2011/11/111123-india-ganges-river-pollution (last accessed February 10, 2015).

Nabian, Nashid, and Carlo Ratti. *Living Architectures*. Cambridge, 2011.

—. "Virtual Space: The City to Come." *Innovation: Perspectives for the 21st Century*. Madrid: BBVA, 2010: 383–97.

Narain, Badri, Kedar Narain, and Christopher N. Burchett. *Kumbh Mela and the Sadhus: The Quest for Immortality*. Vararasi: Pilgrims Publications, 2010. Navlakha, Gautam. "A Show of 'Hindu Power.'" *Economic and Political Weekly* 24.13 (1989): 658.

National River Conservation Directorate, ed. *Status Paper on River Ganga: State of Environment and Water Quality*. Alternate

Hydro Energy Centre / Indian Institute of Technology, Roorkee, 2009, http://www.moef.nic.in/sites/default/files/Status%20Paper%20-Ganga_2.pdf (last accessed February 10, 2015).

Neuhaus, Fabian. *Studies in Temporal Urbanism: The UrbanTick Experiment.* Berlin: Springer, 2011.

Nora, Pierre. "Between Memory and History: Les Lieux de Mémoire." *Representations* 26 (1989): 7–24.

"Norms in Absence." *Economic and Political Weekly* 36.4 (2001): 252–53.

Patel, Vikram, et al. "Chronic Diseases and Injuries in India." *The Lancet* 377.9763 (2011): 413–28.

Paul, Vinod Kumar, et al. "Reproductive Health, and Child Health and Nutrition in India: Meeting the Challenge." *The Lancet* 377.9762 (2011): 332–49.

Pinch, William R. *Warrior Ascetics and Indian Empires.* Cambridge: Cambridge University Press, 2006.

Pradhan, S. "Sangam Attracts Young and Old." *Rediff News,* January 10, 2001.

Project Management Institute, ed. "Perfect Mix of Planning, Teamwork, and Commitment." *Manage*

India 3.1 (2011): n. p.
Rao, Mohan, et al. "Human Resources for Health in India." *The Lancet* 377.9765 (2011): 587–98.

Raza, Gauhar, and Surjit Singh. "Cultural Distance between Peoples' Worldview and Scientific Knowledge in the Area of Public Health." *JCOM* 3 (2004): 4.

Raza, Gauhar, Surjit Singh, and Bharvi Dutt. "Peoples Attitude to Scientific Knowledge: The Context of Culture." *Journal of Scientific & Industrial Research* 54.2 (1995): 108–21.

Reddy, K. Srinath, et al. "Towards Achievement of Universal Health Care in India by 2020: A Call to Action." *The Lancet* 377.9767 (2011): 760–68.

Ringler, Claudia, Joachim von Braun, and Mark W. Rosegrant. "Water Policy Analysis for the Mekong River Basin." *Water International* 29.1 (2004): 30–42.

Rothfork, John. "God with an Elephant Head: Pilgrimage to India." *Prairie Schooner* 62.3 (1988): 92–103.

Rydin, Yvonne, et al. "Shaping Cities for Health: Complexity and the Planning of Urban Environments in the 21st Century." *The Lancet* 379.9831 (2012): 2079–2108.

"Sanitary Reform in India." *The Lancet* 171.4408 (1908): 582–84. Originally Published as vol. 1, issue 4408.

Scardino, Barrie, 1945–, William F. Stern, and Bruce, 1941– Webb. Ephemeral City: Cite Looks at Houston. 1st ed. Austin: University of Texas Press, 2003.

Sclar, Elliott D., Pietro Garau, and Gabriella Carolini. "The 21st Century Health Challenge of Slums and Cities." *The Lancet* 365.9462 (2005): 901–03.

Serwylo, Peter, Paul Arbon, and Grace Rumantir. "Predicting Patient Presentation Rates at Mass Gatherings Using Machine Learning." 8th International Conference on Information Systems for Crisis Response and Management (ISCRAM 2011), Lisbon, Portugal.

Sharma, Vinay. *Health for All through Affordability and Profitability with Public Spiritual Partnership,* http://www.adbi.org/files/2010.12.11.cpp.sess2.5.sharma.paper.health.affordability.pdf (last accessed February 10, 2015).

—. "Motivation Absorbs Magnitude: An Analysis of Health Care Services of Kumbh Mela." 中国公共管理 (2009): 1.

Sharma, Vijay, Sushil Bhadula, and B. D. Joshi. "Impact of Mass Bathing on Water Quality of Ganga River during Maha Kumbh-2010." *Nature and Science* 10.6 (2012): 1–5.

Singhal, Shaleen, Graeme Newell, and Thi Kim Nguyen. "The Significance and Performance of Infrastructure in India." *Journal of Property Research* 28.1 (2011): 15–34.

Sinha, Surajit, and Baidyanath Saraswati. *Ascetics of Kashi: An Anthropological Exploration*. NK Bose Memorial Foundation, 1978.

Soubhy, Saleh. *Pèlerinage à la Mecque et à Médine: Précédé d'un aperçu sur l'islamisme et suivi de considérations générales au point de vue sanitaire et d'un appendice sur la circoncision*. Impr. nationale, 1894.

Steffen, Robert, et al. "Non-Communicable Health Risks during Mass Gatherings." *The Lancet Infectious Diseases* 12.2 (2012): 142–49.

Stille, Alexander. "The Ganges' Next Life." The New Yorker, January 19, 1998, http://www.newyorker.com/magazine/1998/01/19/the-ganges-next-life (last accessed February 10, 2015).

Thackway, Sarah, et al. "Should Cities Hosting Mass Gatherings Invest in Public Health Surveillance and Planning? Reflections from a Decade of Mass Gatherings in Sydney, Australia." *BMC Public Health* 9.1 (2009): 324.

Till, Jeremy. *Architecture Depends*. Cambridge, Massachusetts: MIT Press, 2009.

Tomasi, Luigi. "Homo Viator: From Pilgrimage to Religious Tourism via the Journey." William H. Swatos and Luigi Tomasi, eds. *From Medieval Pilgrimage to Religious Tourism: The Social and Cultural Economics of Piety*. Santa Barbara: Praeger, 2002: 1–24.

Unger, Alon, and Lee W. Riley. "Slum Health: From Understanding to Action." *PLOS Medicine* 4.10 (2007): e295.

Urry, J. *Globalising the Tourist Gaze*. Graz: Lancaster University, 2001.

Vale, Lawrence J., and Sam Bass Warner. *Imaging the City: Continuing Struggles and New Directions*. New Brunswick: Center for Urban Policy Research, 2001.

Vij, Monika. "RS and GIS Based-Risk Assessment, Preparedness and Prevention of Crowd Disasters: A Case Study of Religious Pilgrimage in India," http://cipa.icomos.org/fileadmin/template/doc/KYOTO/26.pdf (last accessed February 10, 2015).

Vlahov, David, et al. "Urban as a Determinant of Health." *Journal of Urban Health: Bulletin of the New York Academy of Medicine* 84, suppl. 1 (2007): 16–26.

Wang, Ya Ping, and Alan Murie. "The New Affordable and Social Housing Provision System in China: Implications for Comparative Housing Studies." *International Journal of Housing Policy* 11.3 (2011): 237–54.

World Health Organization (WHO), eds. "Communicable Disease Alert and Response for Mass Gatherings." World Health Organization, 2008, http://www.who.int/csr/mass_gathering/en (last accessed February 10, 2015).

—. "Ecosystems and Human Well-Being: Health Synthesis." World Health Organization, 2005, http://www.who.int/globalchange/ecosystems/ecosystems05/en (last accessed February 10, 2015).

World Health Organization (WHO), et al. "Global Forum on Mass Gatherings, Rome, Italy 26–29 October 2009." 2011, http://apps.who.int/iris/bitstream/10665/70616/1/WHO_HSE_GAR_SIH_2011.1_eng.pdf?ua=1 (last accessed February 10, 2015).

—. "Hidden Cities: Unmasking and Overcoming Health Inequities in Urban Settings." World Health Organization, 2010, http://www.who.int/kobe_centre/publications/hiddencities_media/who_un_habitat_hidden_cities_web.pdf (last accessed February 10, 2015).

—. "Interim Planning Considerations for Mass Gatherings in the Context Ofpandemic (H1N1) 2009 Influenza." http://www.who.int/csr/resources/publications/swineflu/cp002_2009-0511_planning_considerations_for_mass_gatherings.pdf (last accessed February 10, 2015).

Winston, Diane, and John Giggie. "Introduction Special Issue, Religion and the City." *Journal of Urban History* 28.4 (2002): 395–97.

Zeitz, Kathryn, et al. "Measuring Emergency Services Workloads at Mass Gathering Events." *The Australian Journal of Emergency Management* 22, no. 3 (August 2007): 23–30.

FILM AND VIDEO

Entering the Extraordinary World: Initiation Rites Video. Baba Rampuri. 2012, http://rampuri.com/entering-the-extraordinary-world (last accessed February 10, 2015).

IRHA Symposium. Parts 1, 2, and 3. 2011. https://vimeo.com/ephemeralcity (last accessed February 10, 2015).

Lagos Wide & Close: An Interactive Journey into an Exploding City. Rem Koohlaas and Bregtje van der Haak. 2001, http://lagos.submarinechannel.com (last accessed February 10, 2015).

Kumbha Mela. Michelangelo Antonioni. 1989.

Kumbh Mela: Songs of the River. Nadeem Udden. 2005.

Kumbh Mela: Walking with the Nagas. Julienne Rashore. 2008.

Mystic India: An Incredible Journey of Inspiration. Keith Melton. 2005.

River of Faith: A Film about the Kumbh Mela. Namit Arora. 2013.

Short Cut to Nirvana: Kumbh Mela. Maurizio Benazzo and Nick Day. 2004.

"Worshiping at Kumbh Mela." Poh Si Teng. *The New York Times,* February 10, 2013, http://www.nytimes.com/video/world/100000002055648/worshipping-at-kumbh-mela.html (last accessed February 10, 2015).

WEBSITES

Ardh Kumbh 2007 Allahabad. http://ardhkumbh.up.nic.in.

Clean Ganga Portal. http://www.cleangangaportal.org.

"Eenvoudig Online Verzekeren." *Dajiales.* http://www.dajiales.info.

"Five Stages of Squatting." *Encountering Urbanism* blog. http://encounteringurbanism.blogspot.de/2009/09/five-stages-of-squatting.html.

Ganaga Action Parivar. http://www.gangaaction.org.

GYAN: Green Yatra Action Network. http://www.gyanworldwide.org.

KMP 2001: Kumbh Mela Project. http://www.kmp2001.com.

Kumbh Mela: Hindu Pilgrimage in Contemporary India. http://www.kumbhamela.net.

"Monitoring Committees for Kumbh Mela 2013." *Railway, North Eastern.* http://www.ner.indianrailways.gov.in.

"The National River Conservation Directorate (NRCD)." *Sankat Mochan Foundation.* http://www.sankatmochanfoundationonline.org/save_ganga.html.

Trash | Track. http://senseable.mit.edu/trashtrack.

IMAGE CREDITS

ACKNOWLEDGMENTS

FIELD TRIP
Participants

POOJA AGRAWAL
NAMRATA ARORA
DOROTHY AUSTIN
IWAN BAAN
SATCHIT BALSARI
KALPESH BHATT
CHISTIAN BLASER
JENNY BORDO
AMANDA BREWSTER
CANDACE BROWN
DEREK BROWN
REBECCA BYERLY
RICHARD CASH
SALONI CHATURVEDI
STEPHANIE CHENG
KASHYAP CHOKSI
ISAAC DAYNO
FELIX DEROSEN
NAMITA DHARIA
VINEET DIWADKAR

DIANA ECK
SUE GOLDIE
GREGORY GREENOUGH
REET HAZARIKA
MEENA HEWETT
SUSAN HOLMAN
UMANG HUTHEESING
M. JAVED
DHRUV KAZI
TARUN KHANNA
ANNA KNEIFEL
KATIE KOCH
JIM LASKO
BEN LEWIS
JOHN MACOMBER
NORA MAGINN
OSCAR MALASPINA
NUTAN MAURYA
BRENNA MCDUFFIE
RAHUL MEHROTRA
DINESH MEHTA
DIPTI MEHTA
ALYKHAN MOHAMED

DEONNIE MOODIE
TODD MOSTAK
LARS MULLER
NEIL MURTHY
JUKKA-PEKKA ONNELA
PARIMAL PATIL
LOGAN PLASTER
ANITHA POTTAMKULAM
NICOLAS ROTH
RAVI SAM
RANVIR SHAH
LEILA SHAYEGAN
VAUGHN TAN
RACHEL TAYLOR
FELIPE VERA
GÜNTHER VOGT
MICHAEL VORTMANN
NED WHITMAN
JAMES WHITTEN
TIONA ZUZUL

This book was made possible by the generous
contribution of Vikram Gandhi and Meera Gandhi.

A special thanks to the Prakriti Foundation for
organizing all the supporting events during the fieldwork,
and to Devesh Chaturvedi, Shraddha Dwivedi,
Mani Prasad Mishra, Rajesh Rathore, Alok Sharma
for their generous collaboration in the Kumbh Mela
Workshop at the Harvard University Radcliffe Institute
in August 2013.

RESEARCH and
PRODUCTION TEAM

FIELDWORK

TEAM ON-SITE
Namita Dharia
Vineet Diwadkar
Oscar Malaspina
Rahul Mehrotra
Alykhan Mohamed
Felipe Vera
James Whitten

TEAM OFF-SITE
Chuan Hao Chen
Juan Pablo Corral
Michael Lee
Jose Mayoral Moratilla
Ben Scheerbarth
Johannes Staudt

BOOK PROJECT

TEAM LEADERS
Vineet Diwadkar
Jose Mayoral Moratilla

TEAM
Benjamin Scheerbarth
Johannes Staudt

PARTICIPATING
HARVARD SCHOOLS

School of Arts and Sciences
Graduate School of Design
School of Public Health
Business School

EDITED BY: Rahul Mehrotra and Felipe Vera
COPYEDITING: Sandra-Jo Huber and Jake Starmer
GRAPHIC DESIGN: Hannes Aechter
LAYOUT CONCEPT: Nick Rock
TYPEFACE: Matrix, Apercu
PRODUCTION: Anja Wolsfeld, Hatje Cantz
REPRODUCTIONS: Weyhing digital, Ostfildern
PAPER: Profibulk, 150 g/m²
BINDING AND PRINTING: DZA Druckerei
zu Altenburg GmBH, Altenburg

PUBLISHED BY
Hatje Cantz Verlag
Zeppelinstrasse 32
73760 Ostfildern
Germany
Tel. +49 711 4405-200
Fax +49 711 4405-220
www.hatjecantz.com
A Ganske Publishing Group company

Hatje Cantz books are available
internationally at selected bookstores.
For more information about our
distribution partners, please visit our
homepage at www.hatjecantz.com.

ISBN 978-3-7757-3990-0

PRINTED IN GERMANY

COVER ILLUSTRATION: Dhruv Kazi